TRANSFORMATION MANAGEMENT IN POSTCOMMUNIST COUNTRIES

TRANSFORMATION MANAGEMENT IN POSTCOMMUNIST COUNTRIES

Organizational Requirements for a Market Economy

Edited by
Refik Culpan
Brij Nino Kumar

QUORUM BOOKS
Westport, Connecticut • London

Library of Congress Cataloging-in-Publication Data

Transformation management in postcommunist countries : organizational
    requirements for a market economy / edited by Refik Culpan and
    Brij Nino Kumar.
        p.   cm.
    Includes bibliographical references and index.
    ISBN 0-89930-840-6 (alk. paper)
    1. Europe, Eastern—Economic policy—1989- 2. Postcommunism—
Economic aspects—Europe, Eastern.   3. Free enterprise—Europe,
Eastern.   4. Industrial management—Europe, Eastern.   I. Culpan,
Refik.   II. Kumar, Brij Nino.
HC244.T69859 1995
658′.00947—dc20   94-31461

HC 244 T69859 1995

British Library Cataloguing in Publication Data is available.

Library of Congress Catalog Card Number: 94-31461
ISBN: 0-89930-840-6

First published in 1995

Quorum Books, 88 Post Road West, Westport, CT 06881
An imprint of Greenwood Publishing Group, Inc.

Printed in the United States of America

The paper used in this book complies with the
Permanent Paper Standard issued by the National
Information Standards Organization (Z39.48-1984).

10 9 8 7 6 5 4 3 2 1

*To my wife Oya
and my children Burcu and Alpay
for their continuing support—R.C.*

To my wife Burgl—B.N.K.

Contents

Illustrations

FIGURES

Chapter 8

Chapter 12

TABLES

Chapter 2

Chapter 3

Chapter 9

Chapter 10

Chapter 11

Preface

This book has evolved from our joint research and seminar on foreign direct investment and development in Eastern Europe, held in 1991 while Refik Culpan was spending a term as Visiting Professor at Universität der Bundeswehr, Hamburg, where Brij Nino Kumar was then Chairman of the Department of Business Economics. This was the time when Germany had recently been united and the former socialist part of the world was—as it seemed—awakening after a long spell of oblivion and darkness.

"Transformation" became an important concept at that time, propagated to lead these countries out of the dismal state imposed upon them for decades by a political system that lacked the legitimacy to govern society and the lives of individuals. Transformation is a complex phenomenon affecting all walks of life and has become the object of interdisciplinary research.

"Transformation Management" is a small interdisciplinary area within the vast field of research needed to contribute to the advancement of the former socialist societies. Nevertheless, it is important, considering that economic development is first and foremost connected with the efficiency of enterprises which under socialism had been practically "denaturalized" in the sense that their very constitutive elements such as entrepreneurship, risk-taking, and individual responsibility were systemically missing. Transformation management is about renaturalizing and revitalizing enterprises in former socialist societies.

In this book we wanted to present views from an international prospective about how the problem of transformation was perceived and what solutions were suggested. We invited scholars of management from Europe and the United States to share with us this challenging task. We took into account the risk that an international academic circle would bring not only different views on the problem of transformation management, but also a varied understanding of the term. In anticipation of this, the contributing authors, along with the invitation to participate, were given an idea of the factual problems grouped loosely around a conceptual frame of reference, which Refik Culpan expounds upon in the Introduction. This gave the authors the freedom to write about various problems of transformation management they had been confronted with according to their particular professional background and experience. The task of bringing some order into this diversity and drawing some theoretical inferences needed to satisfy knowledge-constitutive interests is undertaken by Brij Nino Kumar in the Epilogue.

Between the Introduction and the Epilogue, five parts and 14 chapters span a wide range of issues arranged according to the main elements of the concept. These chapters are described briefly below.

Part I presents an overview of the changing market environment and the goals of transformation in the postcommunist countries against the background of former state-owned enterprises.

In Chapter 1, Ronald Savitt discusses the tasks of adopting market-based management, especially from the point of view of newly privatized firms.

In Chapter 2, Alicja Kozdrój-Schmidt and David Van Fleet analyze the strategies and tasks of transformation by providing an insight into the practices and shortcomings of management in Poland. By short-listing the mistakes, implications for future strategy are drawn.

By examining environmental conditions in Chapter 3, William Tullar singles out the tasks and requirements of organizational design needed for accomplishing the transformation process. The special case of American–Russian joint ventures serves as an example.

Parts II to IV comprise the core of the volume. In Chapters 4–12, a detailed analysis is provided of the problem areas hindering the accomplishment of the goals. In the solutions presented, strategies are suggested for pursuing the goals of transformation laid down in Part I. Since management techniques are various and diverse, a systematic approach is taken by classifying them into three pertinent categories: "Structure" (Part II), "Behavior and Personnel" (Part III), and "Process" (Part IV).

In Chapter 4, Darko Deškovicz provides an understanding of corporate governance in Slovenia. Former state-owned enterprises in all postcommunist countries have to transform the central structure of decision-making into more flexible modes suitable to a market economy. The Slovenian model, which includes worker codetermination, can serve as an example.

Michael Gaitanides and Erhard Bredenbreuker analyze the problems of restructuring organizations for transformation in Chapter 5. They discuss the collective combine firm, which was the typical productive organization in former socialistic countries, on the basis of the Mintzberg organization typology. They draw conclusions for restructuring through a case study of a former textile combine.

Chapter 6, by Rolf-Dieter Reineke deals with the structural problems of integrating former combines and firms of postcommunist countries with Western companies through mergers and acquisitions and East–West joint ventures. The issue of combining two different corporate cultures is especially critical and is analyzed in the framework of an acculturation model.

In Chapter 7, Michel Domsch and Désirée H. Ladwig elaborate on personnel development in East–West joint ventures as a means of achieving transformation.

The authors detail training concepts appropriate to the different situations defined by the requirements of the partners involved.

Conrad J. Kasperson and Marian Dobrzynski focus on training and development for a market economy in Chapter 8. Based on the history of management education in Poland, they show the deficits in management. They then investigate into the needs of todays' Polish manager and the ways of meeting them.

In Chapter 9, Arieh Ullmann discusses teaching management as a foreign language, the key role of management education in the transformation process. Besides the lack of familiarity with basic management tools, the managers of Eastern Europe have limited knowledge about the context within which these instruments are applied. The chapter presents observations gathered in Hungary and the implications for effective instruction.

Johann Engelhard and Stefan Eckert show the importance of foreign firms and their mode of establishing business in the transformation of postcommunist economies in Chapter 10. Based on an investigation of German firms, the consequences of patterns of market entry on market performance and, subsequently, the transition of economies are examined. Market-entry strategies are thereby embedded in the different transition policies which Eastern European countries are following.

In Chapter 11, Martin Welge and Dirk Holtbrügge provide an overview of the problems that firms in Eastern Europe are encountering in financial investment and operations and with financial management. Special reference is made to the Belarussian economy, as various available sources of finance are identified and deficits in managerial accounting and managerial finance are discussed.

Chapter 12, by Ulrich Dörrie focuses on restructuring of the technological base in former state-owned enterprises. In most cases, firms in Eastern Europe lag behind the West technologically. Closing the gap in product and process technology is a strategic necessity for transformation. The author shows some trends and strategies in innovation management.

Part V of the volume contains the final two chapters. In comprehensive case studies, overall problems of transformation are presented to round out the analysis of various aspects explored in the previous chapters.

In Chapter 13, Tomasz Mroczkowski et al. present five case histories from the service industry, showing private-sector development in Poland. Based in the city of Gdansk, these firms illustrate the opportunities and risks of establishing small- and medium-sized enterprises by professionals and entrepreneurs. The description of different businesses in a transforming environment is instructive and shows how free enterprise, in spite of problems, develops in such changing environments.

In Chapter 14, William Pendergast deals with transforming management in the Czech and Slovak Republics. Based on the analysis of over thirty case studies, the author shows how companies in the Czech and Slovak Republics face and solve the problems of the "triple revolution" that includes 1) the systemic transformation of the local economy, 2) the modernization of archaic internal operations, and 3) keeping pace with global competition.

A book like this is made possible only with the cooperation of the authors involved. We would like to take this opportunity in thanking each one of them in agreeing to participate in this project with original chapters written for this volume.

Refik Culpan
Brij Nino Kumar

Contributors

Erhard Bredenbreuker is Director of the Treuhandanstalt in Berlin. He has 30 years experience in management, as CEO in industrial companies, and consulting.

Refik Culpan is a faculty member of the School of Business Administration, Pennsylvania State University at Harrisburg. He has published extensively, including several books (most recently, *Multinational Strategic Alliances*) and a large number of articles in academic and professional journals.

Darko Deškovicz is Consultant at Team Training International, Ljubljana, Slovenia. He was a research fellow at the Research Centre of Faculty of Social Sciences (University of Ljubljana). His articles have appeared in *International Review of Sociology, Public Enterprise,* and Slovene journals.

Marian Dobrzyński is Professor of Management at the University of Warsaw. He has taught abroad, including the United States (University of Southern Indiana and Franklin and Marshall College), Algeria (Université d' Alger Centre), and other countries.

Ulrich Dörrie is Akademischer Oberrat at the Institute for Management and Business Administration (Industrial Management), University of Erlangen-Nürnberg. He is a member of the Research Group for Innovation and Technological Forecasting (FIV).

Michel E. Domsch is Full Professor and Chair of Human Resource Management and Labour Relations at the Universität der Bundeswehr, Hamburg. He has edited volumes on human-resource management, organizational behavior, and international management and written a large number of articles.

Stefan Eckert is Assistant Professor at Chair for Business Economics and European Management, University of Bamberg. His research areas include international financial management and market-entry strategies in East Europe.

Johann Engelhard is Full Professor and Chairholder for Business Economics and European Management, University of Bamberg. His research areas include theory of international enterprises, cooperation in East Europe, overseas assignments, and capital structures for foreign subsidiaries.

Michael Gaitanides is Full Professor and Chair for Business Economics and Organization at the Universität der Bundeswehr, Hamburg. He has published extensively in organizational theory and is a consultant for international firms.

Maciej Grabowski is Vice President of the Gdansk Institute for Market Economics, which is supporting the economic transformation process in Poland. He was consultant for OECD and IFC on development of the private sector in Poland.

Dirk Holtbrügge is Research Assistant at the Chair of Management at the University of Dortmund. He has published various articles in such journals as *Aussenwirtschaft, Osteuropa,* and *Osteuropa-Wirtschaft.*

Désirée H. Ladwig is research project leader at the Institute for Human Resource Management and Labour Relations at the Universität der Bundeswehr, Hamburg. She is preparing her Ph.D. on an empirical study about R&D cooperation in small- and medium-sized German firms.

Conrad J. Kasperson is Professor of Business Administration at Franklin and Marshall College in Lancaster, Pennsylvania. He has been a member of the faculty of the University of Warsaw as a Fulbright Professor in 1988–89 and 1992, and has studied Polish management education for the U.S. Government as an aid to the administration of foreign aid to Poland.

Alicja Kozdrój-Schmidt is the author of over 35 publications and presentations in Poland and at international seminars. Her research has led to several awards and grants, including ones from the British Council, the British Academy, the United States Information Agency, and Eastern Washington University.

Przemyslaw Kulawczuk is currently lecturer of economics at the Gdansk University and director of Polish–American Small Business Development Center in Gdansk. He has carried out research projects focused on small business development at the Gdansk Institute for Market Economics and is a nationally recognized expert on private-sector formation and economic transformation. He has published in Polish and English.

Brij Nino Kumar is Full Professor and Chair of Business Economics and International Management at Friedrich Alexander Universität, Erlange-Nürnberg. He has published extensively books and professional articles in international management/business in journals in Germany, the United States, France, and Japan and is consultant to firms and German government agencies.

Tomasz Mroczkowski is Associate Professor at the American University, Washington, D.C., where he specializes in teaching comparative and international management in the MBA program. He was educated at Ampleforth College (England) and the Jagiellonian University, Krakow. Dr. Mroczkowski is an expert on East–West trade and foreign direct investment. Prior to coming to the United States in 1980, he worked for a Polish think tank in Warsaw, specializing in economic policy analysis.

William R. Pendergast is Dean of International Management, Monterey Institute of International Studies. His publications include numerous articles on management education, management in Eastern Europe, and management negotiation.

Rolf-Dieter Reineke was Assistant Professor of Business Administration at the University of Münster and then Senior Technical Advisor at the Organizational and Management Consultancy Division of the German Agency for Technical Cooperation, Eschborn. Presently he is with Gemini Consulting. He has authored a book on acculturation of foreign acquisitions, coedited a volume on management consultancy, and published numerous articles.

Ronald Savitt is John L. Beckley Professor of American Business at the University of Vermont. His work has appeared in the leading journals in marketing, including the *Journal of the Academy of Marketing Science, Journal of Marketing,* and *Journal of Retailing.*

James Sood is a Professor of Marketing and International Business at the American University, Washington, D.C. He has provided consulting services to international organizations, government agencies, and private industry. He has recently been involved in a number of research projects in Poland.

William L. Tullar is currently visiting professor at the Fachhochschule in Worms, Germany.

Arieh A. Ullmann is Associate Professor of Management, School of Management, State University of New York at Binghamton. His fields of interest include strategic management (impact of organizational culture on strategy, business strategy, and government regulation) and international business (Eastern Europe).

David D. Van Fleet is Professor of Management, Arizona State University, West. He is a Fellow of the Academy of Management and has published in the areas of contemporary management, behavior in organizations, military leadership, and organizational behavior. He is a past Editor of the *Journal of Management* and has over 150 publications and presentations, including journals in Australia, Germany, Great Britain, Norway, Russia, and the United States.

Martin K. Welge is Full Professor and Chair of Management and International Business at the University of Dortmund. His publications include 12 books and articles in professional journals such as *Management International Review, International Studies in Management and Organization, Zeitschrift für Betriebswirtschaftslehre, Zeitschrift für betriebswirtschaftliche Forschung, Die Betriebswirtschaft, Zeitschrift für Organisation,* and *Wirtschaftswoche.*

Introduction

Transforming Enterprises in Postcommunist Countries

Refik Culpan

The foundations of recent political and economic changes in postcommunist countries lie in their strong desire to transform their economies from command to market economies. In this transition, much attention has been paid to political and economic reforms at the macro level but less concern has been given to organizational requirements of effective business enterprises in formation. Most of the business publications on postcommunist economic liberalization deal with business opportunities in the region and designing appropriate corporate strategies for Western firms (Quelch et al., 1991). No serious attempt has been made to systematically examine the transformation process in postcommunist nations from the standpoint of business concerns and to suggest essential components of free enterprises as a model for organizations in these formerly socialist countries.

In this transformation process, the critical question is whether firms in postcommunist countries must strive for modern management techniques proposed for or adopted at the Western firms or adopt an intermediate solution to their present problems. We believe that they must transform themselves immediately and radically by adopting the most advanced management tools and approaches available, because this is an excellent opportunity to start from scratch and build the ideal firm, although it is a formidable task. Many German and Japanese firms used such an opportunity after World War II when they rebuilt their enterprises. Ultimately, the competitiveness of formerly socialist or newly established firms will depend upon their performance against not only other domestic but also foreign firms, in an increasingly global market. If the transforming companies do not build solid, effective strategies and structures now, they will suffer later from problems similar to their traditional dilemmas and again ask for a rescue from their governments. To break this vicious circle, they must pursue a radical transformation path by which, despite difficulties, they can build viable organizations.

This chapter examines the organizational imperatives of such a transformation and the necessary ingredients of creating a free-market enterprise in these changing societies. It offers a conceptual model in which the goals and means of building and/or developing a free and effective enterprise can be defined.

First, the chapter outlines the turbulent market environment in postcommunist countries and then reviews the relevant literature describing organizational and managerial characteristics of state-owned enterprises (SOEs) and building efficient and competitive firm strategies and structures. Second, it introduces a conceptual model consisting of goals and means of business concerns in transformation to a market economy and the necessary market infrastructure. Finally, it discusses business implications of such a transformation for both postcommunist and Western companies.

CHANGING MARKET ENVIRONMENT

One major reason for the collapse of communism is its failure in providing a satisfying standard of living for its people because of mismanagement of resources. Consequently, the people and the leaders have turned in frustration and despair to Western capitalism as an alternative way to prosperity. As this apparent revolution takes place, firms in formerly socialist countries seek new ways of structuring and positioning themselves to meet market demand in a timely manner. To develop the new capitalism in postcommunist countries, crucial changes must be made, including moving from central planning to firm planning, from non-competition to free competition, and from mismanagement to efficient management.

At the enterprise level, a strategic revolution must be accomplished to move in new directions. This includes better production planning instead of storming production at month and year ends, diversifying suppliers nationally and internationally instead of only vertical integration, increasing the number of marketers, as well as reducing the number of procurers (Auerbach & Stone, 1991).

Nevertheless, change is the only constant in formerly socialist countries today. In this rapidly changing environment, organizations are striving for creative solutions to their problems. For example, a number of managers at SOEs in Russia and Ukraine have leased some of their enterprises and even engaged in joint ventures with Western firms.

BACKGROUND OF SOEs AND PREVIOUS STUDIES

To understand the necessity of transformation in SOEs, we have to understand the organizational and managerial characteristics of communist organizations. A review of the literature reveals the significant features of these organizations and their managerial behavior.

Rondinelli (1991) reported that "Most manufacturing takes place in huge, inefficient, unproductive state-owned enterprises that are losing their markets in the [former] Soviet Union and other socialist countries. Many are over-staffed and have obsolete technology and deteriorating facilities. Services and retail activities are still provided by state-owned enterprises, but some micro-enterprises and small businesses are now emerging" (p. 27).

In developing the new capitalism in Eastern Europe, Auerbach and Stone (1991) suggest that Eastern European countries should understand the following: more professional management, more customer-focused management, the variety of institutional solutions, "business-style" management with its strengths and weaknesses, continuously evolving private-sector management ideas in the West and their implications for public and voluntary action, organizing power relations in organizations, transition to a consumer-goods-based economy and then to a service economy, and financial sources and institutions affecting the creation and running of organizations.

In recognition of strategic and structural changes, Ivancevich et al. (1992) claim that "whatever the ultimate or next generation political configuration looks like, the managers of the economic infrastructure will be asked to transform their organizations. Soviet managers will need to put together the strategies, organizational structures, appropriate work units, and a set of motivational programs to produce the goods and services that are needed, at a quality level that is acceptable, and on a schedule that is reasonable" (p. 43). In their study, the authors found that the Soviet managers "know that the quality of product is low, and they must improve this part of production if they are to compete internationally. However, they are still faced with a bureaucracy that is rigidly administering the flow of goods and raw materials" (p. 53). The authors note that people who lived through a totalitarian regime have difficulty adjusting to a world of democracy, free enterprise, and risk-taking decision making.

A Harvard study of decision making in the former Soviet Union, as described in the book "Behind the Factory Walls" by Lawrence and Vlashoutsicos (1990) summarized the findings of an American–Soviet team of management specialists. Two American and two Soviet enterprises operating in a similar type of business were studied. The researchers examined the structure and decision making in these enterprises. Interesting similarities as well as differences among American and Soviet enterprises were discovered. For example, Soviet managers adjusted targets downwards to insure the plan's accomplishment and were more involved than American managers in responding to ministry (external) requests. Hierarchy in the U.S. firms is structured as a vertical chain of command. Communication, however, takes place horizontally as well as vertically at all levels. In the former Soviet Union, managers have authority over everyone below them. Communication was conducted on a top-down pattern with little effort to initiate horizontal communication. Subordinates from all levels had the right of direct access to their leaders.

Soviet managers used a paternalistic management approach by involving themselves in such nonwork matters of concern to employees such as housing, medical care, education, and family decision making. The immense authority of Soviet managers was the product of custom, culture, and tradition.

In building strategic alliances between Eastern and Western companies, Newman (1992) asserts that companies venturing into Eastern Europe or similar developing areas should use "focused joint ventures" as used in Peoples' Republic of China to establish a business. Such ventures are effective instruments for behavior modification necessary to transform sheltered production into competitive production. "Each 'focused joint venture' is intentionally inflexible; it succeeds by promptly serving a clear need, and probably has a limited life span. However, adaptability can be attained through a series progression of 'focused joint ventures' " (p. 72).

This review provides us with background information about the salient characteristics of communist organizations and managerial behavior. Bearing this background information in mind, let us turn to introduction of a new model, which we believe must replace the existing organizational and managerial practices.

A CONCEPTUAL MODEL

From the vantage point of postcommunist organizations, the conceptual model of transformation from command economy to market economy includes goals to be achieved and means to be utilized. Of course, such a goals–means interface (see Fig. 1) will be affected by market infrastructure, which sets the foundation for business concerns. Because of the special focus of this volume, we will elaborate on the goals–means relationship but recognize the importance of infrastructure factors. Principal interwoven goals of the transformation can be defined as follows.

Goals

Customer Orientation. The very existence of a business firm depends upon its ability to meet the demands and needs of its customers. This very simple but often overlooked fact distinguishes organizations operating in a market economy from those operating in a nonmarket economy. It also even determines the competitive performance of companies in a market economy, as demonstrated by many Japanese companies. In other words, when firms in market economies ignore this basic principle, they suffer loss of competitiveness, as experienced by many U.S. and European firms vis-à-vis Japanese firms. Paying attention to customers' needs and producing quality and suitable products and services are essential for business competitiveness. Yet SOEs in Central and Eastern Europe, under the central economic plans, have developed production policies driven by central authority rather than consumer needs. The principal responsibility of SOEs has been toward the government, therefore, they have tried to please the government as they implement centrally imposed plans. However, all business success rests on the extent to which companies satisfy their customers (Peters & Waterman, 1982). Hence, SOEs must go through a fundamental change in their business philosophy and organizational culture by placing priority on customer needs and satisfaction.

Self-reliance. The goal of self-reliance is an extension of the first goal of customer orientation. Traditionally, SOEs have been instruments of government policy implementation and have been subsidized by their government. For example, Aeroflot Airlines has been dependent on subsidized fuel, but a typical Western airline must rely on market sources to survive. Under a capitalist system, managers of SOEs or other companies should be aware of the fact that no one will

Figure 1
Goals–Means Model

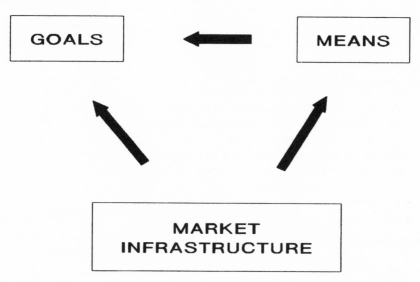

save their money-losing enterprises. Each enterprise should be able to stand on its own feet. The only sources of capital available are equity and credits, which are available according to the enterprise's market performance.

Lean Structure. SOEs are usually rigid bureaucratic structures with over employment. They must undertake major restructuring and downsizing programs to increase efficiency of their organizations. Unless they create lean organizational structures yielding efficient operations, their competitiveness and even survival will be in danger. Big organizations, which are very common in formerly communist countries, unfortunately generate complexity, which in turn leads to obstacles in communication and decision-making processes. At Western firms, a high overhead cost signals a serious problem. Firms should control these costs by cutting the "fat" within the firm. The fat here means excessive number of employees, more layers of hierarchy, high cost of production because of waste, and low machine and labor productivity.

The recommended organizational designs are flexible, organic structures with a matrix organization or divisional organizations with decentralized authorities (Peters & Waterman, 1982). By adopting such structures, organizations avoid accumulating dysfunctional assets.

Total Quality Management (TQM). TQM refers to a management philosophy and practice ingrained in corporate culture leading to satisfying customer needs. It is based on the idea that every task within an organization is a fundamental process.

Hence, managers must integrate strategy, technology, communication, innovation, and human resources in the pursuit of total quality (Hames, 1991; Spiker, 1991). TQM requires 1) customer definition of quality, 2) believing in the impact of quality on productivity, cost, and competitiveness, 3) employee involvement in quality improvement, and 4) a synergistic approach to achievement of total quality (Sarazen, 1991). Furthermore, Hames (1991) claims that there are seven universal principles that need to be present: the customer comes first, the appreciation of quality, teamwork, continuous improvement of processes, employee participation, system leadership, and recognizing the importance of variation within the process. "In today's competitive business climate, the creation of innovation and synergy through cooperative teamwork is not merely a key strategic tool. It is a business necessity—a prerequisite for survival" (Hames, 1991, p. 14). Some might view such fundamentals as luxuries for formerly communist organizations, but the choice must be made for a "transformation," not for a "reform." Only through radical changes can a new organizational system be established. The new system must comprise the following TQM features, which Brown and Svenson (1990) recommend for Western firms as well: vision and values, commitment and participation, quality measurement, continuous improvement, human-resource development, technology and systems utilized, and rewards.

As Porter (1985) pointed out, the success of today's enterprises lies beyond quality production and effective management of all the activities in the value-chain. Thus, Central and Eastern European companies should build a solid TQM base and integrate business activities into a customized model that will work for them.

Innovation. Even firms in many Western countries have learned a lesson that mere survival is not sufficient in a competitive international marketplace. To gain a competitive edge, firms should continuously renew themselves and advance their products and services (Peters & Austin, 1985). Given the rapid pace of technological and global changes, no firm can survive without a deep commitment to improve its product and expand its markets. Four basic types of innovation, in order of originality, include invention (creation of a totally new product, service, or process), extension (new use or different application to an already existing product, service, or process), duplication (creative new application of an existing concept), and synthesis (combination of existing concepts and factors into a new formulation or use) (Howell & Higgins, 1990).

In accomplishing innovation, Central and Eastern European firms can benefit from the accumulated knowledge of their countries in basic and defense sciences. The advanced space and weapon technology in Russia, for example, can offer great opportunities in developing consumer products and services.

We must admit, however, that some serious obstacles to such transformation do exist. For example, the lack of organizational knowledge in Central and Eastern Europe will slow their transition to a market economy. Management skill stands out as the most needed commodity. The long-lasting suppressive communist regime did not encourage development of such virtues as quality-consciousness, self-reliance, and the work ethic. Grasping the basics of business competence will be vital for the successful transition to a market economy.

Means

Privatization. Based on the British experience, Moore (1992) cites "three major factors—the subordination of commercial to political objectives, the fact that survival is not dependent on success, and the failure to harness the power of self-interest—which are the root causes of the poor performance of nationalized industries. Because these ills cannot be cured as long as the industries remain in government hands, the only solution is to privatize them" (pp. 118–119).

Although this is a governmental policy decision beyond an enterprise's discretion, there are important implications of privatization entailing organizational commitments and changes.

Privatization is a difficult task to accomplish even in Western countries because of its political and economic ramifications. It often results in laying off a large number of employees, at a high political cost. The German government, for example, had to soften its stand on selling East German plants to private enterprises by requesting that potential buyers guarantee job security for at least a certain percentage of employees.

Nevertheless, privatization must be accomplished to institute viable business entities. Small enterprises, retail stores, restaurants, and the like can be sold at auction or directly to private individuals. For example, authorities in Ukraine sold 17 small SOEs to eager buyers at the nation's first-ever public auction. Large enterprises can be offered to Western investors first. If acceptable buyers are not found, privatization should pursue a gradual course. SOEs could be turned into corporations, with the government as the majority shareholder for the time being. Top managers can be offered a small percentage (e.g., 5%) of the shares and workers an additional substantial (e.g., 25%) percentage at book value. Although this approach gives government, rather than management, control of an enterprise, eventually the government's majority stake would be sold at free-market prices to investors.

Employee share ownership "has an unrivaled power to teach the responsibilities and rewards of a free society" (Moore, 1992, p. 119). This is an effective way to motivate employees to take an interest in company performance and enhance productivity. It will encourage employee involvement in management of the company and stimulate taking innovative measures to improve the operations, procedures, and outcomes.

In Russia, for example, all medium- and large-scale enterprises—except for those in a few strategic and raw materials industries—were supposed to declare their privatization plans and begin structuring by 1992. However, only 40% of such companies managed to file their paperwork in time for the Russian government's original October 1st deadline. So far, companies are fairly evenly split in selecting between the main options for privatization. The first gives management and workers a 49% share in the concern at a lower price but with fewer voting rights. The second costs more but gives management and workers a majority stake of 51%. "If a company fails to submit its own plan, the government will impose the privatization in which the government has more control" (Wall Street Journal, 1992).

Once a company goes private, government subsidies must end. However, privatized companies may face the dilemma of paying dividends on the one hand, especially when prices are rising, and investing for further restructuring and expansion on the other hand. This is why they should look for foreign financing.

However, it must be remembered that privatization is not a panacea for effective management but a first step in the right direction. Privatization yields transformation in business strategy, organizational structure, and firm performance. After privatization, a new organization and management system should be established, as described above, to achieve the ultimate benefits of privatization.

Relearning. To demonstrate the need for relearning, we refer to the Rondinelli's (1991) observation: "Managers used to operating under socialist principles and with assured markets in the [former] Soviet Union and CMEA (Council for Mutual Economic Assistance) countries fear the removal of state subsidies and the uncertainties of the market. Many are ill-prepared psychologically or administratively to deal with the competition" (p. 30). This observation calls for a transformation in managerial behavior. Thus, managers should be trained in the areas of taking responsibility for decision making and risk taking. They should learn to assess market opportunities, obtain and invest capital in productive projects, use information systems, cash-flow management, and standard systems of accounting. Most importantly, training programs should be designed to make managerial attitudes and behaviors compatible with the goals specified above. As Vladimir Yamkinov, the director of the Stolichnaya Cristal factory in Moscow, stated, "In the current situation, we don't know how a privatized company will work. . . . It doesn't fit any theory we learn in school—not Adam Smith, not Ford, not Karl Marx, and not Lenin . . . " (Wall Street Journal, 1992). Such confusion and ambiguity should be eliminated by formulating explicit organizational objectives and policies. Formerly communist enterprises can get assistance from Western companies in learning market-oriented behavior. For example, Rosshelf, a group of 19 Russian companies, receives financing and support for feasibility studies from the Houston construction and engineering company Brown & Root Inc.

Managerial Entrepreneurship. Rapidly growing numbers of new and sophisticated competitors and a sense of distrust of the traditional methods of enterprise management call for Central and Eastern European enterprises to develop "intrapreneurs," managers with innovative and productive ideas. The enterprises should support innovation and venture development in products and/or technologies in their existing organizational environment. As many companies in the

West have been recognizing the need for corporate entrepreneuring (Burgelman, 1984, Kanter, 1985), organizations in Central and Eastern Europe should infuse entrepreneurial thinking into their bureaucratic structures. Of course, this requires retraining as well as reeducation. A new breed of managers who are educated in Western business values will contribute substantially to this process. Investing heavily in entrepreneurial ways would allow new ideas to flourish in an innovative environment. Four key factors in developing a climate that will help innovative people to reach their potentials include: 1) the presence of explicit goals, 2) a system of feedback, 3) an emphasis on individual responsibility, and 4) rewards based upon results (Scanlan, 1981).

Modern managerial techniques widely used in Western firms such as just-in-time management, quality circles, computer-aided designs, computer-aided manufacturing should be introduced to existing organizations to revolutionize the way that they function.

Strategic Alliances. Central and Eastern European companies may form strategic alliances including joint ventures, licensing and franchising agreements, and marketing agreements with Western firms for a variety of reasons including minimizing transaction costs, accessing Western markets, and augmenting organizational learning. For example, Herzfeld (1991) argues that joint ventures, like transplanted DNA, will become the organizing matter of new life—commercial life and new forces of production that sustain wealth. The Central and Eastern European enterprises can avoid economic disorder through joint ventures with Western companies, "By the force of their action or example, joint ventures will engender a new population of managers: marketing managers, process-technology and information-technology specialists, financial analysts, quality engineers, and business strategists who will lead the (former) Soviet economy into the next century" (Herzfeld, 1991, p. 81).

In this fashion, Uzbekistan plans a 50–50 joint venture with Newmont Mining Corporation to process low-grade gold ore. The joint venture will construct a $75 million facility at the Muruntau gold mine, which is considered one of the world's largest open-pit gold mines. Another example is Russian Wood Express, Inc., a subsidiary jointly owned by American PLY GEM Industries and Russians. They believe that the Siberian forest represents an enormous alternate wood source for the building and forest products industry.

Such strategic alliances will contribute considerably to the development of Western-like business strategies and structures while they enhance their performance in productive efficiency and firm profitability. These alliances will assure successful technology transfers from Western firms to transforming firms.

MARKET INFRASTRUCTURE

Developing ideal goals and providing appropriate means are not sufficient for building a market economy unless market infrastructure exists. Factors in market environment will affect the goal formation and means availability. They include legal and tax systems, banking, telecommunications, transportation, intermediary agencies, and education and training. A legal system should be created in post-communist countries to allow not only private ownership but also regulations on contractual arrangements, labor relations, and other commercial relationships. A tax system encouraging savings and investments and promoting business ventures and entrepreneurship should be adopted. Banks are desperately needed to give credits to new entrepreneurs and existing enterprises. For example, in Kazakhstan, a commercial bank formed as a joint venture between a group of U.S. and Kazak investors will help in financing new business ventures. Telecommunication networks should be developed for information exchange and fast and reliable communication. Western telecommunication giants such as AT&T and Siemens have already been involved in improvement of communication networks in some of these countries. Transportation systems should be improved to carry goods from producers and manufacturers to retailers on time. Intermediary agencies besides banks, such as wholesalers, retailers, brokers, and sale representatives, are needed to conduct market transactions. Education and training systems should be restructured to create new business values, ethics, knowledge, and skills. Toward this end, many formerly socialist countries have established ties with Western universities and consulting firms to provide business and management education and training.

It is not the intention of this chapter to elaborate on the appropriate features of all these factors of market infrastructure, nor is there space enough to cover them in detail. However, the present model accepts the fact that such a market infrastructure must be in place to accomplish firm-level transformation.

IMPLICATIONS OF THE MODEL

As a result of the organizational and managerial changes described above, Central and Eastern European firms will become more efficient in delivering products and services desperately needed by consumers. Moreover, they will become competitive in their national and international markets. The suggestions made in this chapter are for long-term strategic changes that postcommunist firms must go through; piecemeal or remedial solutions cannot produce the desired transformation. As formerly communist enterprises are transformed and new companies are established, they will increase the standard of living for the people in these countries, which is overdue.

From the standpoint of Western firms, Central and Eastern Europe presents an emerging market. For example, 67% of U.S. executives responding to a *Fortune* survey consider Eastern Europe as a major new market, comparable in importance to Western Europe in 20 years (Albert, 1990). Improved organizational structure and performance of Central and East European firms will stimulate more Western business interest in the region. In fact, many Western companies have already invested in this region. For example, such U.S. multinationals as General Motors, Dow Chemical, Eastman Kodak, S.C. Johnson & Son, and Xerox have been involved in such technology transfer. Basically, two kinds of companies will be involved in Central and Eastern Europe—multinational companies such as Olin, Marathon Oil, Warnaco, and TRW; and small- and medium-sized businesses that find special expertise, as well as cost advantages, in Central and Eastern Europe. An example of this latter category is the joint venture of Erie Scientific, USA, a maker of laboratory glass, that opened a microscope-slide venture with a local partner in Budapest. Most of these firms are companies led by people who have Central or East European ethnic or family ties.

However, the investment climate for Western companies in Central and Eastern Europe over the next few years will depend upon the progress of the formerly communist enterprises in transforming their structure and capabilities. Unless Western businesses find suitable counterparts as buyers, partners, or suppliers in Central and Eastern Europe, their initial enthusiasm will disappear. Present and future investments will produce satisfying results when only organizations accomplish their transformation process, which means thinking and acting with market responsibilities.

Western companies need to study market conditions as well as organizational characteristics in Central and Eastern Europe to take advantage of business opportunities there and transfer know-how to them. "Technology and management skills are the primary focus, since Central and East Europe is sadly lacking in both and hungry to acquire them" (Oliver, 1991, p. 11). This raises a host of strategic questions, such as type of technology to transfer (state-of-the-art or mature technology), forms of transfer, and staffing and training requirement for technology transfer. Western firms should be able to address these issues before making any commitment to postcommunist countries.

CONCLUSION

Given the present level of intensive global competition, transforming enterprises in Central and East Europe cannot afford to employ outmoded or low-quality management practices and organizational designs. When they have a chance to rebuild their enterprises, they must do it in a fast, comprehensive, and efficient manner to become competitive domestically and internationally. The success of German and Japanese firms in various industries (e.g., automobiles and steel) has been attributed to their newly built factories that utilized the most recently available technologies after World War II. A similar approach should be utilized by formerly communist enterprises to establish viable business enterprises.

Auerbach & Stone (1991) observe that " . . . the ability to anticipate and lead consumer demand, rather than being several years behind it, is a strong characteristic of successful businesses. This capability grows with experience and is reinforced by success. It cannot be created quickly" (p. 65). This observation is also applicable to formerly communist enterprises. Additionally, it must be noted that there are cultural roots of economic performance (Franke et al., 1991). Of course, changing these cultural roots is a challenging and long process. Nonetheless, postcommunist companies are advised to systematically and persistently pursue the organizational transformation goals defined above and to utilize the means recommended to change their strategy, structure, and performance for competitiveness.

REFERENCES

Albert, M. (1990). Wary hope on Eastern Europe. *Fortune,* January 29, 125–126.

Auerbach, P. & Stone, M. (1991). Developing the new capitalism in Eastern Europe—How the West can help. *Long Range Planning,* 24(3): 58–65.

Brown, M.G. & Svenson, R. (1990). What "doing" Total Quality Management really means. *Journal of Quality and Participation,* September: 32–38.

Burgelman, R.A. (1984). Designs for corporate entrepreneurship. *California Management Review,* Winter: 154–166.

Franke, R.H., Hofstede, G.H. & Bond, M.H. (1991). Cultural roots of economic performance. *Strategic Management Journal,* Summer: 165–178.

Hames, R.D. (1991). Total Quality Management: The strategic advantage. *International Journal of Physical Distribution and Logistics Management,* 21(4): 9–14.

Herzfeld, M.J. (1991). Joint ventures: Saving the Soviets from Perestroika. *Harvard Business Review,* January–February: 80–91.

Howell, J.M. & Higgins, C.A. (1990). Champion of change. *Business Quarterly,* Spring: 31–36.

Ivancevich, J.M., DeFrank, R.S. & Gregory, P.R. (1992). The Soviet enterprise director: an important resource before after the coup. *Academy of Management Executive,* 6(1): 42–55.

Kanter, R.M. (1985). Supporting innovation and venture development in established companies. *Journal of Business Venturing,* Winter: 47–60.

Lawrence, P.R. & Vlashoutsicos, C.A. (1990). *Behind the Factory Walls.* Boston: Harvard University Press.

Moore, John. (1992). British Privatization—Taking capitalism to the people. *Harvard Business Review,* January–February, 115–124.

Newman, W.H. (1992). "Focused joint ventures" in transforming economies. *Academy of Management Executive,* 6(1): 67–75.

Oliver, M.J. (1991). Eastern Europe: The path to success. *Columbia Journal of World Business,* 25(1): 10–14.

Peters, T. & Waterman, R. (1982). *In Search of Excellence.* New York: Harper and Row.

——— & Austin, N. (1985). *Passion for Excellence.* New York: Random House.

Porter, M.E. (1985). *Competitive Advantage.* New York: The Free Press.

Quelch, J.A., Buzzell, R.D. & Salama, E.R. (1991). *The Marketing Challenge of Europe (1992).* Reading, MA: Addison-Wesley.

Rondinelli, D.A. (1991). Developing private enterprise in the Czech and Slovak Federal Republics. *Columbia Journal of World Business,* 26(3): 26–36.

Sarazen, J.S. (1991). Continuous improvement and innovation. *Journal for Quality & Participation,* 14(5): 34–39.

Scanlan, B.K. (1981). Creating a climate for achievement. *Business Horizons,* March–April: 5–9.

Spiker, B.K. (1991). Total quality management: The mind-set for competitiveness in the 1990s. *Manufacturing Systems,* 9(9): 40–45.

Wall Street Journal, October 21, 1992, p. A12.

I

ENVIRONMENT AND STRATEGY FOR TRANSFORMATION

1

Critical Issues of Privatization

A Managerial Perspective

Ronald Savitt

INTRODUCTION

The political and economic changes in Central and Eastern Europe have come
with amazing speed. Nations that many thought would never turn toward market
economies are actively pursuing that goal. All of the economic, legal, political, and
social institutions are facing dramatic challenges, which are beyond the belief of
all who study them. Greatest pressures have been placed on reforming the old
economic structures in order to convert state-owned enterprises to viable private
enterprises. As such, Bulgaria, the Czech and Slovak Republics, Hungary, Poland,
Romania, as well as Russia and the other nations of the former Soviet Union
provide important laboratories for studying management transformation.

Transformation and Privatization

Words such as change, development, transition, and transformation are all used
to describe the movement from the past through the present to the future. Transformation represents the most dramatic and radical of these concepts because of
its scope. It implies a fundamental restructuring of all of the basic institutions in
each of these countries. While the "old system" was clearly defined and understood, the "new order" is only vaguely defined in terms such as democracy and
market economy. While we in the West have a clear idea of what these mean, even
with our own differences, postcommunist nations do not.

Transformation is a total process affecting attitudes, values, and behaviors of
every member of society, though in the West it is more narrowly defined in
economic terms. Economic, political, and social transformations are inextricably
intertwined. They affect and, in return, are affected by one another. For example,
the corporate governance structure of a business develops both from economic and
political objectives and is influenced by societal desires. This chapter acknowl-
edges the larger issues but concentrates on economic transformation, especially
with regard to the development of firms.

At the most general level, economic transformation programs are composed of
four elements; these are:

1. Trade liberalization, including the reduction of import and export barriers.
2. Market-based prices resulting from the elimination of regulations and the advance of competition among buyers and sellers.
3. A convertible and valued domestic currency.
4. Privatization, which aims at converting state-owned enterprises into privately owned and managed firms (Köves & Marer, 1991, pp. 15–33).

While these elements frame the process, each of the nations of the region have selected different strategies for pursuing them and have allocated different priorities among them, with different results.

Privatization has become the central focus of economic transformation throughout the region, with each country developing processes by which to change the ownership base of many of their industries. It is founded on the premise that private decisions will lead to better results than the previous system and represents the major commitment toward moving toward Western capitalism. Each of these countries has approached the process with its own historical perspective with the result that there are a number of privatization schemes including auctions, employee buy-outs, joint stock conversions, joint ventures with foreign investors, and a number of direct-sale options. Some of this has been very successful, some has been questionable, and some has resulted in failure. There is an ever-increasing literature on this process; several studies provide detailed evidence (Kocsis, 1992; Mejstrik & Burger, 1993; Lieberman, 1993).

An important measure of the success of privatization is the degree to which there is a change from the public form of ownership. "The purpose of privatization should be to replace passive–public ownership with active–private ownership" (Ellerman et al., 1992, p. 130). Such a shift, in itself, does not ensure that the privatized enterprises will succeed, though these conditions represent a start in that direction. There is still the need for active–private ownership to exert active, market-oriented management. This can only come about if the new owners either actively participate in the management or engage others who both understand the challenges and have the skills to manage the firm in a market-like fashion. Change in ownership in no way guarantees that the new, privatized firm will be in any better condition to operate in the evolving market economy than the state-owned one that preceded it. All too often the "managers of the past" are the managers of the present and the future, and, as such, in spite of the will to do so, they simply do not have all of the skills needed to manage in the new environment.

Purpose of This Chapter

Most of the efforts toward privatization have been at the macroeconomic level, especially with regard to the establishment of processes to encourage and support privatization. Much less attention has been paid to the management of the resulting enterprises. Underneath the process is the assumption that the new private firms will be able to make their way in the new environment; somehow, management skills will develop from the new market economy or they will be learned as firms begin to interact with one another. Those enterprises which are either purchased outright or are operated through a foreign joint venture may see the greatest infusion of Western management skills. Current experiences of General Electric with Tungsram in Hungary suggest that this does not come easily. There are significant challenges for Westerners in learning about how the old system works as well as significant challenges in changing the attitudes and behaviors of managers used to the socialist system. Those processes may take longer than anyone ever thought. The newly privatized firms may learn new management practices as they begin to compete with others; however, they do not have the resources to replicate the practices of the larger enterprises, especially those with foreign management. What they may do is to look as if they are changing; however, there are significant differences between running advertisements on local television channels and developing, implementing, and operating an integrated marketing plan.

What local firms in these economies may learn in the short run is how to react, rather than to act. There will always be exceptions, much as there are in Western economies, and it will be difficult to explain how and why sophisticated management behavior develops from the past. What we must be concerned with is how to influence the development of management techniques that allow the results of privatization to be successful. This is a topic that has not received the same amount of attention as the process of privatization itself, and until it does the transformation of these economies may be retarded. What makes an economy perform in effective and efficient ways is the quality of management at the level of the individual enterprise. This is a lesson that we are slowly recognizing and one that must be mastered quickly. Some of the issues that need to be dealt with are discussed below.

The purpose of this chapter is to define and discuss the critical challenges that management of these newly privatized firms will confront as they move from their past to their future.

MANAGEMENT AND PRIVATE ENTERPRISE IN PERSPECTIVE

The Framework

It is important to step back to describe the setting in which the management of Western enterprise has developed in order to understand the overall challenge of the process. Management as we know it has evolved over several hundred years in generally open societies. We have grown up, especially since the end of World War II, with freedoms, rights, and responsibilities to wear what we want, spend our money as we please, produce what we want, and do business as we please. This system of values is often described as the "free market." The idea of a free market is based on Adam Smith's "invisible hand," which directly implies the active participation of buyers and sellers. Whether Smith's atomistic world ever existed is less important than the systems that developed in defining roles and expectations through the market. What has evolved and, of course, was missing the socialist system, is a set of premises on which managers can take action. All of this is part of capitalism, which has lead to the economic development we understand.

Economic development of significant magnitude took place in the economies of Central and Eastern Europe under socialism, but the system was based on a different set of principles. They were exhorted to produce without regard to markets but as part of a central plan in which individual decision making and responsibility had to give way to the goals of the state. Their managerial structures and behaviors are vastly different from those in the West. Not only must they learn about the "market experience," they must also learn about the complex practice of capitalism in the twentieth century (Lane, 1991). Today's "free market" or, better yet, "open market," requires more sophistication from managers than the political rhetoric which accompanies it. Economies and enterprises in postcommunist countries must quickly learn to operate in their new markets without having the luxury of the transitions of the eighteenth and nineteenth centuries behind them (Polanyi, 1957). Alfred Chandler's description of managerial capitalism represents the complexity of twentieth century capitalism that must be quickly absorbed and learned: "The market remain(ed)s part of the generator of demand for goods and services, but modern business enterprise took over the coordinating flows of goods through existing processes of production, and distribution and of allocating funds and personnel for future production and distribution" (1977, p. 1).

Privatization in a Chaotic Environment

Privatization in a relatively stable environment with well-established institutional arrangements is difficult enough but especially so in the chaotic conditions of transformation (Moore, 1992). Each of these nations has conditions that would be significant challenges to the most sophisticated Western executive, let alone untested managers. Transformation has resulted in high levels of inflation and unemployment and an exacerbation of shortages of all kinds of goods as well as social and political confusion about what should be accomplished first. Inflation, though not unknown, was not in the realm of individual enterprise decision making, and unemployment was never a part of the mind-set of managers—the central-planning system controlled prices and provided "jobs for all." Shortages that were characteristic of the socialist system remain. They have been magnified by pent-up demand for all kinds of goods and services as well as by production readjustments among many enterprises. Some of the old relationships have been eliminated and new relationships have not been formed. At the same time, well-protected markets are now open to foreign firms, who are providing new products and new ways of doing business. While the chaos of change is significant in itself, what makes it so dramatic is the lack of knowledge of how to deal with it.

Linda Ackerman, an organizational development scholar, provides an interesting perspective for understanding the nature of managerial change required in these firms. She defines three types of change (1986, pp. 1–8). The first is the improvement of what is already in place and forward movement with a general idea of what the path looks like. The second is transitional, in which the organization evolves slowly, replacing current methods with new ones, all within the context of a plan with clearly defined steps. The last, transformation, "is something akin to letting go of one trapeze in mid-air before a new one swings into view. . . . Unlike transitional change, the new state is usually unknown until it begins to take shape . . . " (ibid, p. 2). Though dramatic, the description is appropriate. The enterprise will have no idea of who will own it, how it will be managed, how it will change, and what environment it will face. In essence, the new trapeze may be difficult to catch and may guarantee only limited direction.

CHALLENGES FOR MANAGEMENT IN PRIVATIZATION

Some Basics

Privatization might be an easier undertaking if all the old state enterprises were to disappear and new enterprises were to be created from scratch. Given that this is impossible, Drucker's guidance for thinking about creating viable enterprises for the future is an excellent starting point: "(1) The present business must be made effective; (2) its potential must be identified and realized; (3) it must be made into a different business for a different future" (1964, p. 4).

The Old Management System

The new enterprises will take a variety of forms and shapes, and some will look very much like similar Western organizations, down to charts, language, and methods, but much of the old will be left. Although it is easy to focus on the legacies of the past, it is important to acknowledge that people did work hard, important projects were completed, significant strides were made in many industries, and a wide range of goods and services were provided. While they did not match Western output, this was due more to the nature of the economic system than the abilities of the people themselves.

While there will be challenges in transforming the attitudes and behaviors of managers in the state enterprises, this does not mean on a per se basis that they have nothing to add to the new enterprises. Clearly, they have substantial knowledge about how things worked and, although they did not engage in change, they know about how changes were made. Moving them to a new managerial system is difficult. However, they represent a valuable source of knowledge that should not be discarded or abandoned. In many of these countries, managers come from strong scientific and technical backgrounds and in many cases are much better versed in such topics than similar Western managers. While the technological base may be outdated, it will still be the dominant one, and the change to any new system will be made easier with people who know how it works. Finally, these managers survived the socialist system. Survivability represents an important entrepreneurial behavior that needs recognition. While there are significant negative legacies from the past that must be dealt with, there are also important positive factors that should not quickly be discarded.

Central planning framed the way in which economic decisions were made and represent the key elements that must be changed in the individual enterprise. There are several critical dimensions that must be appreciated. First, managers of enterprises were dependent upon superiors; little could be done without direction and permission from above. The entire economic system worked from the top down and little coordination of performance flowed back through the system. Indeed, the end goals were framed in performance terms, primarily in quantity produced. Second, managers were dependent on subordinates to carry out actions. There were few rewards based on productivity and achievement in the sense we know. Because the managers' tenure was dependent on the way in which subordinates were treated, pressures to be more productive, for example, were not going as successful as giving in to the masses, especially since tenure in the position came from reelection by the subordinates. Third, because managers had no property rights in the activities of the enterprise and because they were evaluated by both superiors and subordinates on "little matters," they adopted a short-run outlook. Facing the fundamental dilemma of income today or income tomorrow, they readily chose the former (Kornai, 1992, pp. 466–468).

Finally, besides attempting to ameliorate the philosophies and the styles of the past, the new enterprises must adapt to the practices of the present. There are several which are at the heart of the process.

Developing a Market Orientation

Before a market orientation can be developed and implemented by an enterprise, fundamental societal conditions must be present. Lane identifies these as:

1. Information networks that freely allow exchange of information.
2. A variety of tastes, values, goods, and services that are substitutable for one another.
3. The coordination of economic exchanges through a price system.
4. A competitive environment.
5. The separation of political and economic authorities (1992, p. 12).

Given that some or most of these conditions will not be present for some time, the tasks of developing a market orientation are enormous. To some extent they will be ameliorated as firms in markets evolve and as society and economy begin to change.

The primary strategic choice for a privatizing firm is to create a market orientation. The starting point for developing a market orientation for a firm is understanding its basic assets. Although the financial assets as captured in financial documents are critical, the most important assets are customers and employees. A market-oriented firm begins by building a customer focus, which means that all employees, regardless of activity or function, recognize that business is about satisfying customers, a point that managers of many Western firms do not fully realize (Narver & Slater, 1990). A fundamental proposition is that the strategy must be defined in this way and that the organization must be restructured to carry it out. For the old socialist firm, this requires a dramatic shift from a centrally controlled production orientation to a market-based process. Preliminary results are only beginning to surface and the results are still mixed (Jackson, 1993).

Developing a customer, not simply selling to a consumer, requires the restructuring of an organization so that all employees regardless of their function understand their role in satisfying needs. This goes beyond the often cited "marketing concept" and gathering information about consumer wants and extends to the provision of goods and services. Market demand must be met with an ever-critical concern for doing better than others are able to do. How this moves from rhetoric to action is not a simple process, even for firms in market economies.

Employees, especially front-line employees such as retail clerks and service workers, must be oriented toward dealing with consumers in the context of "consumer is the only reason that we are in business." In societies in which individual needs and wants have been subjugated to the interests of the state, it is difficult to change well-entrenched values reinforced by well-developed behaviors. Acceptance of what the system provides, rather than demanding what the system should offer, would be a dramatic change in the best of times. Difficult as this is in Western society, it is more difficult when there are few examples and much work needed to undo old attitudes and behavior.

Restructuring Organizations

The second strategic choice is developing an organizational structure to carry out the strategy. This activity goes beyond the traditional analysis of restructuring in privatization, which is a process of defining and then creating viable economic entities from state-owned organizations, which can then be sold. Restructuring is a more complicated process involving creating a management structure that has as its purpose creating a viable enterprise that can operate in a market environment in which the firm participates in financial, labor, resource, and traditional product markets.

The initial step is to create a corporate governance structure. This contains two parts in Central and Eastern Europe. The first entails the creation of the concept in light of the past system, and the second is the choice of a specific form that might work in economies that lack the basic institutions of capitalism such as corporations, banks, institutional investors, and stock exchanges (Frydman & Rapaczynski, 1992, p. 262). The basic question that this exercise deals with is: who has authority and who is responsible for the operations of the firm? It is basically a question that is part of the process of establishing a business in the West, to which little attention is given until the governance structure fails. But it is a radical issue for those whose experience with private property is nonexistent.

The second step of restructuring organizations relates to the operational aspects of the new organization. The basic orientation of state enterprises was to produce and distribute goods and services and to serve specific social functions, including such things as the provision of housing, health care, and recreation. Although enterprises differ among the various economies in the region, they have some important common characteristics. Among these are:

1. They are ("were" is not the appropriate term yet) very large—larger than similar types of firms in Western economies—and each enterprise dominated the industry in which it operated (Hoch, 1992, p. 264).
2. They are highly specialized and have high degrees of vertical integration.
3. They are composed of narrowly organized operating divisions that are not well integrated into working toward a common goal.

Specialization of functions as well as specialization of industries drives the management processes. Solutions within enterprises, such as the integration of production with physical distribution let alone marketing, were never entertained because of the power that managers and superiors would have had to give up to subordinates. Since there were never market alternatives that might be able to provide what the firm needed, enterprise management never had to deal with make-or-buy decisions. They simply made, with the result that there was an ever-increasing demand for resources, which created and exacerbated what has become known as "economies of shortages" (Kornai, 1980). Divisions of an integrated enterprise engaged in extensive hoarding of supplies and to the extent that management was rewarded on a stock basis rather than a flow basis, the various units became more independent of one another.

Management and Planning

What holds an organization together is an information network. In the state-owned enterprise, what information was available was used only as a means of control and that from top to bottom. Little information was shared among departments and very little if any information flowed upward from users back toward producers. Central planning laid out the rules of the game, and for each enterprise activities were connected to an overall plan for the economy. In each sector of the economy, individual enterprises received directives in regard to what to produce, how much to produce, how to produce, and when to produce. Planning did not include the participation of those who had to administer the plan and to make certain it was carried out. It was based on quantitative quotas that were neither connected to demand conditions, on the one hand, nor to supply, on the other.

These quotas are the socialist system's equivalent of the market-based resource-allocation principle.

Planning, in the sense of having control and accountability, really were never part of the central plan nor at the level of the enterprise. When evaluations were carried out they were judgments between the budget and the actual performance, and were regularly subject to revision by showing how production really did meet plans. At the level of the enterprise, accountability was defined in readjusting the plan goals to fit the results. Simply put, plans were always reached, because their goals were rewritten in terms of reality. This history makes it difficult to introduce planning as it is known in Western business. Planning was part of the mechanism through which everything in the old system went wrong.

Understanding Markets and Buyer Behavior

The basic notion of markets as understood in open economies is not well developed at the firm level in postcommunist countries. In the traditional "Soviet system," firms and consumers were all part of one process. Manufacturers did not have to seek buyers, nor did intermediate distributors have to seek final distributors or the ultimate consumers. What we refer to as the marketing channel was no more than a crude logistical system in which each of the succeeding parts played no more than depot roles in the distribution of goods. The idea of market information flowing from the market back through the system did not exist, nor was there any of the promotional activities related with moving goods and services down the system. Wholesalers and retailers served primarily as depots in which merchandise was stored. The practice of buying and selling through negotiation basically did not exist.

Consumer demands were accepted as best known by central planners; hence, manufacturers did not have to worry about adopting products to any known desires that might be held by consumers. The asking of questions obviously had no role to play nor did the reaction of consumers to products. This did not mean that consumers were satisfied but that they were made to be satisfied by what was available. Without the pressure from intermediate and ultimate purchasers and without competition among producers and distributors there was no need to worry about making improvements in products.

As the result of nationalization of industries, they were restructured along lines to at best maximize economies of scale. Industries were highly specialized to gain hoped for production and distribution benefits. With such a format, standardization became critical. The net result was strong vertical industries that had little to do with one another at any horizontal level in what we might conceive of as competitive relationships and a minimization of transactions within the distribution system. This greatly affected and still affects the development of active consumers, especially ultimate consumers in the marketplace. Given economies of shortages and limited choice, market participators became "takers" rather than "formers" of markets. Consumers in the region, in spite of significant changes, still are not aware of their role in an open, market economy. On the other hand, sellers, to the extent that they see opportunities to exploit markets, much as the state organizations before them, continue with their old practices. The basic structural change is that in many cases ownership has moved from the state to private owners. Management has not always changed, giving rise to the one-sided nature of markets (Savitt, 1993).

There is a strong tendency to overestimate the similarities between developing economies and even poorer parts of Western economies and those of Central and Eastern Europe. As enticing as these similarities are, there is great danger in equating them, especially in light of the early success both in consumer and industrial markets since the start of the transformation period. The successes have been real enough, though the underlying reasons reflect factors other than simply a turn toward a market economy. The opening of the market made business look easy; however, what drove much of the success was pent-up demand, especially for Western goods, and the long period of shortages of all kinds. Counteracting the immediate successes has been the dramatic transformation costs noted earlier. High levels of inflation and ever-increasing unemployment rates have dramatically affected purchasing power and will continue to do so for some time. These two factors greatly affect general buyer behavior, which has basically been formulated around "takers" rather than "demanders."

More importantly, consumers of all types in the region have different behavior patterns than those in the West, both in terms of process as well as criteria. They are not fully aware of their responsibilities as participants in a market economy. Although the stages of buyer behavior as a problem-solving activity are universal, consumers go through them differently in various settings. Consumers move through problem recognition, search, choice, and postdecision evaluation, but the emphases and outcomes are different in postcommunist economies. More time is spent searching because of the shortages and limited market information. More time is required than by Western standards and the resulting search does not often reveal an adequate assortment from which choice can be made. Choice does not arise from analysis of alternatives but as a result of what is physically available. There is extensive product substitution without regard to the basic need that sparked the search. Available supply drives the system. For example, clothing is purchased when food was wanted. Postdecision evaluation as a critical element of the process and an important part of the market economy in the context of market power does not exist.

Educating the buyer becomes a fundamental challenge at all levels in the economy. How quickly this is recognized as an important part of the transformation is unclear. Clearly, foreign firms, as they enter these markets, are moving quickly to create favorable conditions through which to bring consumers to them (Savitt, 1993). Whether local firms will get close enough to this perspective is greatly influenced by the degree to which they understand the privatization process and the conditions of the market economy.

PERSPECTIVES

Privatization will only work with effective management. There is no short course to knowing which system will work best. Developing market-oriented firms is the starting point but, like much of the recent history in the region, the final results will be influenced by many factors. The present discussion has proceeded on the assumption that Western techniques can be transported into the region with only minor changes, that is an empirical test whose answer will come only after a great number of experiments. The challenge is to construct them carefully so that they will work, otherwise we may see these firms slip back to their old styles of management. We have high hopes for the success of postcommunist economies without really knowing how to make it all happen.

NOTE

I wish to acknowledge the important contributions of Mr. Carsten Betterman, my graduate research assistant, whose dedicated efforts helped shape a large study from which this chapter is drawn.

REFERENCES

Ackerman, L. (1986). Development, transition, or transformation: Question of change in organizations. *OD Practioner,* December: 1–8.

Chandler, A.D. (1977). *The Visible Hand: The Managerial Revolution in American Business.* Cambridge, MA: Harvard University Press.

Drucker, P.F. (1964). *Managing for Results.* New York: Perennial Library.

Ellerman, D.P., Vahic, A. & Petrin, T. (1992). Privatization controversies in the east and west. In M.P. Claudon & T.L. Gutner (Eds.), *Comrades Go Private: Strategies for Eastern European Privatization,* pp. 117–146. New York: New York University Press.

Frydman, R. & Rapaczynski, A. (1992). Privatization and corporate governance in Eastern Europe. In G. Winkeler (Ed.), *Central and Eastern Europe Roads to Growth,* pp. 255–285. Washington, D.C.: International Monetary Fund and World Bank.

Hoch, P. (1992). Changing formation and privatization. *Acta Oeconomica,* 43: 263–280.

Jackson, T. (1993). Pioneer looks east for profit. *The Financial Times,* April 16, 13.

Kocsis, G. (1992). The uncertain state of privatization. *The New Hungarian Quarterly,* 128: 113–120.

Kornai, J. (1980). *Economics of Shortage.* Amsterdam: North Holland.

——— (1992). *The Socialist System: The Political Economy of Communism.* Princeton, N.J.: Princeton University Press.

Köves, A. & Marer, P. (1991). Economic liberalization in Eastern Europe and in Market Economies. In A. Köves & P. Marer (Eds.), *Foreign Economic Liberalization: Transformations in Socialist and Market Economies,* pp. 15–36. Boulder, CO: Westview Press.

Lane, R.E. (1991). *The Market Experience.* Cambridge: Cambridge University Press.

Lieberman, I.W. (1993). *Privatization in Latin America and Eastern Europe in the Context of Political and Economic Reform.* Paper presented at Lehigh University Seminar on Liberalization, Integration and Privatization. Bethlehem, PA.

Mejstrik, M. & Burger, J. (1993). *Vouchers, Buyouts, Auctions: The Battles for Privatization in Czechoslovakia.* Paper presented at Lehigh University Seminar on Liberalization, Integration and Privatization. Bethlehem, PA.

Moore, J. (1992). British privatization—taking capitalism to the people. *Harvard Business Review,* 73(1): 115–122.

Narver, J.C. & Slater, S.F. (1990). The effect of market orientation on business profitability. *Journal of Marketing,* 54: 20–35.

Polanyi, K. (1957). *The great transformation: The political and economic origins of our times.* Boston: Beacon Press.

Savitt, R. (1993). *Challenges to the Development of Marketing in Central and Eastern Europe.* Working paper, No. 93-003. School of Business Administration, The University of Vermont.

2

Learning from Mismanagement in Polish Organizations[1]

Alicja Kozdrój-Schmidt and David D. Van Fleet

INTRODUCTION

The Polish management system of the 1980s was designed with a belief in the automatic character of a market economy and the effectiveness of competition. However, this was supposed to occur in a quasi-market, without adequate managerial knowledge of market economies. What is more, the most recent experiences with management came from the reform efforts of the 1970s, which were based on "3×S" (self-dependence, self-management, self-financing). This was more slogan than practice (except for self-management, in the form of workers' councils) and was adopted with few changes in the 1980s. Under prevailing conditions, success and advanced reforms through the implementation of a market economy are not very likely.

During the 1980s, inflation and an unbalanced market, in which many enterprises enjoyed monopolistic positions and political and economic authorities sought control over enterprises, there was a need for restrictions, which took a variety of forms. Each system of restrictions bred resistance, a search for ways of bypassing them, pressure from interest groups, and employee protests. These results suggest problems in achieving effective competition in a quasi-market.

Poland entered the 1990s with a new political situation and an economic crisis. After the first parliamentary elections with the participation of the Polish opposition (1989) and in cooperation with Western specialists, the first noncommunist government began to work on in-depth economic reform. The objective was to stop hyperinflation and stimulate privatization. Soon after its election, the new government declared that the State and its agencies would no longer be the owners of all economic enterprises. The government's job was to create conditions for the development of private enterprise in a market economy. Poland started privatization in 1990 (Czarny, 1992; Dietl, 1992; Lipton & Sachs, 1990; Sachs & Lipton, 1990; *Economic Program for Poland,* 1989). It was believed that changes in the business environment would force companies to behave "rationally" and increase production and sales. Unfortunately, the current difficult economic and social situation shows that this belief was oversimplified (Cole, 1992). Privatization alone is not the answer.

For years the Polish economy was mismanaged. A deep crisis in work organization (in invisible and visible forms) developed in Poland. That crisis has become
severe since the end of the 1970s. Now, Poland wants to develop a market
economy. To do so, it must correct basic mistakes and use a managerial approach
to all changes that take place. Poland cannot rely solely on privatization and
self-starting improvement processes. The government will have to direct changes
toward people, who are Poland's greatest assets. Before this can be done, an
economic and market structure must be in place. As a market economy develops,
there will need to be a focus on the development and implementation of managerial practices that effectively utilize human resources.

This chapter will describe and assess past and current management practices,
primarily in state-owned companies in Poland. Implications will then be described
that would better equip Poland for transformation into a market economy.

CAUSES AND CONSEQUENCES OF MISMANAGEMENT
IN POLAND

It has only been the developments of the last few years that have forced on
Poland (and other former socialist countries) an awareness of the imperative of
modern management—to fully utilize human resources. The role of managers is
vitally important; indeed, the management style that an organization uses has been
called "The Ultimate Advantage" (Lawler, 1992, p. 13). Unfortunately, Poland has
tried many overly simplistic answers. For example, among Polish academics one
often heard statements like "it is enough to pay well" or "the wage fund for the
work force must be tied to the enterprise's income." On the other hand, practical
solutions tended to combine ideological guidelines built into state policy.

Attention to human resources is an important but neglected topic in Polish
management theory and practice. During the 1950s its neglect, which led to such
practices as identical pay to all workers on the same job regardless of performance,
became apparent as efficiency and quality plummeted. During the 1960s attempts
were made to deal with low efficiency through the use of sophisticated pay
incentives. Among those were: 1) incentives from profit addressed to both the
whole work force as well as to management personnel in 1961–63; 2) a point
bonus system for white-collar workers in state enterprises begun by the Council
of Ministers in May 1964; and 3) the so-called Gomulka system of material
interest incentives of the Council of Ministers and Central Council of the Trade
Unions in July 1970.

The results of these efforts were meager at best. During the 1970s, it became
apparent that within the then existing social–economic system there was no
possibility for dealing with this problem. On the other hand, there were almost no
effective professional (educated, experienced, etc.), managers.[2] For many years,
the term "manager" was not even used in organizations. Nevertheless, with a view
to upgrading the role of managers in the economy, those interested in this problem
began to use the term "managerial cadres" (kadra kierownicza) with respect to

managing directors, their deputies, and heads of plants. This change, however, did not have much influence; it was just impossible to automatically change "directors" into managers while promotions and jobs were granted only to Party activists (Glinski, 1990b).

Simultaneously, many institutional forms of worker participation emerged: "worker competition," production meetings, and the movement of rationalizers (industrial experts) among shop-floor employees. It may be surprising, but these early forms of workers' activism led to increasing passiveness among managers as well as decreasing their role in managing organizations. Indeed, the emergence of the Party administrative system and workers councils were rather natural developments under these circumstances (Glinski, 1990b). Conditions inherent in the system also made it impossible to implement certain management techniques developed in industrialized countries. Instead of management, Poland had party administration and the whole economy was treated as a centrally operated company regulated by the government and the Communist Party (Glinski, 1987, 1990b,c,d). The occurrence of mismanagement was greatly influenced by the external environment facing business. The Polish external environment, especially its political institutions (Party organizations in companies, trade unions, and workers councils), predominated. These were institutionally anchored to the internal environment, so that both the core and the periphery of organizations were controlled by political and legal elements of the external environment. This created the situation seen as mismanagement in the 1960s by the United Nations Industrial Development Office (UNIDO) and again 1989 by the United Nations Development Program (UNDP) mission to Poland.

THE POLISH RESPONSE TO MANAGERIAL PROBLEMS

Cultures, such as those of Japan (Lincoln, 1989) and other Asian countries (Onedo, 1991), have created conditions for effective management based on their particular characteristics (see also Ishikawa, 1986; Nowakowski, 1987). Others, such as Germany (Welford, 1990), Sweden (Naylor, 1990), and the United States (Porter, 1990), have combined enforcement by managers with participation by employees to establish effective managerial systems. Until now, Poland has done none of this. The following sections touch upon aspects of the practice of management, noting what seems to be recommended for U.S. companies and briefly describing current Polish practices. Descriptions of Polish experience (see Table 1) suggest that many current practices have not been highly successful.

The Manager's Role

Research underscores the role of the manager as a major participant in formulating tasks, evaluating effects, and establishing the consequences of performance. Managers through their knowledge, experience, competence, and commitment, are instrumental in organizational effectiveness. The managerial role has been

Table 1
Mismanagement in Polish Organizations

Management Issue	Typical "Polish Practice"	Suggested "Best Practice"
Manager's Role	Weak leadership Work brigades more powerful than managers	Strong leadership Set example Administer system
Management Practice Involvement	Small economic units, partnership groups, workers councils	Participation and ownership important to commitment
Pay practices	Piece-rate incentives, low wages for equity, nonperformance factors Basic functions: to prevent conflicts, to adjust for inflation, to compensate for working conditions, to retain, motivate, and to facilitate employees' growth	Pay for performance—make visible the link between better performance and better pay. Basic functions: to motivate, to retain, to compensate for working conditions, to facilitate employees' growth, and to adjust for inflation
Job evaluation	Overreliance on UMEWAP, disrupted by government policy, internal and external equity controlled by government	External and internal wage and salary determination within a company's control
Performance appraisal	No real work standards, "pay-giving" standards, subjective judgments and opinions when required[1]	Establish job related standards, compare results to goals, evaluate, use results as a basis for personnel decisions[2]

[1]The performance appraisal objective is to justify wage/salary increments; the results are hardly utilized in a company; linkage to individual reward allocation is extremely weak.
[2]The basic relation should be as follows: performance → appraisal → reward.

compared to the brain and the nervous system as an enforcer of results (Glinski, 1985). Without careful measurement of results and linking wages to results, there is not likely to be an effective system leading to improved performance.

The establishment of such a system can easily result in conflict. When management does not feel strong and consistent support (both substantial and moral), they will become tolerant, yielding, and even tend not to notice unacceptable behavior. This is precisely what happened on a very large scale in Poland. What is more, this also was shown in research conducted on the strongly propagated (by government and Communist Party) brigade system of work organization. The results showed unequivocally that the creation and leadership of highly effective self-management work groups is impossible without specialized managerial knowledge, which cannot be obtained by spontaneous interaction between group members.

Work brigades have received much attention in Poland since 1985. Called "partnership groups," they have become very popular. Within the so-called "second stage of the economic reform," they became not only an important topic but were even treated as the key to the solution of economic problems in the Polish economy. Several specific elements characterize the Polish "brigade system" (see also Kozdroj, 1986a,b, 1988; and *Zespolowe Formy Organizacji Pracy,* 1989):

1. The brigades received the right to determine wage levels for individual members of the brigade or employees from other organizational units of the enterprises periodically involved in cooperation with them.
2. First-line supervisors were eliminated from the brigades.
3. Almost no changes in work organization were introduced (although some elements of job rotation and flexibility emerged).
4. A group piece-rate system instead of an individual one was introduced.
5. Brigades had very strong negotiating positions. The group was used in manipulative ways by its members to gain significant financial rewards.
6. Brigades tended to create their own production plans (they even negotiated contracts independently with clients in some instances).
7. Responsibility along with accountability was delegated to these groups.

This approach, while it had some elements in common with Western autonomous groups and self-regulating teams (Grootings et al., 1986; Aguren et al., 1984) as well as with approaches being attempted in the Soviet Union, extended the power of workers well beyond their jobs and was, as a result, less effective than it could have been. Indeed, just as Employee Stock Ownership Plans (ESOPs) do not seem to be a highly effective way of competing in terms of net income (Park & Rosen, 1990; Gilbert, 1990), the use of employee empowerment over nonjob issues (such as contract negotiations and the actual allocation of financial rewards independent of performance or even goal attainment) proved to be a poor approach to management in Poland. Indeed, this seems to provide anecdotal evidence that the use of empowerment should be contingent upon the situation, as has recently been argued (Bowen & Lawler, 1992).

The brigade system was first of all seen by managers as a way of avoiding restrictions put on the enterprises in terms of compensation. It was a sign or symptom of a belief in the dominating power of monetary rewards and the self-motivation of employees who can thereby experience independence and democracy in their total work environment, not just with regard to their jobs. It is interesting that it was not the first time in Polish "business history" that a repetition of old "well-known slogans" was used to justify change.

Management Practice

Many managerial approaches adopted during the last few years can be characterized as attempts to achieve motivation in the specific situation of "socialist state-owned enterprises" through greater involvement.

Motivation Through Involvement. This involvement is achieved through the use of small economic units, partnership groups, and workers' councils.

"Enterprise small economic units" (zakladowe zespoly gospodarcze) were created, similar to those in Hungary, as elements of the black market. The main idea was to rent machines, raw materials, and facilities to small voluntarily formed groups of employees who were retired, on maternity leave, or worked in their spare time. Every task had its own "price," which was paid to the group. In this way, employees could earn extra money in their own company.

"Partnership groups" refers to the brigade work organization and a wage system based in practice on the group piece-rate system built onto the ideology of participation, industrial and general political democracy, and partnership in an organization.

Workers' councils were created in enterprises and, at this level, employee interests were articulated and control over administrative decisions and actions were carried out.[3] While the literature seems to suggest that greater participation may lead to higher levels of commitment, the Polish experience has been that participation leads to control due to the particular political and social structures in place.

Pay Practices. Early efforts at achieving motivation through payment practices were limited primarily to piece-rate systems tied to close supervision over employees.[4] It was assumed that piece-rates would introduce certain automatic links between wages and efficiency. It is interesting to note that this assumption, made in the West at the turn of the century, was not accepted in Poland until after World War II and then was accepted as the "most fair solution," similar to the socialist principle "to each according to his/her work." But, while this assumption may be appealing ideologically, it has not proven to be very practical, since it continually fails (Albinowski, 1988). It seems impossible to achieve the ideological principle embodied in the assumption because of low wages, inadequate norms, and/or the impact of market forces. In addition, inflation, directive tasks, "worker competition," and the elimination of highly qualified managers and specialists all contributed to its failure.

Piece-rate systems were developed in Poland at a time when knowledge as to their limits was becoming accepted worldwide and other countries were implementing solutions with new, additional elements based on suggestions from recent research and developments in management knowledge (Lawler, 1992, chapters 7 and 8). Piece-rate systems in Poland, then, became popular at the same time that many Western companies started to withdraw from them and began to implement wage systems based on job or skill evaluation (base pay) with incentives (bonuses) for outstanding performance (see for example *Reform in Sweden*, 1977).

At a basic level, management theory and research suggest that to achieve effectiveness a manager should make sure that those who have performed best (with respect to the amount and quality of the effects of work) should always be the most highly rewarded and the most satisfied with the rewards (wages and/or salaries) received (Milkovich & Wigdor, 1991). Employees should see that those who work better really do receive more than those who work poorly or only at an average level (Milkovich & Newman, 1990; Lawler, 1990, 1986).

In a market economy, wages are based on labor markets, prevailing wage rates, the cost of living, productivity, and other factors, both without and within the organization. These factors are the basis upon which strategic, tactical, and operational decisions are made to lead to the achievement of organizational goals. Unfortunately, for many years Polish practices in this area were dominated by central-government regulations. From the central, national level, decisions were reached about a variety of compensation issues including: basic rates and rules of their increase, rigid rules for creating "wage funds" (a company's payroll),[5] fair wages differences, job evaluation, performance appraisal, and fringe benefits.

At the same time, the central government was the only owner and administrator of pension plans and medical insurance. On the other hand, simultaneously, there was the model of "low salaries/wages," which was accepted by authorities as the "socialist philosophy" and the realization of social equity. These conditions led to several side-effects, among which were: a) low work standards (job standardization) that allowed employees/workers to surpass established (given) norms and get higher wages; b) a decrease in quality control and the performance appraisal of work results; c) the habit of working extra on a part-time basis; and, finally, d) disciplinary problems.

This philosophy of "low wages" caused other side effects, too. The most important was an overemphasis on a number of different pay elements not tied to performance (i.e., fringe benefits for time of service or supervisory/managerial position, paid vacation, allowances, etc.). Because employees were legally entitled to those elements of pay, they claimed (asserted in most cases) their right to these elements as a bargaining tool. All elements of employee compensation created, in their opinion, fixed, stable, and, finally, guaranteed compensation. So almost no part of compensation was based on performance. Compensation played a role only in retention; keeping all employees (not just those highly qualified and "valuable" for an organization) became the standard situation.

Even changes introduced in the 1980s had very little influence. These changes were based on the assumption of increased enterprises' responsibility and freedom in creating their own wage policies. Unfortunately, deep economic and political crises resulted in growing pressure on wages not related to the effects achieved by the enterprise as a whole and by individuals performing their tasks ("Place w okresie zmian systemu gospodarczego," 1990; "Raport o placach w gospodarce uspolecznionej w latach 1982–1989," 1990; Czajka, 1990; Krencik, 1989; Koz-droj, 1986a).

Job Evaluation. Most contemporary organizations use two basic methods to determine wages and salaries: job evaluation and performance appraisal (Schuler, 1992; Milkovich & Newman, 1990). Job evaluation provides a "hierarchy map" of different types of jobs in an organization. The methods used in Western companies vary widely and, indeed, in some organizations a "skills" approach is replacing the "jobs" approach (Lawler, 1992, pp. 144–171). Unfortunately, in Poland the UMEWAP-87 system (Universal Method of Job Evaluation) was adopted in 1987 for the whole economy and for all types of organizations. While it is true that Polish organizations were allowed to use somewhat different methods, they could do so on the condition that these could be "transported" into the universal system.

This overreliance on a single, job-based system occurred despite discussions among experts and suggestions and even warnings from Western specialists ("Work and Pay," 1986). What is more, this overreliance was reinforced through a parliamentary bill. The government wanted to keep control over compensation in companies through the use of UMEWAP, but it created a series of management errors in enterprises while overregulating compensation policies and practices.

Overregulation existed for all aspects of compensation—wage level (by controlling wage differentiation between companies and evaluating fairness of wage levels between companies, branches, and industries); wage structure (through state regulations defining possible elements of compensation packages and approval of the job evaluation system used in a company); and individual wage levels (through job evaluation and fiscal control). Companies in such situations were unable to create their own policies and practices. They become "administrators" and "realizers" (producers) of state decisions, and neither executives nor operating managers had responsibility in this area. So state control over compensation prevented the companies' managers and supervisors from exerting influence; every decision and salary recommendation had to have approval and strong justification in state regulations. The situation became much more complicated with growing inflation. In effect, the job evaluation system became "stale" at the very moment at which it was created.

Remuneration in the form of wages is an important motivator, under the condition that wages and the effects of work are linked and are not "modified" by the presence of hard environmental factors independent of the organization and its managers. Unfortunately, this is disrupted by government policy in the area of specific social welfare. It was possible in Poland, because of the existence of the "economy of deficit" and the crippled market that allowed the state/government to manipulate these "rare" goods, creating a special category of employee's privilege (e.g., distribution of cars, apartments, and gardens). Polish organizations were, in effect, rewarding A (Party membership and attendance, acceptance of low wages, etc.) while hoping for B (high quality and performance) (see Kerr, 1975).

Performance Appraisal. The results of work and its evaluation must be part of the "contract" in which a manager and an employee, as precisely as possible, agree upon expectations and obligations. This, on the other hand, requires a model for measuring and evaluating the effects of work (performance appraisal). Performance appraisal is the means by which the contract is "transported" into the evaluation of results and, in the end, how rewards (pay raises, bonuses, promotions, etc.) are determined (Fisher et al., 1990; Lawler, 1990; Lawler et al., 1989).

Determining standards, norms, or patterns of performance on the basis of an analysis of job/task requirements is the starting point in this process (Borman, 1991; Latham & Wexley, 1981). The process should serve to determine future goals and tasks and be conducive to employee self-development (Lawler et al., 1989). This is especially relevant in Poland, in a situation of crisis, where it is necessary to create a framework for measurement and appraisal that reflects the conditions for introducing the basic principles of management (Glinski, 1985).

Such an analysis enables management to determine the critical (from the point of view of the objectives of the organization) behaviors and to formulate effective programs and managerial strategies (wages, training and education, selection, and personnel policy, for example) based on them (Porter et al., 1973). This, then, forms the basis for the realization of the interdependent interests of the company, its managers, and its employees.

In theory, the measurement and evaluation of work performance can include an analysis of the use of resources at particular posts or at organizational units of the company in relation to the effects of work. It is the basis upon which the effectiveness of management is evaluated—the productive use of resources for the achievement of set goals (Glinski, 1990b). Performance is a function of many factors—qualifications and knowledge, motivation to get the job done, the intellectual and physical effort put in, attitudes toward work, accepted work values, the leadership style used by the managers, work methods, working conditions, and rewards. Performance determines the value of the work that has, in fact, been provided. Wages (as an individually valued form of recognition) should be competitive to such an extent as to be attractive to capable and talented people who take advantage of these attributes in their work and perform at high levels.

Unfortunately, the Polish situation falls short of this normative description. Managers have avoided this fundamental function of work—setting standards and performance appraisal. It is interesting that formal documents and procedures were written but not practiced. As an example, consider a very fundamental and "classic" example—work standardization. In 1988 the Institute of Management of the Polish Academy of Sciences conducted research on work standardization in the Polish economy (Kozdroj, 1990). On the basis of statistical analysis, interviews, and a survey of the literature the Institute reached the following general conclusions.

Since 1945 Poland has not had the capability to establish work standards. This does not mean that Polish managers lack knowledge of methods and techniques. It is a situational inability created by a dictatorship of workers interested in keeping the level of their wages high. This situation resulted from rigid basic wage rates established at a low level that stimulated the tendency to establish work standards at a low level, too. Almost all of the time, standards resulted from worker–manager negotiations about the final level of wages. Consequently, such practices led not only to the devaluation of this organizational technique but to the emergence of a pathological situation in this area. For many years there was an aversion to these managerial techniques in Poland. The Institute's study indicated that negative characteristics of work standards worsened over time, while attempts to eliminate or at least reduce those characteristics had little impact. Not only were the standards themselves a sensitive issue but even the reasons underlying them were questioned.

The reluctance to apply work standards was understandable. Action-based verifications of standards as used hitherto had neither fulfilled the basic task of adjusting standards to changing organizational and technical conditions nor been reliable. A widely practiced and spontaneous procedure was to set relatively low standards so that employees could surpass them significantly and earn higher wages. As a result, a new category of "pay-giving" standards was introduced. It should be emphasized that the evaluation of the practice of work standardization by Polish specialists was extremely consistent, and often described as fiction (Kordaszewski, 1982) or denaturalization (Roszkowski, 1986). These descriptions were not surprising, since the average level of work-standard performance for the total economy surpassed, for example, 130% in 1987 and in some sectors even reached 190%, and workers reaching 200% of standard over more than forty years were not exceptions. One wonders whether and to what extent "workers competition" as well as something called the "picture of the leader of socialist workers" (exceeding his standards at least 3 times) had an influence on this phenomenon.

Work standardization is a very specific example and is only one part of performance appraisal. Nevertheless, it shows that Polish managers, on the one hand, were weak and unable to implement and properly use the technique and, on the other hand, that the environment was not conducive to it. But the question is why? The determinants and factors that seemed to account for this included:

1. The system of a centrally managed economy and its implications for management systems and practices in enterprises.
2. The domination of politics in enterprises—the Party organization making the main decisions in enterprises, without responsibility for their results.
3. The wage policy and its implementation.
4. The declining quality of managerial and technical personnel as result of the functioning of the centralized system of administration (instead of management), the criteria for selecting managers, and the system of training (or rather the lack of training) in the field of management.

These factors created managers fully dependent on decisions made by the Party organization ("guidelines") and governmental agencies ("rules"). In the 1980s, there emerged another "partner"—workers' councils and self-government ideology. Workers' councils have been present in Polish organizations since 1956, when they were created for the first time in state-owned companies. They were very active initially, but around 1958 they became passive and were controlled by the Party organization. The revitalization of workers' councils occurred after the strikes of 1980–1981 and then, even during the period of martial law, they had a special role—that of opposition.[6]

THE NEED FOR TRANSFORMATION—THE WAY OUT

Trying to achieve managerial success through involvement seemed like a natural response to the business environment in Poland. Yet that approach and most others have turned out to be less than completely effective because workers were not properly prepared. The new political, social, and economic situation in Poland caused involvement to quickly lose its relevance and even created a natural process by which it may disappear altogether. It is clear that new approaches to management are necessary, both for the "old type" of state-owned companies as well as the "new type" of privately owned ones. Nevertheless, it is worth noting that, while private companies can build their management systems and organization culture from the very beginning, state-owned companies have to deal with established structures, procedures, and constituencies that already exist. Even though the privatization process may be considered as relatively successful and seems to be flourishing, any suggestions about management have to be addressed to state-owned companies, since such companies still dominate the Polish economy.

Specialists from highly developed countries seem to be correct when they advise Poland to introduce modern management, management training and development, and the use of human resources management. Specialists in Poland have a tendency to put more emphasis on solutions involving ownership. Many Polish experts believe in the effectiveness of the "invisible hand of privatization" and of a tight fiscal policy, while others believe in employee shareholding. Meanwhile, managers are more and more in need of "effective management systems." What is needed is a system conducive to the growth of work effectiveness that ensures "social peace" in the company. But, while many managing directors repeat the slogan that effective motivation lies in higher wages, that is only part of the truth.

What should be emphasized is that ineffective management breeds not only social or economic problems but also political problems.[7] Without effective management, it will be difficult to realize the transformation of the Polish economy, which in turn will lead to further political crises. For instance, the present centrally controlled wage policy needs to be relaxed. Basic principles should be established to make up the framework for such issues as labor law and minimum wages, but enterprise managers should make the individual decisions. This means that Polish managers need to be trained in human resource decisions.

Poland needs to develop managers who are highly motivated, experienced, educated, and success-oriented, and who may make decisions independently. The experience and education should, obviously, be linked to market economies, as well. Those managers, then, would ascribe to the following. 1) Managers coordinate the determination of policy in the area of employment and wages; they are the ones who take the leading role in this process and are responsible for its implementation. 2) Job evaluation and performance appraisal, including job analysis and work standardization, are basic instruments for determining the internal wage structure of an enterprise and, as such, are fundamental to the determination of individual wages. 3) Employees are rewarded not for "being employed" or for "coming to work" (membership rewards) but for concrete effects and contributions toward achieving the objectives of the organization (performance-related rewards).

BRINGING ABOUT TRANSFORMATION

How is such transformation to be accomplished, and how long will it take? These questions are very important, very difficult, and may evoke considerable disagreement, particularly while the above-mentioned changes are occurring. Nevertheless, as indicated in Table 2, our answers focus on those questions in what seem to be key areas—the manager's role and managerial practice.

The Manager's Role

Empowerment of Managers. It could be argued that the empowerment of managers is a strategy that could lead to the danger of dictatorship by managers. That is not very likely if the necessary ownership controls are in place. However,

Table 2
Suggested Managerial Changes in Polish Organizations

Management Issue	Recommended Changes
Manager's Role	Engage in training and development to increase leadership
Management Practice	
Involvement	Further reduce the number of state-owned businesses
	Focus on informal participation through modified work teams
Pay practices	Establish merit pay
	Eliminate employment contracts with compensation specifications
	Eliminate "popiwek"
Job evaluation	Allow more labor market variability and flexibility
Performance appraisal	Establish performance standards that are job related, develop objectivity, utilize

empowerment can be a real benefit for companies but both managers and employees need to be empowered and, just as the extent of empowerment for employees should vary with the situation (Bowen & Lawler, 1992), that of managers should, too. Nonetheless, it is necessary to remember that Polish business practice did not have the opportunity to go through all the developmental stages of management that American companies did and so the use of empowerment must be gradual and depend upon the extent of managerial training and development.

Intensive Managerial Training at all Levels. Training should be conducted at all organizational levels from top executives through operational employees. That training should focus on the fundamentals of management and on human resources management with a special emphasis on compensation issues.[8] The translation of basic textbooks by top scholars throughout the world and a series of case studies from Western companies presenting the assumptions, principles, and practices in this area would be the first stage in the realization of this recommendation.

Management Practice

Implementation of Management Knowledge and Practice. This recommendation cannot be questioned. Piecemeal actions currently being taken, primarily by the newly established business schools, are not enough. What is needed is quality, long-term education, not short-term, profit-oriented courses (Fogel, 1991).

Allowing More Variability and Flexibility. More variability and flexibility in the labor market must be permitted. To accomplish this, the existing labor code must be liberalized. Managers need more autonomy, although it would still be essential to monitor discriminatory practices. Changes must be made in regulations concerning severance pay. Downsizing and lay-offs go along with the reconstruction of companies. Because of existing regulations, it is extremely costly for Polish companies to lay off employees. Since these companies are usually in bad financial condition, mandatory severance pay for laid-off employees worsens their situation and extends their recovery period. The lay-off procedure requiring approval of labor unions and workers' councils is another interrelated factor that must be eliminated.

Elimination of Politics in Polish Companies. Politics in Polish companies is still a hot topic (Mapes, 1992), but it must be eliminated. Associated with this recommendation, workers' councils must be modified[9] and informal forms of involvement through Western-type work teams should be implemented. It is tentatively suggested that legislation may be necessary to achieve this goal in state-owned enterprises. If managers are to be responsible and accountable for strategic decisions within a company, they need room for action and for displaying their capabilities.

CONCLUSIONS

These suggestions and recommendations may seem trivial, simple, and obvious to a Westerner. For Poland, they are complicated, complex, and obscure. Nevertheless, we would like to stress that Poland and Polish companies need these and two other kinds of remedies, namely: 1) concentration on internal environment with particular emphasis on changes within the structure and distribution of power, and 2) the development of managerial potential.

The need for the implementation of management knowledge and practice is unquestionable. It is generally a "back to basics" movement. It could be perceived as an overemphasis on the empowerment of managers, although a well-developed board of directors will see to it that the danger of a managers' dictatorship will not develop. Nevertheless, it can be argued that Poland cannot successfully eliminate mismanagement by "jumping into" the futurist picture of effective high-involvement organizations without the necessary fundamentals and minimum experience in basic management practice in a market economy.[11]

NOTES

1. The authors thank Gary Anders and David Bowen, both of Arizona State University West, and John O'Dwyer of the University of Western Ontario, who read and commented on an earlier version of this paper, and two anonymous reviewers for their constructive recommendations. This chapter is an extension of the results of research conducted between 1986 and 1989 by B. Glinski and A. Kozdroj at the Institute of Management, Polish Academy of Sciences, Warsaw, Poland.

2. "In highly industrialized countries, managers are an elite, like political, intellectual, art, and scholarly ones. In the vision of a healthy social structure, this kind of socially competent disposition of social authority to managers is in Poland the main element that is lacking, although not the only one. . . . It has to be added that, in the economy of most of the socialist countries, managerial elites had been consciously driven back to marginal positions by not very clever politicians of the Stalinist style" (Glinski, 1990a, p. 23).

3. This approach was not similar to the German one introduced in the 1950s. "While at the beginning it [the workers' council] was the source and safeguard of a better personnel policy and increased company independence, it later changed into the alternative to management and a factor of political power" (Glinski, 1990b).

4. However, even many early piece-rate systems mentioned changing the patterns of employee–management relations. See, for example, the work of Taylor (Taylor, 1911) or that of the Polish management expert, Adamiecki (Marsh, 1975).

5. Generally speaking, the average compensation and employment in December, prior to a tax year, is the basis for establishing the payroll in the coming year. An increase is possible only in relation to an index based on the inflation rate, which was frequently kept lower through alternations in the "basket of goods" used in its computation. A company may keep 50% of savings achieved through downsizing (although only if the company laid off employees individually and kept lay-offs to less than 10% of the work force; if a group lay-off occurred, other regulations came into play). Payroll includes all money paid to employees, including wages/salaries, bonuses, fringe benefits, and loans. A punitive tax

(called "popiwek") reaches up to 500% for every percent of excess payments over the allowed increase.

6. Labor unions were banned from Polish companies after martial law was implemented in December 1982, while workers' councils were present and active. Nevertheless, this does not mean that the workers' councils were controlled by the government and the Communist Party. For a more complete discussion, see "Still behind bars, 1983" "Poles need more, 1982" and "The institutionalization of martial law, 1982."

7. The intensification of strikes in early 1992 in Poland seems to be a relatively strong argument in support of this thesis.

8. In the area of wages, Polish management must return to and observe the fundamental principles for effective financial motivation—the wages themselves. In the first place, this would entail changing of the present wage policy on the central level to introduce greater freedom for enterprises by having the government formulate only basic principles in areas such as labor law and minimum wages and having individual decisions made by company managers.

9. The concept of the elimination of workers' councils from state-owned companies and the creation of a special kind of supervisory board consisting of representatives of different groups from without and from within a company (including different employee-group representatives) was developed by B. Glinski in 1988 and published in 1989 (Glinski, 1989, 1992).

10. The years from 1989–1992 were spent on changing companies' external environment.

11. For a more complete discussion of the use of mediation and other peaceful conflict-management methods in Poland, see Olszanska et al., 1993.

REFERENCES

Aguren, S., Bredbacka, Ch., Hansson, R. & Karlsson, K. (1984). *Volvo Kalmar Revisited: Ten Years of Experience in Human Resources, Technology, Financial Results.* Stockholm: SAF.

Albinowski, A. (1988). Ekonomia, ktorej mialo nie byc [Economy which was not supposed to exist]. *Zarzadzanie,* No. 10.

Borman, W.C. (1991). Job behavior, performance, and effectiveness. In M.D. Dunnette and L.M. Hough (Eds.), *Handbook of Industrial and Organizational Psychology,* 2nd ed., pp. 271–326. Palo Alto, CA: Consulting Psychologists Press.

Bowen, D.E. & Lawler, E.E., III. (1992). The empowerment of service workers: What, why, how, and when. *Sloan Management Review,* 33: 31–39.

Cole, J. (1992). Poland: Where policy grapples with reality. *Baylor Business Review,* 10: 22–24.

Czajka, Z. (1990). Zasady ksztaltowania plac w Polsce w latach 1919–1989 [Rules of creating the compensation in Poland in the years 1919–1989]. *Studia i Materialy,* Warsaw: IPiSS, No. 12.

Czarny, Z.M. (1992). Privatisation of state industries in Poland. *International Business Lawyer,* 20(3): 151–153.

Dietl, J. (1992). Determinants of private business activities in Poland. *Journal of Business Research,* 24(1): 27–36.

Economic Program for Poland. Outline. (1989). Warsaw: Council of Ministers, October.

Edgren, J. (1974). *With Varying Success—A Swedish Experiment in Wage Systems and Shop Floor Organization.* Stockholm: SAF.

Fisher, C.D., Shoenfeldt, L. F. & Shaw, J. B. (1990). *Human Resource Management.* Boston: Houghton Mifflin.

Fogel, D. (1991). Approaches to management education in reforming economies. *Proceedings—U.S. Competitiveness in the Global Marketplace: A Special Focus on the Service Sector,* October 4-5, 1991, Memphis, TN.

Gilbert, N. (1990). Both sides of the ESOP story. *Personnel,* 67(4): 28–37.

Glinski, B. (1985). *Zarzadzanie w Gospodarce Socialistyczneh* [Managing the Socialist Economy]. Warsaw: PWE.

———. (1987). Variants of the Socialist Economic Management System in Eastern Europe. In J. Child & P. Bates (Eds.), *Organization of Innovation: East–West Perspective.* Berlin: Walter de Gruyter.

———. (1990a). Przedmiot i charakter nauk zarzadzania [Management process]. In B. Glinski & B. Kuc (Eds.), *Podstawy Zarzadsania Oranizacjami* {Essentials of Management in Organizations]. Warsaw: PWE.

———. (1990b). Wspolczesne zarzadzanie—historia i podstawowe tendencje [Contemporary Management—History and Basic Trends]. In B. Glinski & B. Kuc (Eds.), *Podstawy Zarzadzania Oranizacjami* [Essentials of Management in Organizations]. Warsaw: PWE.

———. (1990c). Polska reforma gospodarcza 1982–1988 [Polish economic reform of the years 1982–1988]. In B. Glinski & B. Kuc (Eds.), *Podstawy Zarzadzania Oranizacjami* [Essentials of Management in Organizations]. Warsaw: PWE.

———. (1990d). Centralne kierownictwo strategiczne [Central strategic management]. In Glinski, B. & Kuc, B. (Eds.), *Podstawy Zarzadzania Organicacjami* [Essentials of Management in Organizations]. Warsaw: PWE.

———. (1992). "System gospodarczy lat 90"—"Economic System of the '90s," *Zycie Gospodarcze,* No. 9, March 1.

Grootings, P., Gustavsen, B. & Hethy, L. (Eds.) (1986). *New Forms of Work Organization and their Social and Economic Environment.* Budapest: Vienna Centre and Institute of Labor Research.

Henderson, R. (1989). *Compensation Management.* Englewood Cliffs, NJ: Prentice-Hall.

Hills, F.S. (1987). *Compensation Decision Making.* New York: Dryden.

Ishikawa, A. (1986). Z doswiadczen partycypacji pracowniczej w Japonii [From the experience of workers participation in Japan]. *Polityka Spoleczna,* No. 3.

Kerr, S. (1975). On the Folly of Rewarding A, While Hoping for B. *Academy of Management Journal,* 18(4): 769–783.

Kordaszewski, J. (1982). Patologia systemu pracy i kierunki jego poprawy {Pathology of the work systems and its improvements]. *Przeglad Techniczny,* No. 14.

Kozdrój, A. (1986a). Work groups in socialist enterprises. Conference paper presented at Fourth Workshop on Capitalist and Socialist Organizations, Budapest, June.

———. (1986b). Ogolnopanstwowy system sterowania placami [State system of compensation control]. (interim report). Warszawa: Institute of Management.

———. (1988). *Grupa Pracownicza Jako Przedmiot i Podmiot Motywowania* [Work Group as an Object and Subject of Motivation]. Wroclaw: Ossolineum.

———. (1988a). Rola Srodowiska zawodowego ze szczegolnym uwzglednieniem wplywu kadry kierowniczej na ksztaltowanie postaw wobec pracy [The role of professional environment with particular regard to managerial influence on attitudes towards work]. *Informacje—Ekspertyzy—Propozycje—Metody.* Warsaw: IPiSS, August, No. 14.

————. (1990). Pomiar i ocena efektow pracy [Work measurement and appraisal]. *Problemy Unowoczesnienia Zarzadzania.* Warsaw: Institute of Management.

Krencik, K. (1989). Zakladowe systemy wynagradzania (proba oceny) [Enterprise compensation systems (attempt to estimate)]. *Studia i Materialy.* Warsaw: IPiSS, No. 5.

Latham, G.P. & Wexley, K.N. (1981). *Increasing Productivity Through Performance Appraisal.* Reading, MA: Addison-Wesley.

Lawler, E.E. (1986). *High Involvement Management.* San Francisco: Jossey-Bass.

————. (1990). *Strategic Pay, Aligning Organizational Strategies and Pay Systems.* San Francisco: Jossey-Bass.

————. (1992). *The Ultimate Advantage.* San Francisco: Jossey-Bass.

————, Mohrman, A.M., Jr. & Resnick-West, S.M. (1989). *Performance Appraisal Systems.* San Francisco: Jossey-Bass.

Lincoln, J.R. (1989). Employee work attitudes and management practice in the U.S. and Japan: Evidence from a large comparative survey. *California Management Review,* 32(1): 89–106.

Lindestad, H. & Norstedt, J.P. (1973). *Autonomous Groups and Payment by Result.* Stockholm: SAF.

Lipton, D. & Sachs, J. (1990). Creating a Market Economy in Eastern Europe: The Case of Poland. *Brookings Papers on Economic Activity,* No. 1.

Mapes, T. (1992). Polish daily thrives by refusing to hire communist hacks. Begun by the Intelligentsia, "Gazeta Wyorcza," leaves its competitors smarting. *The Wall Street Journal,* February 7, 1992.

Marsh, E.R. (1975). The Harmonogram of Karol Adamiecki. *Academy of Management Journal,* 18(2): 358–364.

Milkovich, G.T. & Newman, J.M. (1990). *Compensation,* 3rd ed. Homewood, IL: Richard D. Irwin.

————, & Wigdor, A.K. (eds.) (1991). *Pay for Performance.* Washington, D.C.: National Academy Press.

Naylor, T.H. (1990). Redefining corporate motivation, Swedish style. *The Christian Century,* 107(18): 566–569.

Nowakowski, M. (1987). *Japonskie Przedsiebiorstwo na Rynkach Swiatowych* [Japanese Company on Foreign Markets]. Warsaw: Institute of Management.

Olszanska, J., Olszanski, R. & Wozniak, J. (1993). Do peaceful conflict management methods pose problems in posttotalitarian Poland? *Mediation Quarterly,* 10(3): 291.

Onedo, O.A.E. (1991). The motivation and need satisfaction of Papua New Guinea managers. *Asia Pacific Journal of Management,* 8(1): 121–141.

Ouchi, W.G. (1981). *Theory Z: How American Business Can Meet the Japanese Challenge.* Reading, MA: Addison-Wesley.

Park, C. & Rosen, C. (1990). The performance record of leveraged ESOP firms. *Mergers & Acquisitions,* 25(3): 64–74.

"Place w okresie zmian systemu gospodarczego" [Compensation in transition of economic system]. (1990). *Studia i Materialy,* Warsaw: IPiSS, No. 14.

"Poles need more: The lifting of martial law will not be enough to solve the Polish crisis." (1982). *The Economist,* 285 (December 11), 13–14.

Porter, M.E. (1990). *The Competitive Advantage of Nations.* London: Macmillan.

Porter, L.W., Lawler, E.E., III & Hackman, J.R. (1973). *Behavior in Organizations.* New York: McGraw-Hill.

Prokopenko, J. (1986). *Productivity Management. A Practical Handbook.* Geneva: ILO.

"Raport o placach w gospodarce uspolecznionej w latach 1982–1989" [Report on compensation systems in state economy in the years 1982–1989]. (1990). *Studia i Materialy,* Warsaw: IPiSS, No. 2.

Reform in Sweden. Report on New Payment Systems. (1977). Stockholm: SAF.

Roszkowski, E. (1986). *Sluzba Organnizacji i Normowania Pracy* [Organization and Standardization Service Unit]. Warsaw: PWE.

Sachs, J. (1992). Building a market economy in Poland. *Scientific American,* March, 34–40.

Sachs, J. & Lipton, D. (1990). Poland's Economic Reform. *Foreign Affairs,* Summer.

Schuler, R.S. (1992). *Managing Human Resources,* 4th ed. St. Paul: West.

Shama, A. (1993). Management under fire: The transformation of managers in the Soviet Union and Eastern Europe. *The Academy of Management Executive,* 7, 22–35.

"Still behind bars: The lifting of martial law won't free Poland." (1993). *The Economist,* 288 (July 16), 14–15.

Taylor, F.W. (1911). *The Principles of Scientific Management.* NY: Harper & Row.

"The institutionalization of martial law." (1982). *Survey,* 26 (Autumn), 60–67.

Thorsrud, E. (1976). Democracy at Work and Perspectives on the Quality of Working Life in Scandinavia. *International Institute for Labor Studies, Research Series,* No. 8.

Welford, R. (1990). Worker motivation, life time employment and codetermination: Lessons from Japan and West Germany for productivity growth. *The Contemporary Review,* 257(1496): 129–132.

"Work and Pay." (1986). International conference in Poland organized jointly by the Polish Ministry of Work, Pay and Social Affairs, the University of Lodz, and an international organization known as "Work and Pay."

Zespolowe Formy Organizacji Pracy. Oczekiwania i Doswiadczenia [Team Forms of Work Organization. Expectations and Experience]. (1989). Warsaw: IWZZ.

3

Structural Obstacles for Russian/American Joint Ventures

William L. Tullar

INTRODUCTION

This chapter examines the problem of joint ventures of American companies in Russia. The success rate of such endeavors is not precisely known, but the best estimates are that the failure rate is somewhere around 70–80%. Worse yet, most of the ventures don't get beyond the signed agreement. Many reasons concerning conditions in Russia have been cited for this problem: currency problems, bad or anti-Western laws, criminal activity, economic chaos, and political instability, to name the major ones. These are mostly factors that an interested organization cannot change. This chapter suggests a factor that the organization can control: structure. It examines how structure may inhibit or facilitate business and suggests some structural changes that may give subsequent joint ventures a better chance of success.

As of 1991 more than 1000 joint ventures had been established between Russian enterprises and American companies. Yet, of this 1000, fewer than 20 were actually actively functioning and producing revenue (Tullar & Shestakov, 1990). The rest simply existed on paper. *Ekonomika i Zhizn* (February, 1993) reports that the Head of Association of the Joint Ventures and International Organizations in Russia has claimed that the major achievement of the last years is that up to 30% of the joint ventures registered in Russia are really operating, increasing their assets, output, and sales, and successfully competing with the state-run enterprises. Harrigan (1986) asserts that, in general, joint ventures frequently go awry. She cites antitrust problems, sovereignty conflicts, loss of autonomy and control, and loss of competitive advantage through strategic inflexibility. It is the thesis of this chapter that one more category needs to be added when considering joint ventures in Russia: structural incompatibility.

The investment climate in Russia worsened substantially in 1992 compared with 1991 because many officials considered that enterprises with foreign investments should be run just like native firms. Nevertheless, it is clear to most everyone that the existing taxation system, currency situation, and customs difficulties in Russia makes it more effective to invest in any other former Soviet country than Russia. Yet even with such an unfavorable investment climate, 30%

of the joint ventures were succeeding, pouring billions of dollars of needed capital into Russia.

Although the percentage of success of joint ventures is up, it is clear that many of them, begun in hope, are going nowhere. Part of the blame for this lies with the current economic and legal conditions of Russia. The Russians insist on the same demands on joint ventures as they make on state enterprises, and worse still, they often insist on the same structure as native Russian firms. Brooks (1993) satirizes the search for "honest joint venture partners," and he notes that many companies looking for joint venture partners in the Russia, the Ukraine, or Byelorus may have to search through 80 to 100 local enterprises to find one suitable joint venture partner.

Soviet enterprise structure and American (and for that matter most Western) business structure were generally quite different. Although the USSR is gone, its structure of enterprise persists because of the inertia of large organizations and the protection of the remnants of the socialist state. This enterprise structure and the sharp differences between Russian business culture and American business culture, have prevented many Russian/American joint ventures from being successful. Following the theory of Chandler (1962), the thesis of this chapter is that:

1. There is a great difference between the environments in which Western and Soviet (now Russian) companies were formed and developed.

2. These environmental differences have led to very different organizational structures.

3. These structural differences along with the communication patterns they produce have made effective cooperation between American and Russian organizations the exception rather than the rule.

4. The current environment in Russia calls for a structure that is probably not found in Russia or the U.S.

Among the 47,000 or so enterprises left over from the USSR in Russia, the most interesting ones to American companies are the larger ones (Ivancevitch et al., 1992). These enterprises were engaged in a number of high-tech activities, and many of them have R&D staffs and a command of technologies that could really be of use to many Western companies. But in order to make use of these business advantages, it is necessary to be able to make two organizations function well together. While a joint venture is not like a merger, the interface between the two organizations must enable effective communication and cooperation between the two.

Effective communication and cooperation is clearly a problem. In fact, Luthans et al. (1993) conclude that communication with outsiders has not been related to Russian managerial success in the past few years. Their analysis shows that managerial success is predicted overwhelmingly by internal networking, and that the profile of Russian manager activities closely parallels that which one would expect in a large bureaucracy.

THE ENVIRONMENT

The environment in which Russian organizations were conceived and grew was relatively simple and stable. Their macroenvironments were relatively innocuous as far as the kinds of changes they imposed. The political environment changed the emphasis of the organizations, but it was inclined to add new organizations rather than shut down old, inefficient ones. But the environment which most of the Western firms trying to do business in Russia live in is quite different.

Table 1, adopted from Draft (1989), is particularly instructive. If we consider the organizations of the former USSR, we find that almost all of them were simple or complex stable organizations, mostly the former. The pronounced inward focus of these organizations makes for a bureaucratic structure and for a particularly insular type of communication. Such organizations were characterized by few boundary–role spanners. For many of these producers, their connection to the outside consisted mostly of trucks backing up to their loading docks and offloading raw materials or loading finished goods.

In contrast to the situation in the former USSR, most of the American companies, and indeed most of the Western companies seeking joint ventures in Russia, are of either the simple or complex dynamic type. As such, their structure accommodates the requirements for scanning and imitation, departmental coordina-

Table 1
Environmental Complexity and Change*

		Environmental Complexity	
		Simple	Complex
Environmental change	Stable	1. Little scanning 2. Little imitation 3. Operating orientation 4. Few departments with little coordination among them 5. Mechanistic control	1. Some scanning 2. Some imitation 3. Some planning 4. Many departments with little coordination among them 5. Mechanistic control
	Dynamic	1. Some scanning 2. Quick imitation 3. Planning orientation 4. Few departments with some coordination among them 5. Organic control	1. Extensive scanning 2. Extensive imitation 3. Extensive planning 4. Many departments with extensive coordination among them 5. Organic control

*Adopted from Daft, 1989.

tion, and organic control. The planning orientations of formerly Soviet and Western enterprises of the complex dynamic type were probably at least similar in depth if not in substance. But in order to facilitate the scanning and imitation, departmental coordination, and organic control, the Western organizations, and especially American organizations, must be structured properly. If a generalization may be made here, it is that Western organizations tend to be much more organic and formerly Soviet organizations more bureaucratic. However, it is possibly also true that most Western organizational structures would not be appropriate in Russia at this time.

The task environment of the customers, suppliers, competitors, and environmental agencies of Soviet enterprises was much less complicated and had fewer communication requirements. Managers of Western European, Japanese, and American firms are all much more directly concerned with day-to-day operations. Those managers must include representatives of customers, suppliers, and environmental agencies in their daily schedules. This means learning the separate language of each of these and communicating with them on their own terms. The Soviet (and now Russian manager) had and has no such requirements. By the nature of their positions, the task environments for Soviet and subsequent Russian organizations are less intrusive into the everyday running of the business.

The industry/competitive environment for the Soviet organization was, of course, one in which many of them were sole suppliers of the goods they produced. This meant there were no competitors to push them. In the most technologically stable manufacturing niches, there was no pressure to become increasingly more efficient. Continuous improvement is a concept that is still not widely known in Russia. It is instructive to examine the joint ventures being concluded in 1993: many of them are focused around the extraction and use of gold, oil, and diamonds. One must ask oneself why these extraction technologies should have to come from the West. The petroleum and minerals have been in their present locations for some time, so why haven't the local extraction technologies been better developed? American, and indeed most Western, corporations have of necessity established ways of pooling interests, operating authority, and profits long ago so they could develop effective joint ventures (Harrigan, 1986). Part of the lag in Russian exploitation of mineral deposits is due to the technology of organizing.

In the most technologically unstable niches, there were few if any competitors working on the same innovations. Thus there was little pressure to get there faster. Living without competitors in your industry leads to the development of a mindset in which urgency is lacking. The utility of joint ventures for Russia today stems from the import of Western technology and know-how which the organizations bring into Russia.

The macroenvironment of state socialism, and now the transition away from it to a market economy, affects all Russian organizations. Political uncertainty, inflation, and financial uncertainty are features of the macroenvironment for Russian managers. *Ekonomika i Zhizn* (February, 1993) reports that inflation during

1992 amounted to more than 1250%. Most Russian business people can hardly absorb the changes of the last three years. In many cases their need to forge ties with companies outside the country is an attempt to overcome this uncertainty. Thus, Russian managers do have a sense of urgency to make outside ties. However, few Russian organizations have set up systematic ways to build and maintain such ties. In their defense, many of them cannot afford such structures, since changes in their financing schemes (most imposed by the government) are strangling their ability to make such changes and especially their ability to travel outside Russia for purposes of imitation and benchmarking.

Thus the placid Soviet business environment has given way to a much more turbulent and complex business one. Russian enterprises were mostly conceived during the Soviet days and, consequently, their design reflects these origins.

ORGANIZATIONAL DESIGN

Most organizational theorists consider organizational design to have four components: allocation of tasks and responsibilities, reporting relationships, departmentation, and mechanisms of coordination (Narayanan & Nath, 1993). We will consider each of these components in turn and examine Russian organizations.

In this effort, we must recognize that Russian managers are generally not trained as managers but usually as economists, scientists, or engineers. Moreover, the Russian manager "has grown up as a scientist or engineer, not as a professional manager who can go from industry to industry as in the West" (McNulty, 1992, p. 80). In general, management education in Russia (and earlier in the USSR) was quite different than that in the United States. Management education during the last two decades had been reformed, and top-management education was undertaken by the Academy of National Economy. Only second-level and lower management education was handled by the Ministry of Education. Management itself was not considered a profession. Thus, most of the people running the Russian half of a joint venture were educated first as engineers, scientists, or economists, and then their management education was added. If one inquires as to their profession, most of them will respond: "engineer," "chemist," or "economist."

As such, these managers do not share the American manager's interest in structure. Their educations and backgrounds tell them to look for ineffective and inefficient organizations in technology or economics rather than motivating people, communicating properly and applying the most advantageous structure. It is safe to say that most Russian general directors do not think of reorganization as a means of remedying organizational performance problems.

Allocation of Tasks and Responsibilities

Soviet enterprises had a single general director who issued orders and bore responsibility for the firm's results. Decision-making power is still generally in the hands of one man or woman at the top. Soviet law called for strict adherence to and observance of the hierarchy (Ivancevitch, et al., 1992). This concentrates power at the top and makes many of these organizations resemble the classic machine bureaucracy.

Welsh et al. (1993) found that participative interventions with 33 workers in a Russian textile factory produced no significant effect on the production of fabric. Given what we know about the allocation of tasks and responsibilities, this lack of effect is not surprising. The workers expect to be told. They are accustomed to and expect theory X management.

It is also useful to remember that Soviet factory managers often had little control over how many workers they had. In a socialist state, workers were assigned to factories whether they were needed there or not. As Ivancevitch et al. (1992) note, the average Russian factory has over 800 people working in it whereas the average Western factory has around 80. It is hard to imagine that the tasks of the 800 people are closely specified. Moreover, it was and is extremely difficult to hold these workers to meaningful standards of performance or to give pay and/or bonuses based on performance. Thus it is quite difficult for a factory manager to ensure that the many workers in the plant will discharge the responsibilities given them.

Reporting Relationships

As noted above, the Soviets deliberately built bigger and bigger amalgamations of plants, work associations, and farms until they produced large monopolistic combines that often manufactured, distributed, or grew very unrelated things. Although the decision-making power lies at the top of the Russian organization, it is still often impossible for the general director to have a good grasp of all the businesses his or her enterprise is in. Consequently, the many workers work badly, come to work infrequently, and idly walk around much of the time they do come to work.

As an example of the level of centralization, the author once needed a photocopy of a one-page document at a management institute in Moscow. In order to have a single photocopy made in 1990, it was necessary to have a work order signed by the deputy director of an institute of more than 500 engineers and scientists.

Reporting relationships are one way to solve this problems. Power resides at the top. The general director is responsible for all the people under his direction. A survey by the Soviet Academy of Sciences in 1990 revealed that of 1000 Soviet enterprises, more than half employed more than 5,000 and some of them had more than 20,000 workers. Pre-perestroika, fewer than one-fifth of the directors reported that they had the right to make decisions on wages, the introduction of new technology, allocation of funds, and development of the enterprise social fund (Ivancevitch et al., 1992). In other words, most of the general directors had much less authority to make important decisions for their organizations than their American, Japanese, or Western European counterparts do.

Klimova (1991), in a study done at the International Research Institute for

Management Science in Moscow, reported on a survey of general directors in the USSR and other COMECON nations. Her results show that most larger (more than 500 workers) firms had two or more deputy directors. A secondary analysis of her data done by the author also shows that the total value of production (per year) is not related at all to the number of levels in the organization ($r = -.02$) nor is it related to the percentage of workers directly concerned with production ($r = -.07$). The total value of production is related to the percentage of managers in the plant who are line managers, but the relationship is negative ($r = .31$, $p < .001$). However, the best predictors of total value of production is the number of deputy directors in the plant ($r = .48, p < .001$). Apparently, directors of more productive factories have more first reports, but the other factors associated with organizational size don't seem to be related to total value of production.

Departmentation

Generally, Russian factories are organized into departments by function. Since the dominant administrative logic is bureaucracy and since functional departments make for the most efficient reporting relationships, departments are generally concerned with maintenance, production, quality assurance, research and development, and so forth. Again, the Klimova (1991) data point toward departmentation. She found that organizations with a higher proportion of staff managers (heading more departments) had higher total output values and did very little of their production for prenegotiated prices.

Judging from Lawrence and Vlachoutsicos (1990) and personal experience of the author in several dozen factories, it appears as if geographic, divisional, and matrix structures are the rare exceptions rather than the rule in Russian factories.

Mechanisms of Coordination

Klimova (1991) showed that a substantial portion of every general director's time is spent working on planning. Planning was and is very central to the Russian enterprise. This means that much of the coordination is done by bureaucratic control—that is, by sharing the elements of the plan with various deputy directors and supervisors on a need-to-know basis. In fact, Soviet organizations generally did not encourage horizontal communication (Ivancevitch et al., 1992). Therefore, it was very difficult for any sort of organic control system to emerge. The control mechanism followed the general lines of the hierarchy. However, with the power to reward and punish workers mostly absent from managerial prerogatives, the ability to reach planned goals was limited. Compliance with management directives was and is generally grudging and dilatory.

Structure and Joint Venture Problems

If we accept the proposition that many if not most of the joint venture activity was concentrated in the larger Soviet enterprises and continues to focus on the

largest enterprises in Russia, we can then easily see that the organizational structures that Westerners are accustomed to are largely absent. The American manager
seeking to deal with his Russian counterpart finds that the Russian is saddled with
an intractable machine bureaucracy that produces a low per-worker output of
low-quality goods. Moreover, the enterprise contains a great deal of structural
inertia and is extremely difficult to change and maneuver.

These differences in structure make communication problems between Americans and Russians quite frustrating. The communication and structure problems
reinforce each other in a vicious circle. This makes the Russian enterprise even
more opaque to Americans trying to cooperate with it. Americans have their own
models of organization, which feature much different structures. When they attempt to use the Russian organizational structure, they mispredict what will
happen. This often makes for surprising, frustrating results.

Let it be granted here that many of the joint ventures that exist between Russian
and American firms have never been more than paper agreements for two reasons.
First, Russians came west hoping to bring signed agreements back home. Both
sides lost interest because they couldn't see any clear advantages in many of the
agreements that were signed. Second, the economic chaos in Russia is so bad that
Americans in particular and Westerners in general are afraid to invest any
significant amounts of money in Russia. However, there are some joint ventures
in which both sides have made at least some effort but simply weren't successful
in getting things to work. It is in these organizations that the structure by communications interaction effect may have stymied the joint venture.

It is instructive to examine here the problems incurred by American tobacco
companies in Russia. Given the Russian penchant for smoking and the inability of
the Russian tobacco companies to keep up with the demand for cigarettes, it is
remarkable that two of the joint ventures of tobacco companies have already run
into trouble.

The conflict between Dukat (Moscow, Russia), a tobacco factory, and its joint
venture partner, the Liggett Group (USA), was resolved with a compromise
decision of the Moscow city council (Mossoviet). Mossoviet rejected the claims
of Dukat against the American firm. However, the demand to reconsider terms of
the land lease by the Dukat–Liggett joint venture enterprise in Moscow was met
with great protest. Up to the present time, the Liggett Group has invested more
than $6 million in the development of the joint venture (*Izvestia*, January 22,
1993). This couple is not far from the altar and already they're fighting it out in
court. Something's clearly amiss in this union.

Then in Samara, Russia, the Russian–U.S. joint venture cigarette plant is experiencing difficulties with the production of Marlboro cigarettes because of their
high price. The production cost is so high that the enterprise cannot compete with
imported Marlboro cigarettes. In addition customers prefer to buy less expensive
types of tobacco products (*Inzhenerniya Gazeta*, January 12, 1993). Even mighty
Phillip Morris has apparently run into difficulties trying to produce in Russia.
Phillip Morris is a superb marketing organization, so it is hard to imagine they

didn't count the costs of production before they put $6 million into their Russian plant.

Recommendations

Russian organizations must begin to change their organizational structures if they are to survive into the twenty-first century. The environment is such that the large, mechanistic structures that now exist cannot perform well—they are inefficient. Such organizations cannot innovate well. Like an oil tanker floating in a small pond, they cannot turn and maneuver fast enough. Many of them must shed 90% of their employees before they can hope to be competitive, and most Russian managers cannot face the necessity to do this, since such layoffs are extremely difficult to do. Nevertheless, radical downsizing is the current Russian imperative.

If a joint venture is to proceed to the satisfaction of both parties, it must have a structure workable for both. If the joint venture is to perform on Russian soil, then one good possibility is a "skunk works" type organization (Peters, 1987). The classic example of such an organization is Lockheed's research and development facility out in the California desert. Lockheed found it extremely difficult to be innovative and creative within the structure of the production facilities around Los Angeles, so they moved much of their sophisticated R&D effort to a remote location in the desert. The place is a "skunk works" because the accounting and business practices of the place are not in keeping with standard Lockheed practice. Peters has become well known for his "skunk camps," where he teaches managers to do things that make "skunk works" successful.

For Russian joint venture purposes, such an organization would have the form of neither parent and could be set up by an executive committee. Perhaps it would even be necessary for some type of "skunk camp" to be arranged for potential Russian and Western organizational members. Expectations of the "skunk works" would be that it be innovative and creative in making use of the resources on hand. The "skunk works" should aim at getting at least some portion of the Russian organization's products or services up to world standards so that at least part of the joint venture can compete on the world market.

The "skunk works" structure may account for the success Conoco is having with its Polar Lights joint venture to supply ecologically safe oil field equipment to the Ardalinsk oil field complex. The Russian partner in this venture is Archangelskoe Geologia. Conoco has released $700 million of a planned $2.2 billion investment. Oil extraction was expected to start in June or July of 1994 (*Kommersant,* March 5, 1993). At least to outsiders, it looks as if Polar Lights is a small, flexible firm staffed by both Russians and Americans, which will enable it to succeed.

If the "skunk works" is infeasible because of a scarcity of sites where such an organization could be located or because of intransigence on the part of the Russian partner, then perhaps a new division can be created within the enterprise structure. Again, this division could be staffed and structured by a committee composed of members from both the American and the Russian organizations.

However, it will likely be necessary to have a Russian report to the general director. Again, agreed-upon standards of innovation and creativity should be imposed on the division.

Reporting relationships in the new division or "skunk works" should be negotiated by role-analysis techniques and the results should be written down and shared. It is important that common (and perhaps unique) language by arrived at during this process. Much of business Russian consists of terms borrowed from English and to a lesser extent from German. But each new joint venture has to work out and then disseminate the words important to the business the joint venture is engaging in. Both Russians and Americans must learn the new vocabulary, and clearly all of the words will not be English.

Coordination mechanisms must be negotiated between the managers running the suborganization and both sets of senior management. Controls in the new organization should be as organic as the Russian side will allow. Part of the control mechanism must include a lot of horizontal communication. Departments will have to negotiate their requirements of one another without constant recourse to the general director of the organization.

Every effort must be made among American personnel assigned to work with the Russian organization to do the following:

1. Not assume that this is the way we do it at home, so this is how we'll do it here.
2. Understand that American management methods may work in America, but in Russia compromises will be necessary.
3. Understand that all Americans assigned to the project are ambassadors of good will and, as such, must treat their Russian colleagues with respect and deference.
4. Understand that learning at least some of what is a very difficult language is the least one can do. Any effort in this direction is appreciated by Russians.

Even if structural changes in the Russian organization are not possible, prior to the beginning of joint activity, the two organizations should share as much information as possible about themselves so that the communication problems can be minimized. Managers should visit and stay in each other's plants for several weeks at a time. The two organizations should write updated job descriptions for all the managerial and supervisory jobs and share them with the sister organization. The two companies should also exchange newsletters on a regular basis.

For the present, joint ventures are still one of the most attractive forms of cooperation between Russian and American firms. However, the high failure rate will begin to be a factor deterring many future joint ventures with high potential. Understanding the structure of Russian organizations is essential for Americans who seek joint venture partners. The ideal structure for the current very turbulent, complex Russian market is a small organic organization, like a "skunk works," which can refit to handle the vagaries of the market and the environment. Until such organizations are forthcoming with some frequency, failure rates of joint ventures will continue to be high.

REFERENCES

Brooks, D. (1993). Cracking that Post-Soviet market. *Wall Street Journal,* August 24, A22.

Chandler, A. (1962). *Strategy and Structure: Chapters in the History of American Industrial Enterprise.* Cambridge, MA: MIT Press.

Draft, R.L. (1989). *Organization Theory and Design.* St. Paul, MN: West Publishing.

Harrigan, K.R. (1986). *Managing for Joint Venture Success.* Lexington, MA: Lexington Books.

Ivancevitch, J.M., DeFrank, R.S. & Gregory, P.R. (1992). The Soviet enterprise director: an important resource before and after the coup. *Academy of Management Executive,* 6, 1, 42–55.

"Joint venture success rate up." (1993). *Ekonimika i Zhizn,* February, p. 22.

Klimova, E.T. (1991). *Direktor Predpriyatij v Perekhodnij Periyod: Delovoi Portret* (The Enterprise Director in a Transition Period: A Business Portrait). (Tech Rep. No. 92). Moscow, Russia: International Research Institute for Management Science.

Lawrence, P.R. & Vlachoutsicos, C.A. (1990). *Behind the Factory Walls: Decision Making in Soviet and U.S. Enterprises.* Boston: Harvard Business School Press.

Luthans, F., Rosenkrantz, S.A. & Welsh, D.H.B. (1993). An analysis of the activities of successful manufacturing managers in the Soviet Union: An observational study. Paper submitted to *Organization Behavior/Theory.*

McNulty, N.G. (1992). Management education in Eastern Europe: Before and after. *Academy of Management Executive,* 6, 4, 78–87.

Narayanan, V.K. & Nath, R. (1993). *Organization Theory.* Homewood, IL: Irwin.

Peters, Thomas J. (1987). *Thriving on chaos: Handbook for a management revolution.* New York: Random House.

"Polar Lights supplies ecologically safe oil field equipment." (1993). *Kommersant,* January 19, p. 10.

"Problems in the Dukat–Liggett joint venture." (1993). *Izvestia,* January 22, p. 7.

"Problems in the Samara–Phillip Morris joint venture." (1993). *Inzhenernaya Gazeta* (*Engineering Gazette*), January 12, p. 8.

Tullar, W.L. & Shestakov, O.A. (1990). Na pooti k oospekhoo sovmestnovo predprinimatelstva (Toward success in joint ventures). *Moskovskij Biznes,* 1990, 4, 12–13.

Welsh, D.H.B., Luthans, F. & Sommer, S. (1993). Managing Russian factory workers: The impact of U.S. based behavioral and participative techniques. *Academy of Management Journal,* 36, 1, 58–79.

II

STRUCTURE FOR TRANSFORMATION

4

Corporate Governance in Slovenia

Transformation from Self-Management to Codetermination

Darko Deškovicz

INTRODUCTION

In the last five years in Slovenia there has been extensive changes in the area of corporate governance. The political and economic systems have been transformed from a self-management socialist system to a socialist market system and finally to a social market system. Economic agents first changed from self-managing "organizations of associated labor" into social companies (with no known owners) and now they are being transformed into capitalized companies (with known owners). This transformation occurred during the same period in which Slovenia went through the process of becoming independent of Yugoslavia. This was a time of severe economic and political troubles that peaked during the war of independence. The transition from one-party socialist system to a multiparty parliamentary democracy also had an impact on the transformation from the self-managing socialist system to the social market one. Another consequence of this political transformation is the process of privatizing socially owned property, a process that has actually only begun. This period of transformation processes is coming to an end with the stabilization of three key areas: the legal regulation of the process of privatization, the legal institutionalization of capitalized commercial companies, and the management of those companies.

The objective of this chapter is to describe the process of gradual change in corporate governance in Slovenia from a self-management system to a system of codetermination. We will focus on the institutional framework in which act the strategic actors of the process of corporate governance transformation.

ASSOCIATED LABOR HERITAGE

The basic characteristic of the sociopolitical system of the former Yugoslavia was socially owned property, which determined the System of Associated Labor. The major functions of social property were the preservation of the one-party political system, perpetuation of the economic rule of the "working class," and realization of the ideological targets of egalitarian distribution. The concept of social property was based on the assumption of nonconflict or harmonized interests of the employees, companies (in this system termed Organizations of Associated Labor—OAL), and the state. The principle of social property was that neither legal nor physical subjects can be owners of socially owned assets, which were nonproperty or the property of everyone and no-one. The enterprises actually belonged to themselves, without having a real owner. There were three major elements of the System of Associated Labor based on social property, namely the unified form of the OAL, system of workers' self-management, and the role of management.

The Unified Organization Form of the OAL

This dominated the economy, banks, cultural, educational, health, and other institutions at different levels. There were three forms of OAL: the basic organization (BOAL), working organization (WO) and composite organization (COAL). The WO played a major role in the organizational structure of the OAL. In its organizational form the WO resembled a company.

Workers' Self-Management

The fundamental objective of this organizational form of associated labor was directed towards workers' self-management. According to the Constitution and the law, the OALs were managed by the workers. Most important decisions were supposed to be formally made by the workers jointly and directly through referendums, at workers assemblies, and indirectly through their delegates in the Workers' Council. The Workers' Council was the highest self-management body (a substitute for the board of directors) engaged in "managing the work and the business."

Management

Management in the OAL was reduced through self-management to the roles of operational coordinators and technical administrators of individual business tasks. Management (not the classical executive role) was as powerful as it was able to implement business policy by referring to formal and informal political channels. De facto it formulated decisions and had them passed by Workers' Councils. Social property determined the role of management by its nonproperty nature, with the absence of any real owner who would have the right to hire, control, and change management. According to the Yugoslavian understanding of the social nature of property, the managing organ also represented social interests and as such also exerted political control through noninstitutional channels (Warner, 1990).

THE PROCESS OF TRANSFORMATION ASSOCIATED LABOR INTO MARKET ECONOMY

The Political Changes

The political changes that took place at the time when socialism lost its legitimacy in the majority of socialistic states also brought about multiparty systems and started the process of marketization. Towards the end of 1980, attempts to revitalize the inefficient socialistic system resulted in the concept of entrepreneurial socialism, which emphasized the collective character of social property and self-managed entrepreneurship. This was followed by a stage directed towards the transformation of social property by allowing pluralism in ownership, i.e., coexistence of collective and social property. The Law on Enterprises finally replaced self-management with control based on the capital holdings. Slovenia was the first Yugoslav republic (April 1990) to carry out multiparty elections. The changes in the concept of Associated Labor in Slovenia began even before the change of the political system, based on the transformation of the Communist League into a social-democratic type of party and exit from the Communist League of Yugoslavia.

Ownership and Institutional Changes

The real breakaway from the System of the Associated Labor is represented by the Federal Enterprise Law and the Federal Law of Circulation and Management of Social Capital, adopted in 1989. The main intention of the Law on Enterprises was to introduce the market system on the basis of private ownership of productive factors. This was the first time since the Second World War that a law permitted the establishment of enterprises on the basis of private capital. After these legal changes it was possible for those who provided the initial capital to found enterprises rather than through the association of work of the employees. The enterprises were permitted to link up on their own initiative with one another on the basis of autonomous agreements or contracts. The enterprises themselves could also decide about the type of associations and alliances they would form, e.g., capital links, issues of shares, or contributing shares in composite form. Holding companies and other forms of grouping of enterprises were made possible. The OALs were transformed into social enterprises or enterprises with mixed ownership (joint ventures) on the basis of the Enterprise Law. With these legal arrangements, social property was made subject to buying and selling. This led to the beginning of the process of ownership transformation of social enterprises in the former Yugoslavia. Because the law did not prescribe the models and methods of the ownership change of the social enterprises, it opened the door to the so-called "spontaneous" or "wild" privatization.

Changes in the Management of the Transformed Enterprises

In socially owned enterprises, self-management remains the dominant management model, as described earlier, with workers' councils gaining new responsibility to make decisions about the distribution of profits. Self-management control was abolished. The mixed enterprises (joint stock companies and limited liability companies) were required to have the following management organs: shareholder assembly, board of directors, workers' council, and supervisory board. The private enterprises are managed by their owners, and workers only execute their self-management right according to the collective contract. The Enterprise Law did not prescribe the status and prerogatives of the management of private enterprises.

Privatization Process

Late in 1992 the Law on the Transformation of Company Ownership had been passed by the Assembly of the Republic of Slovenia. The law regulates the ownership transformation of companies with social property (social capital) into companies with known owners, either public and/or private, domestic and/or foreign. Methods of transformation of company ownership are the following: internal distribution of shares, internal repurchase of shares, sale of company shares and all company assets, transformation of a company through increase of ownership capital, transfer of shares to the Development Fund. The law puts an end to the "wild privatization" era, and awakens new hopes for normalization of business transactions and foreign investment. The law is a compromise among two basic competing privatization models, the autonomous and distributive privatization, including retaining managerial initiative by autonomously started but externally controlled ownership transformation. It includes possibilities of privatization based on new investments as well as distribution of shares for a considerable portion of assets.

CODETERMINATION AS THE MANAGEMENT SYSTEM OF SLOVENE ENTERPRISES

The Interest Groups

In the political debates over the past two years on the new law on codetermination, three interest groups emerged.

1. The unions took the position that Slovenia had to have "at least as much codetermination as in Germany." Thus, their goal was the German model of codetermination, with the Council of Workers functioning as the central organ of codetermination, with workers' representatives on the Supervisory Board, a Workers' Director, and with unions having the same functions as those in German companies.

2. The second interest group is the "owners" of capital in Slovenia. However, at the beginning (and also at the end) of the parliamentary discussions there was in Slovenia no clearly formed class of capital owners with their attendant association and ties with particular political parties.

3. The management of socially owned companies, the third group, had the key role in the privatization process. During the period of "spontaneous" or "wild" privatization, managers found themselves in a legal vacuum after the virtual collapse of the self-management system and the ensuing absence of clear state controls and the defensive position of the unions. The role of (quasi-) owners was assumed by the management of companies and the Chamber of Economy, who, as the quasirepresentatives of the (future) owners of these companies, represented

the interests of the group of capital owners. This group also opted for the German model of codetermination, but with a pared-down variation (including only 33% instead of 50% worker representation on the Supervisory Board, without obligations to pass information on to workers or to take into consideration the workers' stances, etc.). This interest group was in favor of the model in which management and (future) owners of the socially owned companies took over the leading and decisive roles.

All three interest groups described above lobbied political parties in Parliament. In the end the unions and the current German model of codetermination predominated, mainly because of the absence of a genuine class of capital owners who articulated their concrete interests. In July 1993 the Slovene Parliament passed the Law on the Cooperation of Workers in Management, which took effect on August 6, 1993. This law is related organically (and in time) to the Law on Commercial Companies, which took effect on July 30, 1993.

Main Points of the New Law

According to the new law, worker codetermination differs from the old system of self-management both in terms of institutional regulations as well as the forms of worker participation. The fundamental differences are that:

- Codetermination is no longer a question of workers' responsibility, but rather the new law guarantees workers' certain rights; workers are free to exercise these rights if they decide that it is in their interest to do so.
- Codetermination does not encroach upon fundamental business decisions taken by the company owners.
- Codetermination does not encroach upon major management decisions and has no influence on the appointment of key management positions.

The law regulates worker codetermination in commercial companies (irrespective of the form of ownership) and cooperatives, public service companies, banks, and insurance companies. Workers can exercise their rights to codetermination individually or collectively through the following organs: the Council of Workers, the Workers' Assembly, or workers' representatives in the organs of the company. The law does not touch upon the activities that constitute the form of union disputes. The law even explicitly stresses that worker codetermination does not encroach upon the rights and duties of unions and employer associations, which protect the interests of their numbers. The Council of Workers is not to join in any sort of union dispute. Resolutions concerning the form of the Council of Workers are passed by the Workers' Assembly. Thus the Workers' Assembly is an organ that initiates the formation of the Council of Workers and without which other actions cannot be taken regarding codetermination. In Slovenia (as in Austria and Germany) the law implicitly codifies the practice that without union activity there are no organized Workers' Assemblies, hence there are no procedures to name elective commissions, and no candidacies or elections. Unions are, in effect, the spritus agens in the process of advancing worker codetermination.

The Competences and Roles of Organs of Codetermination

The most important organ of codetermination is the Council of Workers, which is formed when more than 20 workers with active voting rights are employed in the company. The number of members of the Council of Workers depends on the number of employees, from a minimum of three (50 employees) to 13 (600–1000 employees); in companies with more than 1000 employees, the number of members increases by two for every additional 1000 employees. The law also precisely defines the elections, voting commissions, and restrictions related to membership in the Council of Workers. Meetings of the Council of Workers are to be counted as work time. The law also specifies the number of members of the Council of Workers who are to perform their functions for half of their full time work. The employer is to cover the necessary costs for the work of the Council of Workers. The Council of Workers can form committees to handle individual issues under its competence.

The Council of Workers has primarily the following competences: it ensures that laws and other statutes and collective contracts and agreements between the Council of Workers and the employer are administered; it proposes measures that are in the workers' interest; it accepts and takes into consideration proposals and suggestions from the workers when negotiating with the employer; it helps with the recruitment of workers who have a right to special protection (such as the disabled, the elderly, and the young).

The Workers' Assembly is composed of all the workers in the company except managers. The Workers' Assembly is convened by the Council of Workers. The Workers' Assembly has the right to deal with questions under the competence of the Council of Workers; however, it cannot make decisions on these questions. The director of the company can also demand a convocation of the Workers' Assembly. Except for one meeting a year, the Workers' Assembly does not meet during work time.

Worker codetermination within organs of the company is exercised through workers' representatives on the Supervisory Board of the company. The number of workers' representatives on the Supervisory Board is specified in the statutes of the company and cannot be less than one-third of the board members for companies with up to 1000 employees, or less than one-half of the board members for companies with more than 1000 employees. The Council of Workers elects and recalls these members of the Supervisory Board and informs the Shareholder Assembly of these decisions. By Slovene law, the Supervisory Board is an important organ of the company, having the following competences:

- It shall supervise the conduct of the business of the company.
- It may inspect and verify the company's books and documentation, its treasury, the depositors' securities, the supply of goods, and other matters.

• It may convene the General Assembly.

• It may specify that certain kinds of transactions may be performed only with the Board's approval.

The workers representatives on the Supervisory Board represent the interests of all the workers.

A company that employs more than 500 workers must have a Workers' Director, who is recommended to the Executive Management Board of the company by the Council of Workers. The Workers' Director represents and presents the interests of the workers with respect to personnel and social questions. The legal definition of the Workers' Director is relatively unprecise; the actual functions and position of this Director will probably be more precisely formed through practice. A deciding factor in this will be the Workers' Director's performance in situations of conflict, where he will have a dual role, that of the workers' representative and that of a member of the Executive Management Board.

Worker Codetermination in the Company

The law specifies the following forms of codetermination: 1) making suggestions and giving opinions; 2) providing information; 3) group consultation; 4) collective decision making; and 5) the right to veto the decisions of the employer.

1. A worker, either as an individual or through organs of codetermination, has the right to express his opinions and make suggestions related to the organization of his job and the work process, wages, and other issues concerning the work environment. The law also stipulates that the employer must respond to suggestions and questions within 30 days.

2. The employer must provide the Council of Workers with information, above all, on questions related to: the financial standing of the company; development of the company and goals; the state of production and sales; the general economic standing of the company's branch of business; a change in activities; a decrease in economic activities; changes in the organization of production; technological changes; and the yearly accounts and annual reports. Furthermore, the employer must enable the Council of Workers to examine any documentation relevant to the matters listed above.

3. Group consultation. The employer must give the Council of Workers notice (at least 30 days) in advance of passing any resolution and must demand a meeting for group consultation concerning the following questions on status and personnel in the company: sale of the company or a significant part of it; closing down the company or a significant part of it; significant changes in ownership; increasing, decreasing, or reorganizing a large number (10%) of the workers; the passing of acts on retirement benefits, disability, and health insurance; and the adoption of general rules on disciplinary responsibilities.

4. Collective decision making. The employer must submit to the Council of Workers for approval proposals on the following: measures related to worker

safety; workers' use of annual vacation time; guidelines for evaluating work performance and giving workers promotions; rewarding innovative activities; disposition of the housing fund; and vacation facilities and other buildings affecting the standard of living of the workers. The Council of Workers must make a decision on these matters within eight days and the agreement of the Council of Workers is taken to be an agreement with the employer.

5. The right to veto the decisions of the employer. The Council of Workers has the right to pass a resolution vetoing the decisions of the employer if the employer does not inform the Council of Workers before making its final decision and if the employer does not consult with the Council of Workers concerning questions of status and personnel.

As is clear from this concise presentation of the Codetermination Law, the concept is almost a copy of the German institutional model of codetermination. As mentioned earlier, this law is related in content and synchronized with the new Law on Commercial Companies, which went into effect one week before the enactment of the Codetermination Law. The Slovene legal regulations for commercial companies are in a similar fashion modeled after the German legal regulations on enterprises. Slovene joint stock companies, for example, have the same administrative structure as German ones: A Shareholder's Assembly, a Supervisory Board (with workers' representatives), an Executive Management Board, and a Council of Workers. The competences of the individual organs of a company are the same as in German companies. A joint stock company is to be managed by the Executive Management Board for the good of the company, independently and with full responsibility; the Executive Management represents and acts as the agent of the company; if there are several members in the Executive Management, they represent the company jointly, and so on. The competences and responsibilities of the Executive Management Board in relation to the Shareholders Assembly and Supervisory Board are quite similar to German regulations.

CONCLUDING REMARKS

It follows from Clegg's analysis (Clegg, 1990) that in different countries undergoing processes of change there arise different modes of bringing together the key agents of change. These are based primarily on the cultural resources available to the strategic agencies within specific institutional contexts. Slovene commercial organizations find their expression in institutionally framed and culturally embedded terms of relationships that structure the "field of force" in which they are constituted. The key factor that can shed light on whether the transformation of Slovene companies will be successful is how the organizations and their key (strategic) actors are embedded in the broad context of institutional phenomena (as described in this chapter) and in the environment of the organizations. Thus, in the future, the suitable objects of analysis of (successful) transformation will be the diverse forms of calculations and modes of agreement between the strategic agents within which are constituted networks of organizational relations. The actual form that organizations take depends on the specification of these features (Clegg, 1990, p. 152).

If we look at the case of the transformation of Slovene companies from Clegg's perspective, the crucial factor is not that the manager, union representative, or organization follow the German model. Rather, it is the Slovene contribution to normal ways of accounting for actions, calculating strategy, reaching agreements, and mapping cognitively that is important (Clegg, 1990, p. 150). Managerial and organizational actions depend upon specific (nationally variable) institutional frameworks. "It is framed within more or less tacit understandings, as well as formal stipulations, which enable different agencies to do not only different things but also the same things distinctly in diverse contexts" (Clegg, 1990, p. 151). On the basis of these conclusions, we can suppose that what happens in Slovenia within the "German" institutional administrative framework will happen in a "Slovene" manner. In other words, the German model of codetermination will have Slovene adaptations and consequences. This can already be observed in actions of two strategic agents in Slovene companies—management and the unions.

In recent years increasing numbers of Slovene managers have taken a negative stance on worker participation in management. According to surveys, in 1990 53% of the managers were still of the opinion that worker participation in management was a way of attracting workers to and getting them more involved in the goals of the company; hence, it was necessary for the success of the company. A year later, only 32% held this view. At the same time, the percentage of those who believed that worker participation in management was actually harmful to the success of the company increased from 16% in 1990 to 32% in 1991 (Kavčič, 1992, p. 70). After the Codetermination Law was passed, one of the managers of a large concern wrote the following in an open letter to the Presidents of Parliament and Government: "I am surprised by the lack of interest of the owners and the professional managers in the Codetermination Law. I recommend that we set it aside, at least temporarily, or that we at least state clearly when it will be again necessary to implement worker self-management. With a detailed analysis of certain articles of the Law, I can justify the conviction that the Law does not mean the implementation of codetermination to achieve better results, but rather it merely increases costs and blocks quick and effective business decisions" (Duhovnik, 1993).

One important characteristic of the many Slovene unions is that they are not united (in addition to two large, competitive unions, there is an ever increasing number of smaller professional or specialized unions). This weakens their stand against the state and the employers. Another characteristic is that the union operations go from "the top down," with less attention paid to conditions in the company. In the process of privatization in Slovenia, the unions will find themselves in a position of quasiowners of companies. The majority of socially owned companies will be privatized (in part or completely) with the method of internal (workers') purchase. By this method, the majority owners of smaller and middle-sized companies will be the workers, who will then have the dual role of being owners and codetermining workers. Such companies will be less attractive to private (or foreign) investors, and so the union representatives and functionaries of worker codetermination will play the main role. How they will deal with the realities of a market economy remains an open question.

Another open question is how the new private owners will deal with coownership and worker codetermination. What kind of modus vivendi for the administration of these companies will exist between the various types of owners (workers, the state, investment funds, domestic and foreign private investors)? What sort of relations will there be between management and the different unions? How will the organs of codetermination function? All of these questions will be answered in practice in the coming years. At the same time this will be a challenge for the researchers, who, working in a unique laboratory called Slovenia, will have a unique opportunity to observe the historical process of transformation of the administration, ownership, organization, and structure of Slovene companies.

REFERENCES

Clegg, R.S. (1990). *Modern Organizations.* London: Sage.
Duhovnik, J. (1993). Odprto pismo predsedniku DZ Hermanu Rigelniku in predsedniku vlade dr. Janezu Drnovšku. *Dnevnik,* August 24.
Kavčič, B. (1992). *Delavci in upravljanje podjetij.* Ljubljana: Enotnost.
Law on Commercial Companies. (1993) *Slovenian Business Report,* 3(30): 13–60.
Warner, M. (1990). Management versus Self-management in Yugoslavia. *Journal of General Management,* 16(2): 20–38.
Zakon o podjetjih (Law on Enterprises). (1989). Ljubljana: Gospodarski vestnik.
Zakon o sodelovanju delavcev pri upravljanju (Law on the Cooperation of Workers in Management). *Uradni list Republike Slovenije,* 3(42).

5

Restructuring Organizations for Transformation

Michael Gaitanides and Erhard Bredenbreuker

INTRODUCTION

Restructuring organizations for transformation basically means taking into account one of the main characteristics of the planned economy: the impossibility to draw boundaries between organizations and the industrial environment. From this point of view, the typical kind of organization, the combined firm (collective combine), is discussed. For the interpretation of this organization in former socialistic countries, the Mintzberg typology is used. Restructuring means, therefore, going back to the archetypes. This process of restructuring is illustrated by examining the case of the Textima Combine.

THE OVERALL ECONOMIC ORGANIZATION OF THE NATIONAL ECONOMY AS A STARTING POINT FOR TRANSFORMATION PROBLEMS

Centrally Planned and Controlled Production

The problem of organizational transformation in former socialist states can only be understood against the historical background of the overall industrial organization and the control system of centrally administrated national economies. The term "organization," which in the western private-sector context always relates to an enterprise, is not directly applicable to economic units or entities of the planned-economy system. Similar to problems of differentiating between economy and politics, it is difficult to draw a line between the economy of individual enterprises and the national economy. Subsequently, it is not possible to differentiate on market-economy lines between organizations in terms of inner and outer organizations or between system and environment. This can be clearly demonstrated by the example of former German Democratic Republic (GDR).

As early as the late forties the "Soviet Military Administration in Germany" (SMAD) took over all property rights of the confiscated and expropriated firms in the Soviet Occupied Zone. In 1954, the control of the industrial branches was centralized and assigned to the ministries, e.g., the Ministry of Heavy Industry, Ministry of Engineering Industry, or Ministry of Light Manufacturing. Local supply and service enterprises remained the responsibility of the commune. The control organs of the economic units were as follows (Marr, 1989, p. 52).

1. The Government Planning Commission. This was an organ of the Council of Ministers that developed strategic targets for the products of the industrial branches and for the regions, including the distribution of resources. In addition to the drawing-up of national economy plans, international supplies and services had to be coordinated, in particular with the Council for Material Economic Assistance (CMEA) countries. These plans were preset by ministries, central state organs, and districts.

2. Ministries and other Central State Organs. The 25 ministries had vertical control authority in the branches of industry assigned to them. They held the planning authority in these branches and were responsible for the fulfillment of production targets. Cross-sectional tasks were performed by the central state organs, for example the Office of Prices, the National Bank, the State Office for Work and Wages, the Office for Industrial Design, and the Office for Standardization, Measurements, and Product Control.

3. Territorial Organs. District and area councils coordinated their resources with the control and planning decisions made by the ministries. They had direct control responsibility only for local firms (e.g., housing construction and agricultures).

Collective Combines as Units of Production

Collective combines were economic units responsible for research and development, planning, production, and distribution of a whole product range. In the end, about 200 collective combines had a share of more than 90% of the industrial production. In centrally controlled industries there was a direct line of command from the minister in charge through director-generals and directors of firms to the foreman on the factory level.

Part of the collective combines were assigned the role and the competences of "Associations of State-Owned Enterprises," thus paring the way to a high degree of concentration within one branch of industry. The vertically integrated collective combine represented the typical form of a combine. It was responsible for the exploitation of natural resources, manufacturing, and selling of the final product. Not only was it responsible for research and development and production and distribution, but it also included construction operations, fulfillment departments, and subcontractors, especially those that contributed decisively to the final product. Due to general shortage of qualified independent suppliers, even complex operating equipment had to be built by the collective combines themselves. They, therefore, also had to maintain engineering works. For example, a parent firm had to procure lathe-cut parts required for gearwheel production within its combine form. Moreover, the combines were also responsible for the running of social facilities, e.g., for recreation and holiday homes or hospitals. Often the combine owned large estates and sometimes ran farms (Fig. 1).

Figure 1
Firms in a Combine

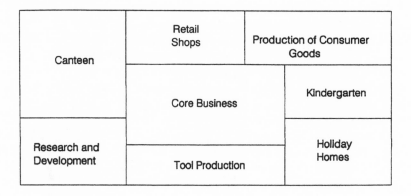

A combine's productivity plan was drawn up as a "closed production process," which ultimately was supposed to lead to an almost autonomous system from the economic point of view. As competition between combines was also avoided, each of them had its own suppliers and satellite firms.

The combine's structure was predominantly shaped by the parent firm comprising the actual core business. Products were manufactured in production plants that were especially designated for this purpose. Besides these plants, the parent firm maintained production units for supplies.

Unity of the combine's management was achieved through uniting the office of the director general of the combine with the office of operating manager of the parent firm (Fig. 2). This joint office not only guaranteed a tight linear organization, but also ensured that all resources and production capacities were exclusively used for the benefit of the core product. Progress in the field of science and technology had to be translated into action as soon as possible, and the combine had to respond to changes in the market (export markets).

The enormous production diversity was regulated by a centralized and disproportionately large administrative superstructure, resulting in a poor economic efficiency with respect to innovation capabilities, market and customer proximity, flexibility, and costs (Bühner, 1992, p. 190).

To sum up, initially the firms were characterized by the following situation:

- Direct linear linkage to the ministry in charge.
- Functional organization of the collective combine and its parent firm.
- Tayloristic understanding of organization, marked by an extreme division between planning and practice, strong centralization of the decision-making system, sluggish official channels, and low flexibility.

Figure 2
Basic Structure of a Collective Combine (AUTORENKOLLEKTIV 1983: 206)

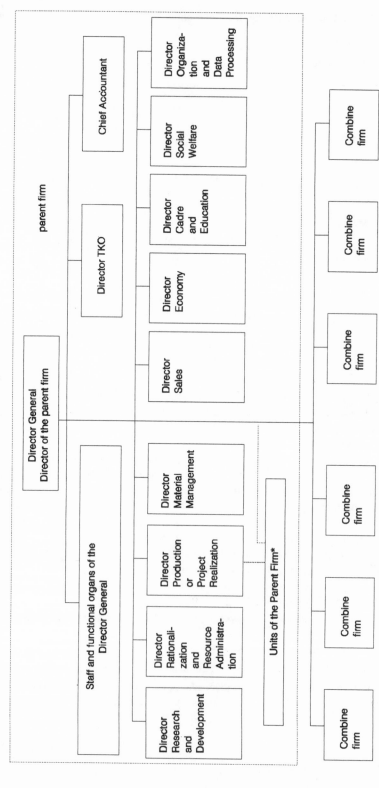

*Variations in the assignment of parent firm units.

Source: Used with permission from Walter de Gruyter & Co., Berlin.

- Extreme vertical and horizontal integration that did not only include subcontractors and distribution outlets (shops), but also many unfamiliar activities, such as the production of consumer goods by combine firms or the running of social institutions.
- Excessive manpower in the functional areas as well as in the combine firms.

The Collective Combine as an Organization Type

The Mintzberg Configuration as Concept of Analysis. Now we will try to establish the typical characteristics of a collective combine as compared to organizations in the private sector. For this purpose we will refer to Mintzberg's structural configuration types (Mintzberg, 1979, p. 299).

Mintzberg describes five basic parts of organizations (Fig. 3). According to their dimensions and scope, five configuration types of organizations can be identified (Fig. 4):

- The "simple entrepreneurial organization," marked by direct control and a predominant strategic apex.
- The "machine bureaucracy," marked by standardization of work flow and technostructure.
- The "professional bureaucracy," marked by the capabilities of its employees and operating core.
- The "divisionalized organization," marked by standardization of the output and by its middle line.
- The "adhocracy," marked by mutual adjustment and supporting units.

Figure 3
The Five Basic Parts of Organization (after Mintzberg, 1979, p. 20)

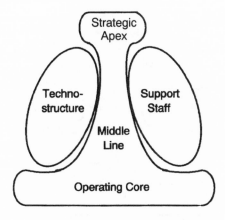

Figure 4
Organization Types According to Mintzberg (1979, p. 14)

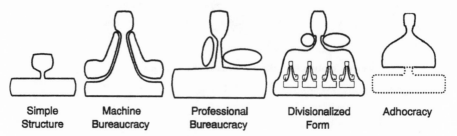

| Simple Structure | Machine Bureaucracy | Professional Bureaucracy | Divisionalized Form | Adhocracy |

The Classification of the Combine. To which of these types do collective combines correspond? A simple and unambiguous classification is impossible. The collective combine seems to be a combination of "machine bureaucracy" and "divisionalized form" (Fig. 5). The strategic apex, middle line, technostructure, and support staff in combines correspond to the "machine bureaucracy" model, while the operating core seems to fit into the "divisionalized form." The Collective Combine typically shows the characteristics of both configuration types.

1. Contingency factors
   - Stable and simple environmental conditions
   - Variety of products and markets
   - External direction and control
   - Obsolete production with a low degree of automation
   - Old and large organization

Figure 5
The Collective Combine as Organization Type

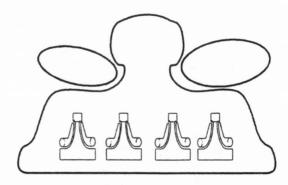

2. Critical functional area
   - Technostructure
   - Middle line management
3. Main design factors
   - Strong vertical and horizontal specialization
   - Vertical centralization and limited horizontal decentralization
   - Functional organization and inferior grouping according to products (combine firms)
   - Strong formulation of expected behavior
4. Primary coordination mechanisms
   - Standardization of output ("plan fulfillment")
   - Standardization of work processes.

However, the combination of the structural characteristics of the "machine organization" and the "divisional organization" model in the collective combine did not result in an accumulation of the respective advantages or competitive strengths.

The economy of scale advantage, characteristic of the "machine bureaucracy" could not be achieved in the collective combine due to small production lots in the divisions (combine firms), resulting in high unit costs. By the same token, the flexibility akin to the "divisional organization" could not be reached, as there was no appropriate decentralization and no scope for action for the middle management.

In contrast to the divisionalized organization, the collective combine did not content itself with a small technostructure and a slender middle management. On the contrary, it showed the structural characteristics of the "machine bureaucracy." The structural type collective combine could only exist as long as it was possible to absorb environmental instability. With the marketing side being taken care of by the central plan, it was mainly the procurement function that could cause difficulties in the execution of the plans because of short supplies. Supply fluctuations were countered by increasing domestic production. With increasing self-sufficiency, the collective combine was able to gain more stability. From this point of view, this type was not inefficient in the given conditions.

Basic Principles of the Organizational Transformation Process

With the collapse of the political and economic system the organizational type collective combine faced a completely changed environment. Central planning in forms of bulk, quantities, and costs became meaningless or was replaced by market mechanisms. The procurement objectives changed, too. On one hand, there was now free access to Western supply markets; on the other hand, the internal supply system collapsed. The previous stable environment, partitioned for means of economic autarchy, was now exposed to a very high dynamism and turbulence.

Organizational transformation must begin within the changed environmental conditions. Several measures seem necessary for organizational transformation.

Reducing the Organizational Type Collective Combine to Organizational Archetypes by Means of Corporate Divestment or Liquidation of Operating Units. To begin with, it seems reasonable to preserve the collective combine in its fundamental structure and to operate the parent and the individual combine firms in the form of independent incorporated companies. Often, in this phase, the firms are converted into subsidiary companies (Private Limited Companies, "GmbH") of a holding corporation ("Aktiengesellschaft"), which is in the possession of the Government Trust Agency responsible for privatization (Treuhandanstalt).

The following questions must be answered (Bühner, 1992, p. 197). Can the available technological base be used for building up an operational core competence? Can the financial resources that are necessary for building up the core competences be procured from unrelated combine parts? Are the necessary resources also to be provided by a third party (e.g., Treuhandanstalt)? Can the operational core competences of other enterprises be harnessed by strategic alliances or joint ventures?

The legal and organizational decentralization achieved in this phase already permits decentralized decision making as well as the delegation of responsibility to individual managing directors. However, it seems that many former suppliers are not competitive enough with regard to costs to exist in external markets because of small size and obsolete technology. Whether they are able to survive or not depends on their internal exchange of supplies and services. On the other hand, the original parent firms increasingly rely on the external supply of components in order to be able to offer competitive products themselves.

Furthermore, a major step lies in the definition and concentration of the core business. This does not necessarily have to be confined to the former parent business, as the relevant decision-making criteria are now the sales possibilities and the available product technologies. Moreover, corporate divestment of the suppliers is to be initiated.

Finally, "privatization," the selling of individual companies unable to exist on their own, must be enforced. Manufacturing scope and integration have to be reduced to a normal degree. Also, the internal interconnection of services must be reduced as far as possible.

Corporate divestment of small suppliers and former service departments is done through management buy out. In this case, the "simple structure" seems to be the appropriate organization form. However, the product range of the newly established core business as well as the relevant suppliers, provided that they could not be sold or made independent, are maintained in the "divisional form."

The remaining part of the original "machine bureaucracy" can only be maintained in exceptional cases. Such cases occur at best in branches of the primary sector with continuous production processes. Examples are the exploitation of natural resources and their processing as well as steel production and energy generation.

The best chance of survival lies in the concentration of business on a vertical core segment and in getting rid of satellite firms. Even so, in many of these branches there is a risk that continuously unprofitable concerns permanently dependent on subsidies are created.

The "professional bureaucracy," too, can be the result of restructuring. Especially in those cases where research and development capacities are to be maintained for economic and research policy interests, this organization form can prove to be useful. An impressive example for this is "Jenoptik" in Jena, where thousands of demanding jobs in the former Combine of Karl Zeiss Jena are subsidized in order to produce product innovations in the field of optical electronics and to exploit the results commercially on a long-term basis. Corporate divestment in the sense of organizational transformation means giving a new structure to the individual combine firms according to their new environment.

Balancing of Structural Deficits Caused by Requirements of Market Mechanisms. Organization of the former parent firm (technostructure and middle-line management) may not have been oriented towards market requirements. In addition, individual functional areas may have to be staffed by responsible and qualified executives. The new organization has to be free of redundant functions on the one hand and supplemented by new necessary ones on the other (Fig. 6). The central departments on the combine's managing level will have to be restructured and the overhead costs reduced to a justifiable extent.

Transformation Success. Up to now the success of the restructuring measures could not be conclusively assessed because of the relatively short time of transformation. Nevertheless, some signs of development are traceable (Nölting, 1993, p. 98). Strategic investments are more successful than just expansion investments (additional purchase of manufacturing capacity) or pure financial projects. Foreign investors with independent operations are especially successful. Takeovers for the most part are only successful in local, regional, and Eastern markets. In Western or interregional markets they are not competitive enough or are hampered in entering the market.

ORGANIZATIONAL TRANSFORMATION IN PRACTICE: THE CASE OF THE COLLECTIVE COMBINE TEXTIMA

The organizational restructuring as described above will now be analyzed in context with a case study of Textima. This case study is divided into two sections. First, the structure of the Textima Combine is explained by discussing briefly its production and supply organization. Then, the Combine's transformation into a joint-stock company and the disengagement of its individual companies by "privatization" is described.

Figure 6
Enlargement of the Actual Organization According to Steinberg (1991, p. 52)

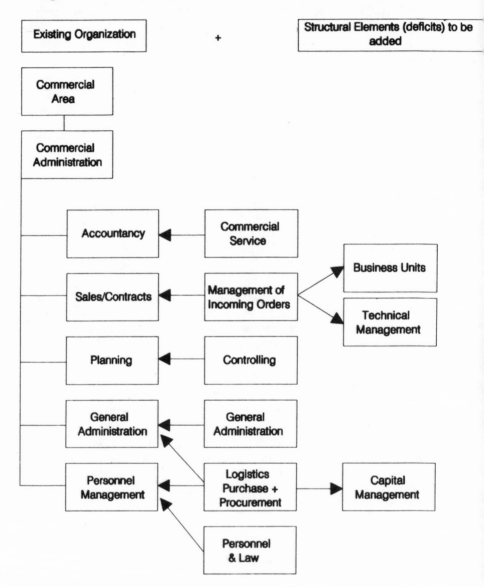

Description of Textima

The Combine's Business Areas. The Textima Combine was an engineering and construction enterprise engaged in the development, planning and production of machines and installations for the textile industry. It produced machines for all phases of textile processing: spinning, stitching and knitting, weaving, textile cleaning and finishing, and ready-made clothing.

According to these phases of textile processing, the following product groups made up the Combine's production programme: spinning machines for natural and artificial fibers, stitching and knitting machines, weaving machines, textile finishing machines, textile cleaning machines, and machines and equipment for the clothing industry.

Organization of the Combine. The Textima Combine comprised 30 individual state-owned firms, which on their part maintained 36 plants. Organization and administration of Textima was in the hands of the Combine's management. Its major task was the development of long- (5 years), middle- (1 year), and short-term plans (quarterly and monthly) on the basis of the proposals put forward by the individual plants. The overall plan of the Textima Combine had to be co-ordinated with the Ministry for Machine Tools and Processing Construction Engineering.

In order to guarantee a high capacity utilization, the approved Combine plans were sent back in the form of planning targets to the individual state-owned firms. If these individual firms were not employed to the capacity prescribed by the Combine central plans, external orders had to be obtained to meet the official planned targets.

Besides the production of core products, production of "technical consumer goods" was imposed on the Combine in order to make up for the chronic shortage of consumer goods in the GDR. In Textima some of the state-owned firms were especially designated for this purpose.

The Combine's Supply Organization. Textima could not set planned targets for other firms of the combine. In order to maintain a certain standard of quality and productivity, Textima, like all combines in the GDR, had integrated as far as possible all necessary manufacturing processes, including production of items in small lots. This made it independent from external subcontractors, even though inefficient in many cases. In case of specialized items, production was restricted to core parts and assembly. In addition to the combine's assembly manufacturers there was also an intensive exchange of parts between the manufacturers of the final products for better utilization of the machine capacity. This led to a production depth of the Textima Combine of nearly 80%.

The following figure illustrates the production depth of Textima (Fig. 7). Figure 8 illustrates the organization structure of the Textima Combine. The aforementioned Consumer Goods Division and the Division for Parts and Assemblies are on the same organizational level as the core divisions.

Figure 7
Manufacturing Penetration of the Textima Combine. Open columns = total amount of blueprint parts;
solid columns = blueprint parts produced in the combine

Number of the
original blue-
print parts of
14 products

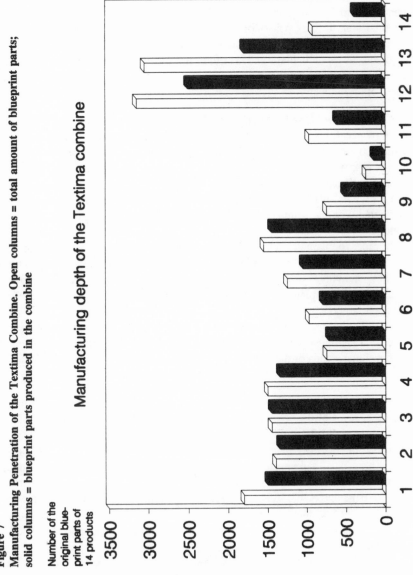

Manufacturing depth of the Textima combine

Figure 8
Organization of the Combine According to Product Groups (1989)

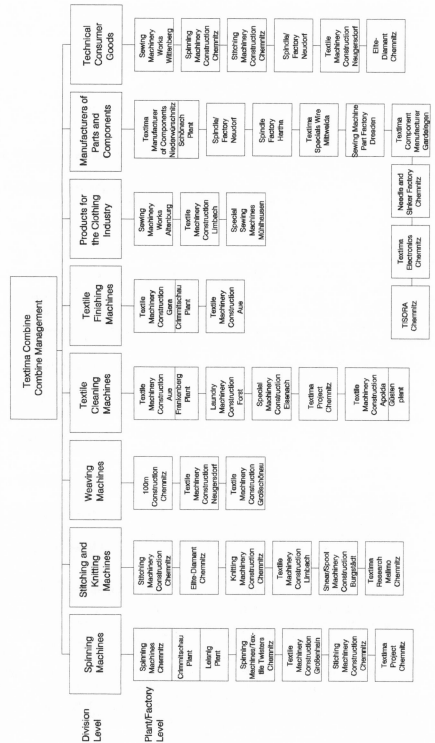

Transformation and Privatization

Transformation into a Corporation ("Aktiengesellschaft"). The first phase of the transformation process consists in giving the combine firms a new legal form. On basis of the Transformation Regulation Act of March 1, 1990, the Textima Combine was converted into Textima Corporation ("Aktiengesellschaft") on June 28, 1990. After the transformation, Textima Corp. comprised a holding company and 31 subsidiaries organized as limited companies ("GmbH"). The shares of the limited companies, which basically corresponded to the capital stock of former state-owned firms (SOFs), were held to 100% by Textima Corp.

For different reasons, a part of the former combine firms was detached from Textima and directly subordinated to the Treuhandanstalt. Some of these companies are listed below.

Textima Combine Firms	*Direct Treuhandanstalt Shares*
1. SOF "Sewing Machinery Works," Altenburg	Sewing Machinery Works Ltd., Altenberg
2. SOF "Textima Project," Chemnitz	Textpro Engineering, Ltd., Chemnitz
3. SOF "Washing Machinery Construction," Forst	Washing Machinery Construction, Ltd., Forst
4. SOF "Special Sewing Machinery Works," Mühlhausen	Special Sewing Machinery Works, Ltd., Mühlhausen
. . .	. . .
39. SOF "Textile Machinery Construction Apolda Plant," Güsten	Textile Machinery Construction, Ltd., Großschönau
40. Former Combine Management	CREATIV Marketing and Public Relations Agency, Ltd.

Between July 1990 and June 1993 parts of some more corporations were released from state ownership. In the end, more than 40 corporations were privatized.

Privatization. The second phase of the transformation process consists of the following necessary steps (Witt, 1993, p. 1167): to align the organization on the basis of business units; to grant the business units autonomy; to eliminate redundant levels of hierarchies; and to reduce the central overheads.

Right after the foundation of Textima Corp. in mid-1990 (first phase), the second phase had to be started. Extensive discussions arose in the company's Supervisory ("Aufsichtsrat") and Executive Boards ("Vorstand") about the right approach regarding privatization and reorganization of the group. The prevailing opinion expressed was that only individual enterprises not belonging directly to the core business should be privatized into independent companies, while the remaining corporation with most of the subsidiaries should first be reorganized and then later be taken to the stock market. Another suggestion was to dismantle Textima Corp. and build two new separate groups.

The main dispute was whether priority should be given to reconstruction or to privatization. This issue has, in fact, also been debated very controversially by the public, which has followed with keen interest the pros and cons of both alternatives. In contrast, the Treuhandanstalt has always held the opinion that both measures were complimentary to each other in the sense that privatization was the best mode of reconstruction.

Indeed, in practice the Treuhandanstalt has had only a few cases where conflict arose. In the case of Textima Corp. this problem was posed in connection with the privatization of Malimo Machinery Construction. The question was whether Malimo should be first merged with other Textima companies in order to achieve productions synergies and thereby subsequently pave the way for a much quicker privatization.

Making a decision on this issue is generally a very delicate task that has to take into consideration the advantages and disadvantages of both alternatives very carefully. Of course, in each case the individual situation has to be taken into account. In doubtful cases the Treuhandanstalt always gave priority to privatization.

After lengthy discussions in the Supervisory and Executive Boards as well as in the relevant committees of the Treuhandanstalt during 1991 and 1992, agreement was reached on a concept of complete corporate divestment directed towards privatization through various modes. For this purpose a special team was formed within the corporation; it privatized three enterprises through direct negotiations in coordination with the Treuhandanstalt. All other privatizations were carried out directly by the Treuhandanstalt. These events are listed below in chronological order.

Supply Organization of the Corporation. The structure of supplies and subcontracting relationships within the corporation—although thinned out considerably by divestment—corresponded in 1991 to a great extent to the exchange relations within the former collective combine. This was due to Textima's unchanged product range. However, modifications occurred with regard to modernized electronic control equipment. Large assembled parts were not any longer developed within the corporation but purchased as complete components from outside. Figure 9 gives an overview of the product and supply structure within the corporation in 1991.

The ongoing process of privatization within the corporation made it difficult to realign the product range on an overall and corporate basis as most of the innovations were worked out in the individual companies, guided by cost aspects of the market. Depending on the product, the scope between the prices that could be obtained on the market and the cost of manufacturing had to determine the framework for new developments of the individual companies. Therefore, new

Figure 9
Organization of the Textima Corporation According to Product Groups (1991)

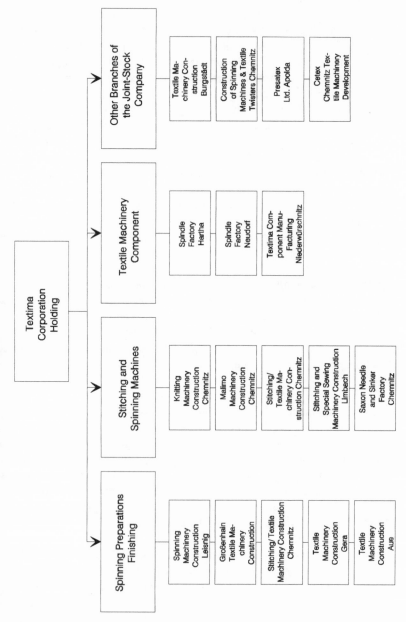

product developments were not guided by the production facilities within the corporation.

Owing to the general pressure of costs, procurement from within the corporation fell increasingly behind in favor of the less expensive market offers. Corresponding to this, manufacturing depth within the corporation has decreased continuously. Even so, in contrast to West German companies, the remaining companies of the former Textima Combine still held by the Treuhandanstalt are interconnected with each other to an exceptionally high degree. Maintaining traditional internal supply relations gives the firms an opportunity to utilize their capacities at reasonable levels. This would otherwise not be possible because of their inability to secure their own markets. From the cost point of view, further corporate divestment of the subcontractors can only be done gradually.

SUMMARY

After the transformation of Textima Combine, more than 40 firms have been privatized since July 1, 1990. At the same time, these companies had to be adapted through extensive reconstruction to the requirements of the market economy. Originally, it was proposed to structure Textima Corporation in the form of a textile machinery corporate group and to officially quote the shares on the stock exchange. But because of the disappointing economic growth of the Combine firms and the limited synergy effects within the corporate group, this type of privatization did not seem to have much success potential. So Textima Corporation was divested completely, internal supplier relations were largely given up, the holdings liquidated and the individual firms privatized separately. On July 1, 1993 just 5 of the 40 combine firms of Textima Corporation were in the hands of the Treuhandanstalt. Three companies were liquidated. The other companies were sold to private investors.

REFERENCES

Bühner, R. (1992). *Management-Holding, Unternehmensstruktur der Zukunft.* Landsberg: Verlag Moderne Industrie.
Marr, H. (1989). Zur Entwicklung der Leitungswissenschaft in der DDR. In R. Pier (Ed.), *Westliches Management—Östliche Leitung*, pp. 37–79. Berlin: De Gruyter.
Mintzberg, H. (1979). *The Structuring of Organizations.* Englewood Cliffs, NJ: Prentice-Hall.
Nölting, A. (1993). Hinter der Kulisse, *Manager Magazin*, 23(6): 96–115.
Steinberg, C. (1991). *Praxisbezogenes Umstrukturierungsmanagement vom Plan zum Markt.* Stuttgart: Schäffer Verlag. Düsseldorf: VDI-Verlag.
Witt, C.D. (1993). Wandel der Aufbauorganisation im Transformationsprozeß ostdeutscher Industrieunternehmen, *Zeitschrift für Betriebswirtschaft*, 63(11): 1157–1168.

6

Merging for Transformation

Rolf-Dieter Reineke

INTRODUCTION

Mergers, acquisitions, joint ventures, and the problems of integration they can imply are highly topical. To date, however, they have been discussed in a rather one-sided way from the financial, strategic, and legal angles. The applicability of the concept of acculturation, as used in cultural anthropology, to the problem of merging corporate cultures, is examined. Based on this concept, the potential for and constraints on influencing the transformation process in the context of the postcommunist countries are considered.

**STATUS OF MERGERS, ACQUISITIONS, AND JOINT
VENTURES IN POSTCOMMUNIST COUNTRIES**

Almost all corporate headquarters in the Western industrialized nations are currently engaged in setting up business activities in the postcommunist countries (PCCs). In 1991, direct investments in Eastern Europe by German corporations alone (not including the former GDR) totalled DM 1.482 billion. In 1992 this figure grew to DM 1.605 billion, thus already surpassing German direct investments in Southeast Asia (Handschuch, 1993, p. 15).

Though there are opportunities in the PCCs, there are also considerable risks arising from developments that have in some cases taken place at breakneck speed and from the often unfavorable legal and economic framework of these countries (Gelb & Gray, 1991). The management of opportunities and risks can often only be performed from a local base, where the individuals involved are familiar with the specific circumstances.

In many cases, it is therefore appropriate to combine Western expertise and capital with a precise understanding of the Eastern market and conditions in one organizational unit. This is achieved in the form of a merger, an acquisition, or a joint venture with a location in the PCC. Joint ventures in particular are a popular choice for entry into the Eastern European market (Smith & Rebne, 1992, p. 190). The management problems of these three forms of corporate cooperation are very similar. They all involve a merging of Eastern and Western resources, and henceforth will be referred to under the generic term M&A, or newly-combined corporation.

What will not be addressed here are direct investments of Western corporations in PCCs in the form of new businesses without any participation by an Eastern enterprise. This form of internalization is currently being vigorously pursued by German corporations in particular, e.g., in Hungary, the Czech Republic, and Poland (Fischer, 1993, p. 8–10). The prime motive in this connection is cost-cutting; the goods produced are mostly reexported to Germany, and any strategic interest on the part of the respective PCC in breaking into the market is a very secondary consideration. As soon as the advantage of low costs ceases to apply, the factory is simply moved to a country where labor costs are lower.

In this chapter, "merging for transformation" will be understood as an evolutionary process designed to combine the resources of Western and Eastern corporations with the goal of achieving long-term integration. The main objectives of an integration of this nature as seen from the perspective of a western corporation, are increased corporate growth and quick improvement of their own market position in the PCCs, overcoming of tariff and nontariff trade barriers, and spreading of business risk over several countries.

Numerous studies on M&As show a clear discrepancy between pursued and actually achieved goals. A high percentage of the M&As analyzed in these studies, which from the economic angle should have been successful, were nevertheless a failure (Business International Corp., 1987, p. 83; Finkelstein, 1986, p. 13). This leads to the conclusion that the existence of conditions conducive to economic success is a necessary but not a sufficient precondition for a successful M&A.

This is especially true in case of M&As that are not merely short-term financial investments but lasting ventures of strategic importance. In this instance, and especially if the integration of the two parts of the new company is close and has been planned on a long-term basis, the contact between the different corporate cultures is intimate. In the M&A process, the significance of the corporate culture is often neglected. Frequently, the cultural aspect is only considered as it were after the event, when the failure of the efforts towards integration is explained by a cultural misfit (Schein 1985: 36). Corporate culture as understood here is defined briefly as a set of collectively shared values, internalized norms, and patterns of thought and behavior within a corporation. M&As and the problems of cultural integration which they can imply, are very important for the transformation process in the PCCs.

When attempting to examine the integration process in M&As, the concept of acculturation borrowed from cultural anthropology and the U-curve hypothesis used in this context seem to be helpful (Nahavandi & Malekzadeh, 1986; Sales & Mirvis, 1984). In the following, the potential and usefulness of the concept with respect to M&As will be discussed. Also, certain instruments that may be helpful in influencing transformation in the context of the PCCs will be examined.

THE CONCEPT OF ACCULTURATION IN THE CONTEXT OF EAST–WEST M&As

When analyzing long-term processes of cultural adaptation concerning individuals or groups, exponents of both cultural anthropology and cross-cultural psychology have used the concept of acculturation as a basis of analysis since 1880 (Berry, 1983, p. 65). The term acculturation can be defined as follows (Redfield et al., 1936, p. 149): "Acculturation comprehends those phenomena which result when groups of individuals having different cultures come into continuous first-hand contact, with subsequent changes in the original cultural patterns of either or both groups."

In the course of the acculturation process, two formerly autonomous cultural systems exert an influence on each other. Although it is true that this influence is caused by exogenous factors originating from the respective opposite group, it nevertheless produces dynamics of internal adaptation (Berry, 1980, p. 217). Although some cultures have proved to be more resistant to cultural influences than others, it can be taken as a fact that a long-term intercultural contact generally causes a process of cultural adaptation. The cause and the form of the process can be different in each case, but the phenomenon of acculturation can always be observed and is independent of the type of culture (Segall, 1979, p. 185).

Dominance and Conflict in Acculturation

In M&As that take place for strategic reasons and not as mere short-term financial investments, different corporate cultures collide. In addition to this, the process also involves a collision between different national cultures ("macro-cultures") when foreign companies are involved. Given a U-shaped acculturation curve, an appropriate adaptation of values, norms, and patterns of thought and behavior of the two parts of the newly combined company is achieved.

As a rule, the extent of cultural adaptation is not equal in both of the corporate cultures involved but depends on which of the two actually prevails and is dominant. Thus, in his empirical research on the integration of foreign acquisitions, Lindgren (1982, p. 69) found that changes in the corporate culture of the parent company can be observed only rarely and only in connection with large-scale acquisitions. In most cases, the dominance of the acquiring company results from the ownership and the relative size of the parent company vis-à-vis the acquired subsidiary. Moreover, in the PCCs, the notion is widespread that "modern" or "Western" patterns of thought, values, and norms have to be adopted because the "old" patterns have historically led to failure. On the other hand, this notion can lead to resistance among many employees who are afraid of "cultural imperialism."

The Western partner of the company is consequently dominant in many cases and the Eastern partner adapts itself to the corporate culture of the Western part of the company to a greater extent than vice versa. The dominance of one part of the newly combined company is a crucial reason for conflicts that occur in the course of the acculturation process. "The apparent domination of one group over the other suggests that what happens between contact and change may be difficult, reactive, and conflictual rather than a smooth transition" (Berry, 1983, p. 66).

In organization research, observed negative consequences of conflicts are:

• Destruction of positive relations between parties as a result of permanent tension.
• Instability of the organization.
• Misallocation of resources.
• Biased or reduced information flows that lead to diminished perception and quality of the decisions made.

Positive aspects of such conflicts are also observed. Examples of such incidents are:

• Discussion of myths and traditions that have not been questioned so far.
• More mutual understanding between the parties.
• Mobilization of resources.
• Disclosure of or the creative search for alternative courses of action resulting in improvement of the future cooperation.

By the same token, conflicts that occur in an M&A cannot be considered as being only negative either. The cultural adjustment, e.g., to a synergetic type of corporate culture (Adler, 1980) will not be possible without thinking about new forms of cooperation.

Also, an increasing convergence of values and behavior in corporate and national cultures in the acculturation process cannot, a priori, be considered as positive or negative. If these patterns are largely compatible, the conflicts, e.g., in the socialization of new employees and in the external relations of the company, will be less marked than in the event of considerable divergences between corporate and national cultures. The divergence of the corporate culture from the national values and norms can, however, also lead to competitive advantages (Bleicher, 1986, p. 783).

Phase Model of the Acculturation Process Based on the U-Curve Hypothesis

The phases of the acculturation process have so far been mentioned only implicitly; this dynamic aspect will now be examined more closely. The starting point is the concept of phases of cultural adaptation as developed in cross-cultural psychology and cultural anthropology.

As shown in Fig. 1, acculturation varies according to different phases of cultural adaptation. The degree of cultural adaptation can be equated with the success of

Figure 1
The Phases of Acculturation

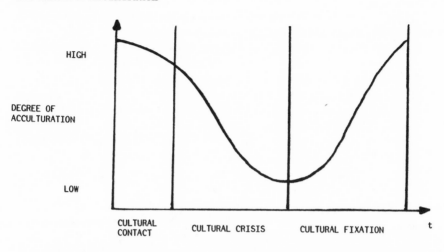

the acculturation process which, in turn, is determined by certain factors. Hypothetically, the following determinants can be assumed to be factors of success [the factors are discussed in detail by Reineke (1989, pp. 60–80)]:

* The corporate-cultural distance between the two companies involved.
* The motivation for corporate-cultural adaptation.
* The achievement of objectives of the M&A.
* The corporate-cultural flexibility.
* The reduction of uncertainty.

Roughly speaking, the U-curve hypothesis states that after an initial positive adaptation, which is due above all to curiosity about the new culture, a crisis in adaptation follows. Once this crisis has been overcome, a process of growing adaptation can be observed (Furnham & Bochner, 1986, p. 131).

In the context of the East–West M&A the model can be described as follows: The phase of "cultural contact" begins when the Eastern and the Western companies hold their first discussions regarding the cooperation, which includes the negotiations about the contract; this phase ends when the plans for the M&A are ready for implementation. If the results of the negotiations are considered to be positive by the Eastern company, and provided there is no further immediate contact between the two, e.g., by an "invasion" of delegates sent by the Western company right after the conclusion of the contractual negotiations, a sense of eager expectancy in the former often prevails. At the same time, uncertainty about the future of the enterprise grows.

These events can lead into the "crisis phase" if methods practiced and systems used in the Eastern company up to that point are suddenly modified or abolished as a result of the influence of the Western company. The intensive interaction between the Eastern and the Western company brings out clearly the cultural differences. Conflicts often arise regarding the appropriate course of action. A high degree of uncertainty within the newly established joint company and "culture shock" are often the consequence, and these result in a cultural crisis. Two typical symptoms at the management level are wavering on the part of many managers in accepting the dominant company and looking for another job with a different company (Jemison & Sitkin, 1986). In the case of "culture shock," the degree of acculturation is, at least temporarily, low. The adaptation curve may take a functional (U-shaped) course and the degree of acculturation subsequently rise. On the whole, depending on the general setting and the instruments available and applied (see below) this process can last several years.

The general observation with regard to the cooperation between companies from the Western industrialized countries and the PCCs is that dominance in negotiation power of the Western company will have to be anticipated in the years to come. Whether or not this will also inevitably involve a cultural dominance, which results in "cultural crisis," and whether "cultural fixation" will follow, can only be established through further empirical studies. The pace at which initial euphoria in former East Germany following the collapse of communism so obviously wore off as Western norms and dominating behavior came to be better known indicates that the U-curve hypothesis is a sound basis on which to proceed.

In the following, an attempt will be made to examine how the process of acculturation can be influenced positively in the sense that the "cultural crisis" phase is reduced to a minimum and "cultural fixation" is achieved. This means effecting a transformation of two corporate cultures into an integrated whole while taking into account the specific prevailing conditions in the PCCs.

INSTRUMENTS FOR MANAGING THE TRANSFORMATION OF CORPORATE CULTURES IN THE CONTEXT OF THE POSTCOMMUNIST COUNTRIES

The spectrum of opinion on the extent to which corporate cultures can be influenced in the sense of a conscious "cultural management" ranges from the view that a planned development of corporate cultures is impossible to a purely mechanistic belief according to which a corporate culture can be changed at will. The former position is less plausible in view of the fact that human beings always have the ability to question and adjust their own thought and behavior patterns, as well as those of others. In principle, this also applies to corporations. But there are also a number of arguments against the latter extreme position of unlimited possibility of changing corporate culture. For instance, because of problems in precisely defining and measuring corporate cultures, attempts to influence culture can have unforeseen results. A planned development of corporate cultures is therefore only possible on a limited and long-term scale. Figure 2 illustrates conceivable approaches for managing corporate-cultural change. In the following sections, several examples will be examined that are of particular relevance in the context of M&As in PCCs.

Strategic Instruments

The strategic considerations that motivate the Western company to enter into a M&A with an Eastern company are based on different patterns of thought and behavior than in "normal cases." A central problem for Western companies is the fact that the Eastern company has not functioned in a market economy, so that, in many cases, its corporate strategy cannot take into account market conditions and the notion of competition.

Strategy workshops and intensive project work are good forums for achieving a common understanding of the strategy and the objectives being pursued. A shared vision of the cooperation can make a considerable positive contribution to the acculturation process. In the context of the PCCs, however, some problems should be noted:

Figure 2
Instruments of Influence on Corporate Culture

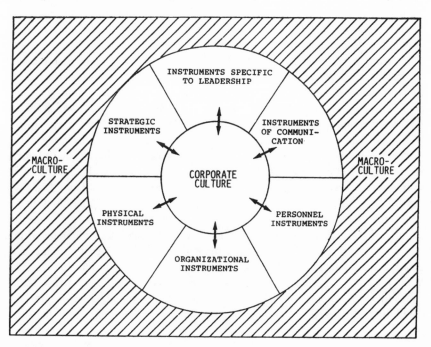

- In many cases appropriate structures needed to mediate team spirit are lacking.
- There is a marked tendency to make "grand gestures." Merely formulating strategies is often considered to be sufficient and equivalent to implementing them (similar to the Party Congress resolutions) (Schmid & Boback, 1992, pp. 3–5).
- Due to the dynamic changes in environment, there is a danger that interests underlying alliances will also shift frequently (ad-hocism).
- The fear of losing one's job is also widespread among managers in the PCCs that as a rule they prefer conservative strategies for the new ventures (Vansina, 1993, p. 11).

Instruments Specific to Leadership

The style of leadership will inevitably affect the corporate culture. The way management solves problems and sets priorities will determine the thought and behavior patterns of the workforce. The kind of influences that will be accepted by the workforce will in turn be determined by the values and norms already embedded in the corporate cultures of the two cooperating corporations.

The socialist concept of democracy tends to favor an autocratic style of management, which does not exist in the West. Management behavior in the East is also greatly influenced by the prevailing understanding of right and wrong as defined by the law, which can be summarized as follows: anything that is not prescribed as compulsory is felt to be prohibited. This understanding of the role of the law is therefore rather prescriptive and as such a constraint. On the other hand, the legal system in the West is based on proscriptions: anything not expressly prohibited is permissible. This fact should be taken into account, for instance, when drawing up joint management principles.

Imposing Western management behavior on the Eastern managers in the new ventures formed by M&A would therefore be difficult in the context of an Eastern, i.e., formerly socialist, national culture. On the other hand many managers from the PCCs also have other qualities, such as a capacity to improvise, which for the foreseeable future are of major significance for entrepreneurial activity in the PCCs and thus a valuable asset within a synergistic corporate culture.

There is a great temptation for Western managers to fill the management vacuum created by the collapse of the old system in the East with tested Western solutions. At present, managers from the PCCs tend to underestimate their own capabilities and performance, which, in view of the adverse conditions under which they have to operate, are often quite respectable. At the same time, an attitude of skepticism vis-à-vis any kind of ideology (including ideologies from the West) is widespread. One of the main reasons for this is that many new concepts have failed and led to even further deterioration (Vansina, 1993, p. 13). Many managers from the PCCs have resigned in the face of the immense actual and anticipated problems. The management team of an M&A can gain new credibility if their actions can improve the situation of the workforce in the short term.

Organizational Instruments

The changes within many M&As will often be very clearly manifested in the organizational structures and procedures of the new venture. The relationship between organization and corporate culture is one of interdependence: the formal structures and procedures are an expression of the value system and norms of the corporation. The symbolic significance of many changes therefore also have an impact on the acculturation process. Conversely, the corporate culture is also influenced by the existing or former structures.

In the former GDR, for instance, structural models were in most cases based on the staff-line system (Pieper, 1989, p. 215). A structure of this type tends to lead to norms and behavior patterns that favor hierarchy. Although staff-line systems are also used quite widely in Western countries, they are in many cases found in conjunction with matrix solutions or team-oriented structures based on collectivist norms.

In organizations in the former GDR, the structure of operations was often controlled through elaborate and detailed regulations (Pieper, 1989, p. 238). There was barely any delegation of responsibility. Inspections were regular and detailed (Kiezun, 1991, p. 84). Many of these rigid systems could only be kept viable through informal networking among the workforce. In M&As, adjustment to other systems and standards often leads to considerable problems. According to several case studies (Ebinal, 1992, p. 1071; Kröger, 1993, p. 101; Kaiser & Tamm, 1992) this is especially the case in the accounting and controlling functions, where the Western partner almost always has to insist on changes. These systems, including the data processing systems, often require forms of organization and management that in many cases can only be established within the framework of a long-term process.

Personnel Instruments

Especially during the initial phase of M&A, active and passive layoffs as well as intracompany transfers contribute considerably towards the integration of corporate cultures, resulting in both potential for risk and a positive outcome of the acculturation process. If a cultural change is desired or necessary, the replacement of key managers is often unavoidable. In many cases it is not possible to bring about the necessary change in thought and behavior among the older generation of managers in the PCCs, many of whom were loyal members of the Communist Party. Attempts to establish a new identity often lack credibility and fail to meet with the acceptance of broad sections of the workforce. When filling vacant positions, it is useful to emphasize basic attitude and orientation as selection criteria. Difficulties arise in the adjustment process when managers who possess specific expertise or are reference persons for many employees leave the company. The void leads to a disorientation among the workforce, which is very difficult for new managers to remedy.

With regard to personnel development, further training is one important instrument for integration in addition to a reorientation in performance appraisal and career planning. A key aspect in many PCCs is the continuous development of an understanding of sales and marketing principles with a view to achieving a high degree of customer orientation within the newly formed corporation. Previously, in the context of the "seller's market," attention was focused on meeting planned targets.

Finally, modifying the incentive system in the Eastern company is in most cases inevitable. In the PCCs, meeting planned targets was of prime importance. "Socialist competition" involved intercompany comparison with respect to the meeting of targets, focusing less on competition between individuals (Lück, 1990, p. 34). Appropriately designed bonus and profit-sharing systems might create an environment that also fosters other values and norms.

Negotiation and Communication

The success of new joint corporations is closely linked to communication in and outside the organization. Key aspects here are the style of communication and information policy before and after merger of the Western and Eastern companies.

The first phase in which the two sides get to know each other involves a process of building trust and confidence as well as interpersonal relationships. Initially, this is handled by the top management of the Eastern company. In many cases it is necessary to be first accepted as a "friend" in order to be able to establish a viable base for business. Russia is a prominent case where negotiations are opened by laying out very general joint "grand schemes." This does not necessarily mean that the Eastern side also intends to implement these projects in detail. However, if the Western partner shows a certain reservation at this point, he is often perceived as someone not willing to support and stick to joint decisions. The logic of this thinking is analogous to that of the Party resolution and the notion of solidarity attached to it (Schmid & Boback, 1992, p. 4).

Quick and rash judgments should be avoided just as much as attempts to preach or criticize. In conflicting situations, adopting a form of metacommunication has proven to be quite useful. This means addressing openly the communication behavior practiced by both sides and the value systems on which they are based. This does, however, presuppose a minimum degree of established interpersonal relationships. In this respect, the managers involved in the cooperation must see themselves as "cultural ambassadors." To prepare for such meetings it is often a good idea to secure the services of appropriately trained consultants. To this end, procedures have been developed such as the Rapid Organizational Appraisal (Kievelitz & Reineke, 1991). Based on this scheme, an analysis of the two involved corporate cultures can be conducted within three to six weeks at reasonable cost and with an adequate degree of precision, so as to produce valid conclusions for the integration process.

One particular problem is language. Words are often used in the West in an entirely different context, and there is the chance that will be distorted in translation. One excellent example of this type of misunderstanding is the commonly used term "corporate culture." Schmid and Boback (1992, p. 7) report on an incident in a workshop where Eastern participants became very reserved as this term was used. After clarification it turned out that it had been understood by the Easterners in a value-laden sense. Evidently, they got the impression that Eastern and Western cultures were being compared at the ideological level.

Misunderstandings and rumors arise between and within Eastern and Western companies as a result of communication problems. There is a tendency to elaborate "worst-case scenarios" in which each side assumes the worst of the other (Bastien, 1987, p. 19).

Apart from using good communication and transparent information policies, symbols can also be employed to promote the acculturation process. Employees often attach symbolic significance to things that might otherwise be presumed unimportant, such as a company kindergarten or car park regulations. Corporate design also falls into this category (colors, architecture, logo).

When western managers come across services or other activities within a company that are unrelated to the core business (e.g., hairdressers, bank branches, and shops), as is often the case in Russia, they often recommend their immediate removal. In so doing they overlook the fact that the boundaries between private and work life are far less clearly defined in PCCs than in the Western industrialized countries. This overlapping is an adaption to poor infrastructure. Many goods and services are unavailable; consequently the company has to make up for what public- and private-sector institutions cannot provide (Schmid & Boback, 1992, pp. 8–10). A sudden shutdown or removal of such company-run facilities has a devastating effect on workforce motivation.

"Symbolic management" of the acculturation process therefore requires a precise knowledge and understanding of the meaning and interpretation of the symbols used. As the interpretation of symbols is highly culture-specific, the risk of misunderstanding is great. There are already numerous examples of the symbols used having achieved just the opposite effect of what was desired.

CONCLUSION

Within the framework of M&As in PCCs, different corporate cultures, which are characterized by their respective national cultures, come into contact. The application of the concept of acculturation has proven useful in facilitating integration. It is possible to apply this approach in order to broaden the perspective on this issue, which to date has focused only on financial, strategic, and legal aspects. Before a merger, acquisition, or joint venture between a Western and an Eastern company in the PCC can be considered, the elements of the two corporate cultures should be examined with regard to their compatibility and potential for change.

Basically, the phase model of acculturation has a descriptive function. The knowledge that results from these reflections can be helpful when attempting to influence the transformation process. It is not possible, however, to derive detailed recommendations for shaping the process. The usefulness and the limitation of this model for coping with the problem of acculturation in M&As therefore has to be judged analogously to its importance in other phase concepts developed in business administration.

REFERENCES

Adler, N.J. (1980). Cultural strategy: The management of cross-cultural organizations. In W.W. Burke & L.D. Goodstein (Eds.), *Trends and Issues in OD: Current Theory and Practice*, pp. 163–184. San Diego: University Associates.

Bastien, D.T. (1987). Common patterns of behavior and communication in corporate mergers and acquisitions. *Human Resource Management*, 26(1): 17–33.

Berry, J.W. (1980). Social and cultural change. In H.C. Triandis & R. Brislin (Eds.), *Handbook of Cross-Cultural Psychology*, vol. 5, pp. 211–279. Boston: Allyn & Bacon.

Berry, J.W. (1983). Acculturation: A comparative analysis of alternative forms. In R.J. Samuda & S.L. Woods (Eds.), *Perspectives in Immigrant and Minority Education*, pp. 65–78. Lanham, MD: University Press of America.

Bleicher, K. (1986). Unternehmenskultur und strategische Unternehmensführung. In D. Hahn & B. Taylor (Eds.), *Strategische Unternehmensplanung: Stand und Entwicklungstendenzen*, 4th ed., pp. 757–797. Heidelberg: Physica.

Business International Corp. (1987). *Acquisition Strategy in Europe*. Geneva: Business International S.A.

Ebinal, M. (1992). Joint Ventures in der GUS—dargestellt am Beispiel der Salamander AG. In B.N. Kumar & H. Haussmann (Eds.), *Handbuch der Internationalen Unternehmenstätigkeit*, pp. 1067–1073. Munich: C.H. Beck'sche Verlagsbuchhandlung.

Finkelstein, S. (1986). The acquisition integration process. In J.A. Pearce II & R.B. Robinson (Eds.), *Academy of Management Best Paper Proceedings*, pp. 12–15. Chicago: Academy of Management.

Fischer, U. (1993). Frust mit Fossilien. *Management Wissen*, 9: 8–10.

Furnham, A. & Bochner, S. (1986). *Culture Shock: Psychological Reactions to Unfamiliar Environments*. London: Methuen.

Gelb, A.H. & Gray, C.W. (1991). *The Transformation of Economies in Central and Eastern Europe: Issues, Progress, and Prospects*. Washington, DC: The World Bank.

Handschuch, K. (1993). In der Armutsfalle. *Wirtschaftswoche*, 35:14–19.

Jemison, D.B. & Sitkin, S.B. (1986). Corporate Acquisitions: A process perspective. *Academy of Management Review*, 11(1): 145–163.

Kaiser, K.-A. & Tamm, A. (1992). *Osteuropa auf dem Weg zur Marktwirtschaft: Zehn Fallstudien mit Lösungsansätzen*. Wiesbaden: Gabler.

Kievelitz, U. & Reineke, R.-D. (1991). Die Analyse von Organisationskulturen: Eine Herausforderung für die Feldforschung. In G. Assmann, K. Backhaus & J. Hilker (Eds.), *Deutsch–deutsch Unternehmen: ein unternehmenskulturelles Anpassungsproblem*, pp. 301–320. Stuttgart: C.E. Poeschel.

Kiezun, W. (1991). *Management in Socialist Countries: USSR and Central Europe.* Berlin: Walter de Gruyter.

Kröger, F. (1993). Restrukturierung zur Privatisierung. *Zeitschrift für Betriebswirtschaft.* Ergänzungsheft 1/93: 97–107.

Lindgren, U. (1982). *Foreign Acquisitions: Management of the Integration Process.* Stockholm: EFI.

Lück, G. (1990). *Die betriebliche Arbeitsmotivation in der Bundesrepublik Deutschland und in der Deutschen Demokratischen Republik.* Wiesbaden: Deutscher Universitäts Verlag.

Nahavandi, A. & Malekzadeh, A.R. (1986). The role of acculturation in the implementation of mergers. In J.A. Pearce II & R.B. Robinson (Eds.), *Academy of Management Best Paper Proceedings,* pp. 140–144. Chicago: Academy of Management.

Pieper, R. (1989). Leitungswissenschaft und Managementlehre: Ansätze eines Vergleichs aus Sicht der Managementlehre. In R. Pieper (Ed.), *Westliches Management–östliche Leitung: ein Vergleich von Managementlehre und DDR-Leitungswissenschaft.* Berlin: Walter de Gruyter.

Redfield, R., Linton, R. & Herskovitz, M.J. (1936). Memorandum for the study of acculturation. *American Anthropologist,* 38: 149–152.

Reineke, R.-D. (1989). *Akkulturation von Auslandsakquisitionen: Eine Untersuchung zur unternehmenskulturellen Anpassung.* Wiesbaden: Gabler.

Sales, A.L. & Mirvis, P.H. (1984). When cultures collide: Issues in acquisitions. In J.R. Kimberly & R.E. Quinn (Eds.), *Managing organizational transitions.* Homewood, IL: Irwin.

Schein, E.H. (1985). *Organizational culture and leadership.* San Francisco: Jossey-Bass.

Schmid, B. & Boback, P. (1992). *Gedanken zur Kulturbegegnung bei der wirtschaftlichen Zusammenarbeit mit Rußland.* Unpublished paper of E.U.L.E. Consult, Wiesloch.

Segall, M.H. (1979). *Cross-Cultural Psychology: Human Behavior in Global Perspective.* Monterey, CA: Brooks/Cole.

Smith, N. & Rebne, D. (1992). Foreign direct investment in Poland, the Czech and Slovak Republics and Hungary: The centrality of the joint venture entry mode. *The Mid-Atlantic Journal of Business,* 28(3): 189–211.

Vansina, L. (1993). Minimalbedingungen für Veränderungen im Osten. *Organisationsentwicklung,* 1: 4–17.

III

BEHAVIOR AND PERSONNEL DEVELOPMENT FOR TRANSFORMATION

7

Transformation through Joint-Culture Ventures in the Formerly Socialist Countries

A Human Resource Perspective with "Cultural Model"

Michel E. Domsch and Désirée H. Ladwig

INTRODUCTION

This chapter discusses the transformation process in the former socialist countries within a framework of East–West joint-culture ventures from a human resource management point of view based on a special "cultural model" developed by the I.P.A. Institute for Human Resource Management and Labour Relations in Hamburg, Germany. The discussion is specifically focused at personnel development in the context of a "new culture" within the East–West joint-culture venture. The model offers a detailed situation-oriented description of relevant market constellations and offers ideas for transformation development training.

THE TRANSFORMATION PROCESS IN EASTERN EUROPE

The radical transformation process in the former socialist countries entails massive economic, political, and social changes. Situations of extreme change, especially of such complex nature as has been witnessed in the former socialist countries, have the inherent danger that the process of constructive transition may result in an uncontrollable, chaotic crisis. Alarming crisis indicators are reported in the media almost every day. Some of these signs are:

Political indicators

• Political instability characterized by a power struggle for political leadership between reformers and old-line Communists.
• Constant predominance of "old-line executive cadres" in all the important positions in society, as well as in management.

- War-like conflicts (civil wars) due to ethnic tensions.
- Lack of entrepreneurial orientation of state policy, exemplified by a very reserved privatization policy and restructuring measures.

Economic indicators

- Declining production.
- Decreasing turnover and exports.
- Shortage of finance and of foreign currency.
- Increasing unemployment (Bowles, 1991).
- Lowering of real income due to galloping inflation.

Business management indicators

- Waning willingness and ability of employees to think and act in an entrepreneurial way (Standing, 1991).
- Insufficient management potential (most managers belong to the ranks of the old-line executive cadre).
- Decreasing possibilities of selling domestic products on the home market resulting from the preference for "Western products."

In view of these developments the willingness of Western companies to invest in the former socialist countries has been and is still declining (Domsch, 1992; Kiezun, 1991).

THE PERSONNEL MANAGEMENT SITUATION IN VIEW OF SPECIFIC TRANSFORMATION PROBLEMS

The East–West Joint Venture from a Cultural Viewpoint

From the point of view of actively participating in the economic transformation process in the formerly socialist countries, East–West joint-culture ventures offer opportunities for development (Pfohl et al., 1992; Uebele, 1991). In this context a joint venture (Weber, 1989; Zentes, 1992) is defined as a jointly managed enterprise that is founded by two or more separate economic and legal entities and jointly managed. The decision for establishing an East–West joint-culture venture has so far only been discussed on a empirical level (Bleicher & Hermann, 1991; Fröhlich, 1991; Ost-Ausschuß der Deutschen Wirtschaft, 1991; Shenkar & Zeira, 1990); whether, for instance, one joint-culture venture partner's line of business, company size, ownership relationships, prevailing organizational structures, and applied technologies would be compatible with the other company's character- istics. In practice it becomes apparent that the success of a joint-culture venture does not only depend on tangible, economic factors but also on the persons working in the joint-culture venture—the culture and social skills of both joint-culture venture partners. The objective of this chapter is not to supply yet another contribution to the discussion about corporate leadership and organizational culture (inter alia, Dülfer, 1991; Hofstede, 1990; Lattmann, 1990; Schreyögg, 1991; Weinshall, 1991). Instead this is an analysis of specific human resource management aspects, especially in personnel development, within the framework of what we call a joint-culture venture (JCV).

Initial Problems in Human Resource Management

The human resource management problems in question, which are becoming apparent in this period of radical change, can be expressed as the *lack* of the following:

1. Objective setting and success monitoring with regard to individual or group performance of employees and executives in order to increase productivity and tap the performance potential at its optimum.
2. Performance-based payment schemes (low wage levels for highly qualified jobs and taking bonus systems with extra payments of up to 200% for granted).
3. Human resource management incentives, both monetary and nonmonetary, to increase the identification with the company and motivation of the employees and executives.
4. Quality management to reach the Western quality levels of products and services.
5. New corporate and leadership cultures. "Old boy" networks and predominance of old cadre hinder constructive restructuring processes.
6. Flexible organizational and communication structures. Highly hierarchically oriented communication and line structures still dominate and hinder the necessary organizational and personnel development.

However, these shortcomings do not apply equally to all the former socialist countries. The transformation strategies and their success are as varied as the complexity of the transformation process itself (FAZ GmbH, 1992; Frankfurter Institut, 1992; Heiduk et al., 1991; Jeffries, 1992; Kremer & Weber, 1992). Poland and Hungary, for example, are much further on their way towards a market economy than, for example, Albania or Romania. This means that for all human resource oriented transformation strategies, situation-based conflicts and potentials of each of the partners of the joint-culture venture have to be taken into consideration individually. It is up to management science to carry out extensive empirical research to contribute to creating a "real world based on past and present heading towards a new future" (Kirsch, 1991; Pearce, 1991).

The decision of Eastern and Western companies to establish a joint-culture venture (e.g., an American and a Polish company decide to produce chocolate in a new enterprise in Warsaw) means founding a JCV, because the corporate culture of the American company and the corporate culture of the Polish company will be fused with one another.

Principles of Personnel Development in JCVs

In terms of personnel development problems within the context of transformation, the following principles apply to JCVs.

1. Both cultures join to form a new culture in the JCV.
2. The success of personnel management actions depends on the market culture.
3. Personnel management in Eastern Europe is restricted here to the diagnosis of market-power potential for the planning of personnel development management.
4. Within a JCV various levels (country, enterprise, group, individual person) and their interrelationship in this "market" are to be taken into account.
5. Partners in the JCV are enterprises/institutions, groups of persons, and individual persons from the former socialist countries, and Western countries, which jointly plan, realize, and evaluate personnel development measures.

THE MARKET CULTURE MODEL WITHIN
A TRANSFORMATION PROCESS

Description of the Model

The market culture model, developed at the I.P.A. Institute for Human Resource Management and Labour Relations, tries to characterize, analyze, and support the JCV within the transformation process in East–West joint-culture ventures.

Culture in this context can no longer be seen as a collective (long-term) programming of human actions (cf. Adler, 1991; Hofstede, 1980; Kumar, 1991; Weinshall, 1991; and their respective comprehensive lists of references) because, due to recent chaotic and turbulent developments, all Eastern European countries are going through a process of deep change wherein common values have been destabilized in all aspects of society, e.g., forms of living, behavior patterns, education systems and values, political development, social stratifications, economic development in terms of type and scope, etc. Therefore, it is more useful and realistic to talk about culture chains or culture networks in the individual countries where transitional cultures (at country, enterprise, group, and individual levels) are strung like beads.

The following aspects of market culture are to be taken into account in the model.

1. The supply situation.
2. The demand situation.
3. The market-level situation.

The supply situation of the model describes the cultural development power of the East European joint-culture venture partner from the point of view of Western personnel developers. The demand situation describes the cultural development power of the Western joint-culture venture partner as personnel developer (e.g., training institutes, personnel development divisions of Western enterprises involved in a joint-culture venture, etc.). The supply and demand situations can each be defined by four variables:

- The interest potential (IP)
- The diagnosis potential (DP)
- The evolution potential (EP)
- The realization potential (RP)

Figure 1 shows the content of the variables in connection with the supply situation. The variables themselves may be differentiated according to "high" (h) and "low" (l). With these variables the cultural development power of both partners (suppliers and demanders), within the framework of personnel development, can be described.

In a "cultural portfolio" a specific supply situation (Fig. 2) or demand situation (analog to Fig. 2) can be described. In general, there are 16 different constellations. A connection between the configurations of the supply and the demand situations of the culture represents the market culture conditions of the explanatory model. By differentiation between the 16 supply situations and the 16 demand situations, one obtains 256 possible market constellations. Assessing each variable according to three degrees of variation—high, medium, and low—results in 6,561 possible market situations. If, in addition, one distinguishes (only) between the four levels—country, enterprise, group, and individual person—the market situation quadruples to a much higher amount of possible market constellations (Fig. 3).

Taking into account the problem of different demanders and suppliers from different Eastern and Western countries in a specific market situation enables additional expansion. From the point of view of the demanders, there could be competing enterprises that would like to take over a certain East European enterprise or there could be competing personnel development institutes coming from one or more countries. Similarly, identical or similar aspects could affect the suppliers. In this case the market culture situation should be described in an extended framework in order to cover each relevant market constellation. The number of possible constellations shows how situation-specific personnel development must be.

For an easier diagnosis of the potentials of the joint-culture venture partners, the visualization in a "radar diagram" (Fig. 4) may be used. There are two radar profiles, one for the Eastern and one for the Western culture development power. By comparing both of the radar profiles, the respective differences in potential can easily be evaluated for each individual variable and every examining angle. Decreasing potential differences makes development training concepts easier to understand and more functional.

Figure 1
Market Culture Model Developed by I.P.A. (Institute for Human Resource Development and Labour Relations), Hamburg, Germany

Supply Situation		
Explaining Variable	**Degree**	**Short Definition**
IP^S Interest Potential (Supply)	high (h) / low (l) — IP^S	Actual willingness of the East European partner (country, enterprise, group, individual person) to bring about target-oriented changes including employing personnel development activities within the framework of a "cultural joint venture" together with the Western partner (country, enterprise, group, individual person)
DP^S Diagnosis Potential (Supply)	high (h) / low (l) — DP^S	Actual capability of the East European partner to sensitively perceive and appreciate cultural situations and their developments in his own domain and that of his Western partner in order to be able to subsequently contribute in a situation-relevant manner to the shaping of a "cultural joint venture" including employing personnel development measures
EP^S Evolution Potential (supply)	high (h) / low (l) — EP^S	Actual capability of the East European partner to design, continously adapt and further develop a "cultural joint venture" with the Western partner while at the same time also taking personnel development measures into account
RP^S Realization Potential (Supply)	high (h) / low (l) — RP^S	Actual capability of the East European partner to realize the developed concept of the "cultural joint venture" together with the Western partner in terms of contents, methodology, didactics, politics, etc. ,giving special consideration to personnel development measures

Transformation Development Training Concepts

Personnel development programs that guide, accompany, and help develop the transformation process have been developed worldwide with different facets, intensities, objectives, and measures (Pieper, 1993). The problem of many programs is that they are too Western-oriented, and thus are often applied in a

Figure 2
I.P.A. Supply Model

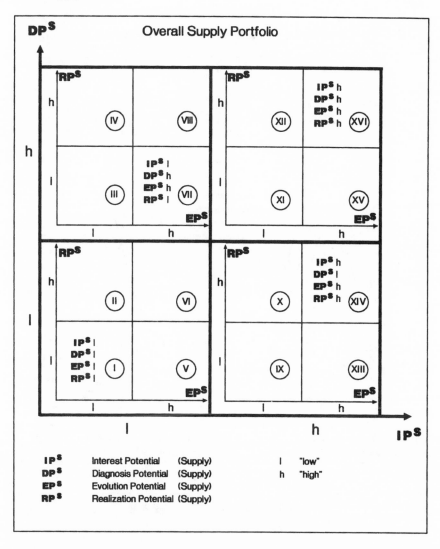

nonculture-sensitive way. In order to reduce the danger of a misguided trans-formation process, the two joint-culture ventures partners should carry out a detailed diagnosis with the help of the above-mentioned model. Suggested means of carrying out this diagnosis are interviews, company analyses, discussions, and problem-solving workshops in which both partners participate. Only after com-pletion of this initial evaluation is it possible to develop a specific transformation-development program.

Figure 3
I.P.A. Market Constellations Model

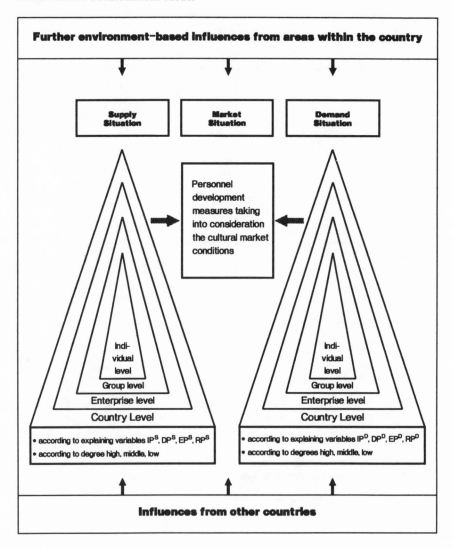

The Western partner has to discuss and decide with the Eastern joint-culture venture partner as to what extent and with which means these differences in potential should and can be reduced. A total merger as in a culture amalgamation can be just as undesirable as a total imposing of the stronger partner's culture on the weaker partner. The approach to transformation-development training must take the following aspects into account.

Figure 4
I.P.A. "Radar Diagram"

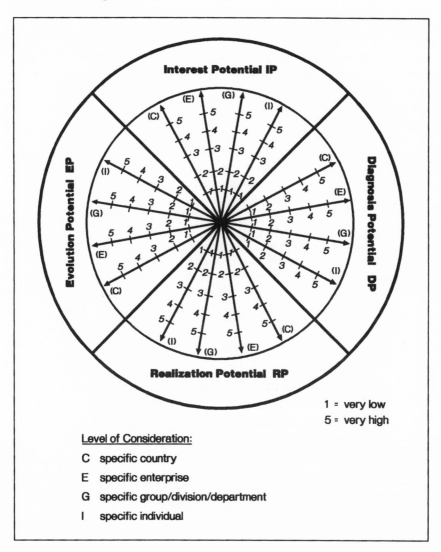

Interest Potential IP

Evolution Potential EP

Diagnosis Potential DP

Realization Potential RP

1 = very low
5 = very high

Level of Consideration:

C   specific country
E   specific enterprise
G   specific group/division/department
I   specific individual

Objectives of Development. Should the transformation-development training only reduce the diagnosed differences in potential and/or should the partners' total potential level be increased? If yes, to what extent? To answer this question, the strategic objectives of the transformation process within the joint-culture venture would have to be assessed.

Type of Training. With a view to reducing the differences in potential, a specific training program can be developed. If only major differences in potential are diagnosed, then special training program can be developed specifically for this purpose.

Target Groups. At which level will the training concept be applied? Will all the employees be involved, or only the executives? Are interface managers necessary to act as group trainers ("family" training) and should they be entrusted with passing on these ideas?

Content. What will be the main content of the training program, for example, transferring new production methods or training for transformation social competence? Will, for example, new ways of cooperation, quality circles, mentorship, and coaching be jointly initiated and created within the framework of corporate-development projects (Bergemann & Sourisseaux, 1992)?

Transformation Agents. How will the people acting as trainers, tutors, coaches, group trainers be selected and appointed? Fully qualified transformation agents will only be available in exceptional cases. Does one decide to cover the demand by engaging external specialists, or does one invest in one's own employees under the motto "train the trainers (process transformation agents)." The latter alternative offers the advantages of stronger identification with the transformation process and an increased sense of responsibility. The group trainer can be a key person in guiding his working group and the respective different departments through the process.

Concept of Time. Which measures should be applied and for how long? Is there only one initial phase, a so-called preparatory phase, or will the transformation process be accompanied by personnel-development measures on a long-term basis? This way a transformation process in a joint-culture venture can take many years (Bergemann & Sourisseaux, 1992; Briggs & Harwood, 1992; Weber, 1991).

Site of Development. Will the chosen employees of each of the joint-culture venture partners be trained separately or in joint activities? Will this take place at a neutral venue or at each other's premises?

Power Structures and Culture Compatibility. Who decides on the actual implementation of the transformation process? Does the Western partner dominate the Eastern partner on the basis of material superiority? Will the transformation process be carried out in awareness of the different cultures or not?

Evaluation. Which activities will be initiated, and under consideration of which interdependencies? Which organizational measures have to be prepared? How will the success be determined and monitored? What about the training effectiveness (Black & Mendenhall, 1990)?

The phase model in Fig. 5 shows an example of the implementation of a possible transformation-development concept. It is possible to differentiate the concept according to compulsory and voluntary activities, as well as main and parallel activities. The exact, company-specific configurations of such a phase model can be compiled in a situation-specific way, tailored to the given transformation framework.

Of course, new developments due to external and/or internal influences and

Figure 5
I.P.A. Phase Model

Phase	Contents	Parallel Activities
1st phase	Situation analysis (status and development) using the "I.P.A.-Culture Market Model" conducted at the location of the East European and Western partners	
2nd phase	Planning of the personnel development program within the framework of the "cultural joint venture" with the participation of "suppliers" and "demanders" incl. technical and power promoters	• Information and communication regarding the progress of process
3rd phase	Training of Eastern and Western process managers, trainers, moderators, coaching teams etc. within the framework of a start-finish concept	• Network environmental activities (association, circle, etc.)
4th phase	Selection, grouping, briefing of participants on the spot	
5th phase	Personnel development (separately and jointly) at the location of the Western partner (6 to 12 months) supported by learnshop concepts, learning partnerships and in accordance with the dual system	• Process controlling incl. evaluation with feedback, adaptation etc.
6th phase	Personnel development at the location of the East European partner, especially within the framework of "family training" using trained and experienced personnel developers	• Supervision
7th phase	Sponsorship programs for personnel development (Go-Together Program, Twin Assignment Program)	
8th phase	Personnel development for specialists and executives (input seminars)	
9th phase	Eastern specialists and executives train other co-workers (transfer training)	
10th phase	Work-Together in the "cultural joint venture"	

changes call for processes of adaptation. That is why such a phase concept cannot be seen as a path, but only as a dynamic guideline. Factors calling for adaptation and adjustment include:

- The differences of "supply" and "demand" potential are seen to be too great and as unsurmountable.
- Rapidly changing hard skills (technology, budget, etc.)
- Changing soft skills during the transformation process (intolerance towards failure, insufficient or decreasing willingness to jointly develop the process).

PROSPECTS

The transformation process in the former socialist countries is difficult. Many inhabitants of the Eastern European countries are worse off now, a few years after the fall of communism, than under the old regime. Functioning concepts for a successful transformation process are missing or have not yet been successfully implemented. Supporting activities and the transfer of money from Western countries have failed or disappeared. Mafia-like organizations are booming, crime has increased at an alarming rate, and civil wars have destroyed the once thriving economies. All these developments give political ammunition to the opponents of the reform who call for boycotting the transformation process.

The above-described market culture model is in the process of being transformed into a questionnaire to be used for an international empirical study. The model is useful not only for analysis and diagnosis of East–West joint-culture ventures, but also to all kinds of intranational and international joint-culture ventures researchers.

REFERENCES

Adler, N.J. (1991). *International Dimensions of Organizational Behavior,* 2nd ed. Boston: Kent.

Bergemann, N. & Sourisseaux, A.L.J. (Eds.). (1992). *Interkulturelles Management.* Heidelberg: Physica.

Black, J. & Mendenhall, M. (1990). Cross-culture training effectiveness: A review and a theoretical framework for future research. *Academy of Management Review,* 15: 113–116.

Bleicher, K. & Hermann, R. (1991). *Joint Venture Management.* Stuttgart: Schäffer/Poeschel.

Bowles, P. (1991). Work, employment and unemployment in the Soviet Union. *Review of Income and Wealth,* 331–336.

Briggs, N.E. & Harwood, G.R. (1992). Training in multinational business. *International Journal of Intercultural Relations,* 6: 341–354.

Domsch, M. et al. (1992). *Unternehmensführung in Polen* (Business Management in Poland). Munich and Mering: Hampp.

Dülfer, E. (1991). *Internationales Management in unterschiedlichen Kulturbereichen* (International Management in Different Cultural Areas), (2nd. ed.). Munich and Vienna: Oldenbourg.

FAZ GmbH Informationsdienste/Dredner Bank AG (Ed.). (1992). *Osteuropa-Perspektiven. Polen, Tschechoslowakei, Ungarn* (Perspectives of Eastern Europe. Poland, Czechoslovakia, Hungary), (2nd ed.). Frankfurt/Main: FAZ.

Frankfurter Institut für wirtschaftspolitische Forschung e.V. (1992). *Zur Wirtschaftsreform in Osteuropa* (On Economic Reform in Eastern Europe). Bad Homburg: Author.

Fröhlich, A. (1991). *Ost–West Joint Ventures. Ziele und betriebswirtschaftliche Probleme.* Baden Baden: Nomos.

Heiduk, G. et al. (Eds.). (1991). *Deutsch–Polnische Joint Ventures. Ergebnisse einer Befragung* (German–Polish joint ventures. Results of an inquiry). Hamburg: Steuer und Wirtschaftsverlag.

Hofstede, G. (1980). *Culture's Consequences: International Differences in Work-Related Values.* Beverly Hills: Sage.

Hofstede, G. et al. (1990). Measuring organizational cultures: A qualitative and quantitative study across twenty cases. *Administrative Science Quarterly,* 35: 286–316.

Jeffries, I. (1992). *Industrial Reform in Socialist Countries—From Restructuring to Revolution.* London: Routledge.

Kiezun, W. (1991). *Management in Socialist Countries.* Berlin: de Gruyter.

Kirsch, H. (1991). *Personalentwicklung im Ost–West-Umbruch* (Personnel Development in the Radical Change between East and West). Wiesbaden: Dt. Univ.-Verlag.

Kremer, M. & Weber, M. (1992). *Transforming Economic Systems: The Case of Poland.* Heidelberg: Physica-Verlag.

Kumar, B.N. (1991). Kulturabhèngigkeit von Anreizsystemen (Cultural dependence of incentive systems). In G. Schanz (Ed.), *Handbuch Anreizsystem,* pp. 127–148. Stuttgart: Poeschel.

Lattmann, Ch. (Ed.). (1990). *Die Unternehmenskultur. Ihre Grundlagen und ihre Bedeutung für die Führung der Unternehmung.* Heidelberg: Physica.

Ost-Ausschuß der Deutschen Wirtschaft—in Zusammenarbeit mit dem Bundesministerium für Wirtschaft (Eastern Committee of German Industry and Commerce—in Cooperation with the Federal Ministry of Economic Affairs) et al. (1991). *Investitions-und Kooperationsführer "Polen"* (Guide for investment and cooperation in Poland). Cologne: Author.

Pearce, J.L. (1991). From socialism to capitalism: The effects of Hungarian human resources practices. *Academy of Management Executive,* 5: 75–88.

Pfohl, H.-Chr. et al. (1992). Joint Ventures in Ungarn. Gesetzliche Rahmenbedingungen und Ergebnisse einer empirischen Untersuchung. *DBW Die Betriebswirtschaft,* 52: 655–673.

Pieper, R. (1993). *Managment training in Osteuropa.* Wiesbaden: Deutscher Universitäts-Verlag.

Schreyögg, G. (1991). Die internationale Unternehmung im Spannungsfeld von Landeskultur und Unternehmenskultur (The international enterprise in the area of tension between national culture and enterprise culture). In R. Marr (Ed.), *Eurostrategisches Personalmanagement* (Eurostrategic personnel management), vol. 1, pp. 17–42. Munich and Mering: Hampp.

Shenkar, O. & Zeira, Y. (1990). Interactive and specific parent characteristics. Implications for management and human resources in international joint ventures. *Management International Review* (Special Issue), 30: 2–22.

Standing, G. (1991). Wages and work motivation in the Soviet labor market. *International Labour Review,* 130: 237–253.

Uebele, H. (1991). Joint Ventures zwischen Betrieben der UdSSR und der Bundesrepublik Deutschland (Joint Ventures of USSR and German companies). In H. Albach (Ed.), Joint Ventures. Praxis internationaler Unternehmenskooperationen (Practice of international enterprise cooperations). In: *ZfbF-Ergänzungsheft,* pp. 89–124. Wiesbaden: Gabler.

Weber, R. (1989). *Joint Ventures.* Zurich: Rüegger.

Weber, W. (1991). *Defizite internationaler Management Trainings.* Chur: Rüegger.

Weinshall, T.D. (Ed.). (1991). *Culture and Management. Managing Culture in Different Countries.* Berlin: de Gruyter.

Zentes, J. (1992). *Ost-West Joint Ventures.* Stuttgart: Poeschel.

8

Training and Development for a Market Economy

The Case of Poland

Conrad J. Kasperson and Marian Dobrzyński

INTRODUCTION

The transformation of Poland's economy from command to market driven rests heavily on the shoulders of industrial management. Not surprisingly, the sudden shift on January 1, 1990 created a great deal of turbulence for which managers were most often ill-prepared. Since then, however, a great deal has been learned about Polish management and managers and about management training both in-place and needed in order to continue this economic transformation.

It must be remembered that in the history of industrial management there has never been as extreme or ambitious an undertaking as that engaged in by Poland. If lessons are to be learned, Poland is the perfect source for this learning. These lessons should be understood by anyone who will participate in the transformation of other socialist economic systems to capitalism or, at least, market-driven economies.

The Western perception of Polish management is not a pleasant one. In a brief summary of the "traps and opportunities" in Eastern Europe, Searing (1990) writes that "trained management talent is in very short supply." He sees this as a problem for potential investors. His is not the only concern, as articles on the quality of management in the newly transformed economies of Eastern Europe have regularly reported. In addition, business schools are considered a "growth industry" in Europe, both in the Eastern and Western areas. Claude Rameau, dean of INSEAD claims that there are few good-quality graduate business schools in Europe, but new ones are starting (*Chicago Tribune,* 1991). The tradition of developing the general manager in a university setting is an American, not European one. Yet it is this training venue that is seen as the one with the greatest potential endurance and as a major supplier of management talent over the long haul.

Recently, the American Assembly of Collegiate Schools of Business organized a conference in Moscow at which the deans of several of the major American schools of business met with Russian and East European educators to discuss the establishment of business schools. Topics included the development of a curriculum, finances, and selecting a faculty (Bennett, 1992). Unfortunately, Eastern Europeans do not have the luxury of the time needed to develop and implement new Western type management schools. The transformation is well underway and managers are needed now. While the general perception is not encouraging, the fact is that there is a history of management training and development in Poland that should be recognized and on which new programs should be based.

It must be remembered that Polish managers performed quite well within the command economic system. Rather than blame managers for the ineffectiveness of the economy, one must really assign blame to the system, itself. Managers were simply unprepared for the new economic system because of its extreme difference from that with which they were familiar. For example, marketing, while taught in some schools, was somewhat irrelevant when the economy of shortages meant that anything produced could easily be sold. In the prior system, managers needed to deal with production systems and the unique problems associated with the power systems in place. But they were familiar with and interested in management theory and practice from both a socialist and free-market perspective. For this reason, one should be quite optimistic about Polish management and treat the accepted perception with some skepticism.

The intent of this discourse is to give the reader a sense of the history of Polish management education, management problems that resulted from the "cold turkey" transformation (which are important to the subject of management education), a status report on Polish management as of this writing, the market conditions for management education, and how management-education programs appear to be evolving. We summarize our ideas as possibilities for education and training.

Our data, presented here in the form of a collection of case studies, were gathered mainly through observations of numerous programs and institutions.

HISTORY OF POLISH MANAGEMENT DEVELOPMENT

The Management Tradition

Poland has a long tradition of management education, which began in the late 19th century before Poland returned to the world scene as a state. During the 1920s, the Scientific Institute of Management (TNOiK) was created. It had two charges: develop management training programs and publish *Przeglad Organizacji (Organization Review),* a monthly journal on management and management training that is still being published. This institute closed after World War II, but was resurrected in 1956. By the early 1960s it was publishing books on management, and in 1964 began producing texts and manuals on what is known as organization theory, e.g., the works by Zieleniewski (1964). Under its auspices, numerous books by Western authors were translated into Polish, such as the works of Drucker, March and Simon, and Likert.

In 1964, academic programs began at the Main School for Planning and Statistics (SGPiS) and other university-level economics schools that focused on management and organization theory. These programs included management topics such as organization theory, marketing, and finance, somewhat similar to those which were also being taught in Western universities, but within the context of a communist system.

In 1972, the School of Management was organized at the University of Warsaw. The curriculum of this program was the equivalent of a combined undergraduate- and M.B.A.-level program and included courses in law, quantitative methods, computer information systems, organization theory and behavior, economics, accounting, finance, and marketing, taken over a five-year program of study.

In addition to the programs found in Poland's universities, management training was also developed by the various ministries as a response to Poland's law on management training. While the ministries often contracted the actual teaching out to independent suppliers, the government, as represented by the ministries and their branches, understood the necessity and value of further development of managers.

Along with this, the Main Center for Management Development, created in the early 1960s with assistance from the ILO (International Labor Organization), had developed numerous programs with modern facilities, libraries, technologies, and Western trainers and faculty members. One of the outcomes of this center was the development of training materials and techniques for Polish managers, but based upon Western practices.

Past Reforms and Developments

There have been several series of economic reforms in Poland; the last under the communist government began in 1980, with the change in government due to the social pressures created primarily by Solidarity. Stage I is probably most notable for the period of martial law; Stage II began about 1986 and led to a shift in organization design from centralized, ministry-directed systems to decentralized ones. This impacted the university system as well as state-owned industries. This decentralization, plus the opportunity for the inclusion of foreign investors in the Polish management system, meant that managers were quickly forced to understand new techniques for the evaluation of their performance. New variables, such as profits, return on investment, and the like, quickly entered the lexicon of management. Most managers, however, were trained as engineers whose only "management" responsibility was to keep the production process moving. Since the development of central planning, for example, market analysis, financial performance, and the like were simply unimportant to the manager of the typical state-owned enterprise. Stage II, however, made it clear that these new ideas were going to stay. In fact, legal and financial reforms had put Poland on a clear path away from centralization (Gajl, 1988).

Universities also faced the prospect of decentralization and a new era of management. At the University of Warsaw, entrepreneurial members of the faculty of the School of Management began discussions with the local management of ICL, a British computer manufacturer to whom these academics had served as consultants, concerning a possible new educational enterprise. This was envisaged as a private, joint-stock venture that would deliver a M.B.A.-type curriculum; it ultimately became Międzynarodowa Szkoła Zarzadząnia of the University of Warsaw (International Business School). This new breed of educational enterprise received a sudden shot in the arm when the entire system was abruptly altered in late 1989.

In summary, Poland has a long history of management education within the context of its command economic system, as well as the period prior to World War II. While the ability of an individual manager to use his knowledge of management theory may have been limited due to the command economic system, it was, nevertheless, a subject which had been taught in the universities for several decades and the subject was neither foreign nor new.

MANAGEMENT PROBLEMS AS A RESULT OF ECONOMIC TRANSFORMATION

Change of Environment

In 1989, as a result of deteriorating economic conditions, funding for universities and ministerial education programs began to shrink rather dramatically. Suddenly, the collapse and replacement of the communist government resulted in the legal mandate that management of Poland's state-owned enterprises had to step down due to political reasons, thereby leaving a void in management expertise. Along with this, the freeing of historic constraints on the economic system made it clear to Polish management that it needed to upgrade itself to Western standards, particularly in the areas of marketing and accounting, if it was to take advantage of this new economic era. A plethora of new management education programs sprang up (Kasperson, 1990). Many of these programs were funded by grants from euphoric Western governments, such as the British Know-how Fund.

The sudden change of course for Poland has meant that the security and predictability of the previous economic system has given way to the uncertainty and dynamics of the new market-driven system. The transformation of the economy was based upon several strategic moves, all of which affected managers of all business firms. Laws on taxation, privatization, commerce, and foreign trade, have changed the context of business dramatically. The old umbrella of the central planners has disappeared and the chaos of free market mechanisms has replaced it.

Critical Issues for Management Development

In this context, managers of firms of virtually all sizes and industries have had to confront a new set of managerial problems, each of which implies a particular educational need. The following is a partial list of the questions managers are trying to understand and answer:

1. How do I maintain a positive cash flow? A restrained money supply as the means to control inflation has meant that customers are slow to pay their bills and the firm slow to pay its taxes plus the subsequent interest and penalties for slow payment.

2. How do I reduce my payroll? Large state-owned firms were saddled with large, inefficient hierarchical structures, with many of the workers idle due to dramatically reduced sales. Despite the obvious need to pare down the structure, laws have been enacted that make it difficult and costly to reduce the workforce. This not only reduces efficiency, but causes cash flow problems, too.

3. How do I sell my product? Many firms had been producing products for which there was no market—the state simply bought the "stuff." The state will not do this any longer, so the product must be brought to a true market. Unfortunately, many managers focused only on production targets because that is what the state—the "employer"—wanted. Now, they must learn marketing.

4. How can I find a foreign partner, but, as a result of the Polish government's desire to quickly privatize enterprises, avoid being "given" to him? In the process of privatization, the methods used to calculate the value of the firm have often yielded "golden" opportunities for Western investors because of the economic decline in Poland. While one way out of the current economic problems of the firm is to join with a more wealthy Western investor, the amount of the investment is often too low to erase the already accumulated cash flow problems. Wealth, to the Polish partner, has been measured in modern technology and distribution-channel access, as well as financial resources. But it is the financial resources that affect accumulated debts.

5. How should I deal with people inside and outside the company? In the previous era relationships were formal, understood, and stable. In the current conditions power relationships are unclear and unstable. Now the manager must determine new relationships based on unfamiliar dynamics.

6. How should I modernize my products and production technology? Most managers are only beginning to understand that the customer is an important ingredient in the decisions about product design. Furthermore, they are learning that long production runs of single products do not match the customers' wishes; that the production must ultimately be sold. We know of one company that only discontinued producing chess sets when it had no more room for storage.

7. Should I expand into other businesses—diversify? Many managers see diversification as a simple way to take the uncertainties out of business when this is often the most inappropriate and risky thing to do. If it appears that diversification makes sense—the first question is one of feasibility—then how to do this takes on new meaning.

8. How can I avoid paying a too heavy tax burden? Currently, Poland's businesses, particularly state-owned enterprises not yet privatized, must pay quite heavy taxes, including "dividends" on the assets of the firm. In fact, even if a firm

is incurring a loss it may have to pay income taxes—a somewhat illogical situation. There may be ways to reduce the tax load, but there are both positive and negative factors that must be weighed for each approach.

9. How can I get a cheap loan? This is seen as the way to answer question 1, but most managers realize that there is more to both questions than what appears on the surface.

10. How can I fight against "gray market" firms that use bribes to get an order and pass the order to another firm for production? There has always been a black market in the communist system, but in the new system there is also a second economy made up of unregistered firms that pay no taxes but operate "out of the garage," so to speak. This "benefit" gives the gray market firms a competitive advantage that, although unfair and illegal, must be recognized. New models of how one creates competitive advantage must be learned.

11. How should a state-owned enterprise be privatized? This is one of the most fundamental questions that is being continually asked by not only business managers, but politicians.

All of the above questions require education and training. Since the transformation began in 1990, many programs have been developed (many have also disappeared from the scene) that have attempted to deliver this education, and a fairly clear picture of what has drawn institutions to the education market has emerged. As stated above, there is a long history of management education in Poland. In fact, Poland has a well-educated work force.

In order to fully comprehend the possibilities for management development, however, we should know what has happened thus far, and why institutions and organizations have engaged in education, either as trainers or students.

DYNAMICS OF MANAGEMENT EDUCATION SINCE 1990

As of June, 1992, there were about 70 institutions in Poland involved in management training and development. They included academic institutions, professional-training programs, plus organizations that offered professional training in conjunction with other services, such as accounting firms (Lakińska et al., 1992).

Academic Programs

Academic institutions that offer traditional undergraduate and graduate education in management have maintained their curricular focus but have attempted to expand their offerings in accounting, marketing, and strategic management. They have done this in the face of diminishing funding. Some schools that had traditional ties to socialist economic theory have even changed their names as a response to new market conditions, e.g., SGPiS, the Main School for Planning and Statistics, is now SGH, the Main School of Commerce, which was its original name when it was created in the 1920s.

The same "general" courses are taught in Polish business and economics schools as in business programs within Western universities. The education system parallels the Western system, particularly the American, with both undergraduate and graduate (MBA) curricula. Because of the importance associated with the term "MBA," programs were created that declared themselves MBA, but should have been categorized as management-development programs (Kasperson, 1990). Within the past year, the boundary between programs has become clear and stable.

In order to legitimize their programs, some schools have affiliated themselves with Western institutions. For example, the International Business School of the University of Warsaw now offers a program in conjunction with the University of Illinois—Urbana/Champaign, in which students receive a diploma from the University of Warsaw and a MBA from the University of Illinois. National Louis University has established a Polish branch to teach business subjects and to train Polish teachers (*Warsaw Voice,* 1991). There has also been a surge of programs for American students in Poland under the general heading of "study abroad," such as the program of The American University at the Adam Mickiewicz University in Poznań.

As of 1990, there was a severe shortage of teachers and modern teaching equipment (Kasperson, 1990). Since demand for business classes has, in the very recent past, grown dramatically and several new business Schools have been created (such as those in Poznań, Katowice, Kraków, and Wroclaw), the number of adequately prepared business teachers is insufficient, especially in the subjects that have held historically low priority or have changed with the economic transformation, such as accounting, finance, money and banking, and marketing. In addition, due to the lack of government funds, salaries for the teachers have suffered serious setbacks in buying power, which were exacerbated by Poland's hyperinflation. This has resulted in a significant exodus of business and technical faculty to consulting firms, foreign firms, and to Western Europe and North America, where salaries have kept pace. Those that stayed rely more on a second job for a substantial portion of their income. This job could be more accurately described as the first job, yet the professor refuses to leave his position in the university. Some of the best-known entrepreneurs in Poland are professors on the one hand and business people on the other.

On the positive side, new business teachers may be relatively easily provided, as they can be recruited from disciplines with a close kinship to business, such as economics, the other social sciences, and engineering. They can and are being trained quickly. In fact, it is from these disciplines that many of the current teachers have been transplanted. For example, the Warsaw Polytechnic University, a school known for its engineering curriculum, has developed a business program specifically addressing the needs of engineers for management knowledge.

By 1993, the shortage of teaching equipment was not considered an issue. Modern teaching software, however, is needed but in insufficient supply. This includes computerized management simulators, strategic analysis aids, computerized marketing-mix analysis tools, and the like. Although these packages are available from the West, they should be tailored to fit the Polish situation.

Other funding needs include video laboratories with videos, computers with relevant business software, and even overhead projectors. This kind of equipment was supplied to the Polish universities during the past two years with Western assistance, but demand has skyrocketed at the same time that funding has declined.

In 1993, one major change in university-level education was the introduction of tuition for certain classes of business students. For example, students are required to pass a series of examinations in order to be accepted into the university, but some students have been allowed to take extramural courses at the university by paying tuition. In addition, some of the specialized graduate-level courses require tuition. This has become a new source of funding for the universities, is not illegal, and has not caused any backlash from the students.

In summary, Polish academic institutions have little to learn about the content of general business education, but have much to learn about the use of various software systems and other pedagogical ideas routinely used in the West.

Professional Management Training

New programs have surfaced in the area of education, development, and training of working managers. Many of these new programs are a result of the unfettered free-market system. Until mid-1992, anyone could pass for a business consultant if he or she possessed any computerized software that could be used to impress a prospective client. People and organizations in the market for training have become much wiser, however, and are now very watchful for the training "carpetbagger." Successful educators now need the stamp of approval from a respected agency or client.

One good sign is that numerous professional programs have been developed that have endured the test of time and appear stable and viable. One example is Międzynarodowa Fundacja Rozwoju Rynku Kapitałowego i Przekształceń Własnościowych w R.P.—Centrum Prywatyzacji (the International Foundation for the Development of Capital Markets and Ownership Transformation in the Republic of Poland—the Center for Privatization), founded in 1990, which offers a wide variety of courses for consultants, potential stockbrokers, candidates for supervisory boards, and the like. Along with education and training it publishes several journals and newsletters in both Polish and English.

As in the West, Poland needs to develop professional organizations that can certify that their members have met a standard level of competence and ethics. For example, accountants and auditors hired by the major Western accounting firms are now being required to become certified by either the ASSA (Great Britain) or AICPA (U.S.). Poland is attempting to develop a similar certification system for its professions within business in order to insure that quality of training and education meets a standard set by industry. Responsibility for the creation of associations that protect the true professionals belongs to the members of the association, but Western colleagues are assisting in their creation.

Consultants are expected to provide "how-to" knowledge. At this time, there is still a grave shortage in Poland of individuals who really know modern management techniques in market-driven economic settings. This shortage is lessening, but assistance is still badly needed. The Polish Chamber of Commerce (Krajowa Izba Gospodarcza, or KIG) has become a major supplier of management training. Until recently, the larger cities in Poland had their own chamber, but within the last two years, as a result of the terms of the 1989 act about chambers of commerce, these were merged into one coordinated body. In addition to training, it is also a source for information, trade fairs, and trade missions—new ideas in Poland (*Warsaw Voice*, 1992).

The major complaint of Polish participants who have been in training programs provided by Western consultants has been the excess teaching of general knowledge either already known by the Polish managers, or easily learned from available handbooks. That is, Western consultants were unfamiliar with the history of management education in Poland and/or the recent laws that impact on the practice of management.

The important weakness of Polish management is the lack of acquaintance with management software such as computer networking, electronic mail, voice mail, distribution logistics, production control, and the like. These can be put into everyday use only with Western assistance because there are few Polish experts.

Recently, the trend has been to form trade or interest consortiums designed to offer specific, need-driven education and training packages. For example, in November 1992, the Free Enterprise Transition Consortium was established in Kraków. It is funded by a grant from the U.S. Agency for International Development (AID) to link outside technical approaches with local expertise, and is developing case studies, tailored training, and a resource center. One of the technical resources is the Peace Corps Business Advisors, which has over 250 volunteers in Poland (U.S. Department of Commerce, 1992).

Several institutions have been formed with close links to industrial firms. For example, Centrum Promocji Kadr (the Center of Management Promotion), which was established in 1989, is a kind of subsidiary of Pol Kaufring, one of the largest joint ventures in Poland, which includes Kodak (U.S.) and Laboratoires Garnier (France). It offers specialized courses for foreign and domestic companies, intensive language training, computer courses, and management courses, plus it has a modern hotel as part of its facilities. While this organization has become successful due to both quality programs and good capitalization, it is now looking for affiliations with Western organizations that will enhance credibility, which is already quite high, and give it another source of qualified instructors. As of 1993, the Center of Management Promotion had become affiliated with the London Chamber of Commerce and was looking for a university link.

In summary, management training and development in Poland can be divided into four categories. 1) Traditional university-level education, now in the process of being upgraded but suffering from high student demand and a lack of funds. 2) New Western-style MBA programs, often done as a joint venture between Polish and Western institutions. Unlike public universities, these require tuition from all students. 3) Management/executive development programs that address specific topics and are often taught by Western consultants or professors. 4) "Wishful thinkers," who have dreamed up a concoction of business English, a business link of some sort, and a hope that qualified instructors can be found. In 1990 this latter group was rather large, but as of the end of 1992 was virtually extinct as the heady days of early 1990 have now given way to the cold realism of the present. A form of Darwinism has eliminated many of the less well-developed management-education programs (*Financial Times,* 1992).

This appears to be quite similar to management education in Russia, where there are three types of schools: state business schools, private business schools, and private consulting firms offering education. As in Poland, the line between the state and private schools is becoming quite blurred (Puffer, 1993).

Survey of Management Educational Needs

In order to determine what managers felt they needed in the way of development, a survey was administered during the second half of April and first half of May 1992 by the Polish Confederation of Employers to a sample of its members—top managers of several firms that varied in size, number and location of branches, and legal status. Since the size of the sample was modest ($n = 65$), the survey might not be considered statistically reliable, but the data that were gathered, combined with personal observations made by the authors, provide a picture of reality.

The respondents identified the following issues as immediate education, or knowledge, needs:

1. Cash flow—how to get money for current operations (working capital). In Poland there is a problem of cash *embouteillage;* that is, firms may not pay their debts because of slow payment of their receivables by their clients—a kind of chain reaction.

2. Tax policy—how to avoid excessive tax costs. For example, state-owned enterprises in Poland pay for insurance on payroll at a rate of 47%, plus a very high tax when salaries increase over certain preestablished limits (popiwek tax), plus fixed dividends on assets, which are payable even if the firm is incurring a loss.

3. Maintaining market share. Since there is intense competition from foreign as well as small private Polish firms operating at lower production costs due to tax exemptions, no tax on excessive employment, and/or no compulsory dividends, it is very difficult for state-owned enterprises to maintain their market share. Similar concerns over competitiveness have been expressed by Russian managers (Panevin & Van Fleet, 1993).

4. Power relationships. The power of the top executive depends to a great degree on his personal style and his relationships with power centers. This is due to the many legal constraints which impact on state-owned enterprises, such as

unions (sometimes several within the same firm) and employee councils, which have the right to dismiss the CEO and to sell, or protect against sale, any part of a firm's assets. This power distribution has had the effect of extinguishing any long-term perspective, since CEOs have had to "fight" for the survival of their firms and for their personal position, both of which have been unstable. Issues such as company mission and strategy are not the current subjects of their attention, although they should be.

The training in which the sample employers participated corresponded only partly with the firms' problems. The training subjects (in declining order) related to computer operation, corporate restructuring, taxes, technical training for engineers, and export techniques. Respondents declared that, besides the topics mentioned above, they were willing to participate in and send their employees for training concerning marketing, accounting, new technologies, and creating a small business. The last topic was important to managers who were close to losing their current jobs.

When asked which training forms the managers preferred—short in-house presentations, 2–3 day conferences, 1–3 weeks off-premise conferences, or courses several months long—it appeared that all varieties were acceptable, although the preference was for short (half to one day) informative sessions at the site of the firm. Obviously, the preferred form and time of training depends on its purpose and topic.

Most of the managers declared that funding was easily available for training. Surprisingly, this statement does not correspond with the conviction expressed by many training officers, who said that the market was, at that time, limited because enterprises could not pay for the education of their employees.

Concerning the motivation of participants, managers were willing to participate in training that provided them with specific knowledge seen as indispensable for maintaining their current position. Another important motive was certification, which increased the chances of training participants who may soon be on the labor market and felt insecure in their current positions.

Responding companies had accepted offers from a wide variety of training institutions, including universities, professional associations, branch training centers, private firms, and foreign assistance. There is no clear preference for any specific training institution; the choice depends on the topics and on the former experience of clients of a specific firm.

However, a market exists for training in some topics not mentioned by the respondents. This includes small-business establishment, economic and organizational issues relating to specific industries, such as the construction industry, and modern technologies. Surprisingly, there was a lack of demand from top managers for management technology issues, such as computer assisted cost and quality control, writing business plans, portfolio analysis, and network planning methods. It seems that managers leave the technical management expertise to consultants or, in the worst case, probably have never heard about some of those techniques.

INFLUENCE OF WESTERN EDUCATORS

Motivation of Western Educators

Western academic institutions, consultants, and business educators have come to Poland for two main reasons: to profit by simply shipping their existing programs to the new Eastern European market, or to enhance their prestige in their home market by being able to add Poland to their list of clients, that is, to make themselves more marketable at home.

Small consulting and/or training firms have seen the situation as very lucrative. Much of the earlier training costs were borne by Western governments through grants. By taking advantage of these grants, the firm could both earn money and enhance its reputation. A typical example of this is a one-week seminar sponsored by the IDA-EC PHARE Programme (a part of Agencja Rozwoju Przemysłu S.A., or Industrial Development Agency) using a grant from the European Community. The program centered on liquidation of state-owned enterprises. (Liquidation is a term describing the sale of a state-owned enterprise either as a collection of assets or as an operating business.) The program was held at a conference center in Konstantin, about 10 km south of Warsaw, and the participants stayed at the center. Three consultants from the Netherlands presented the material in English by using a simultaneous translator. The students included those who wished to become liquidators (individuals who are instrumental in the sell-off of state-owned enterprises), representatives of relevant ministries, or representatives from industry. The total cost of the program was borne by PHARE and amounted to something in excess of US $50,000. The authors attended this particular seminar and discussed the effectiveness of the program with both the educators and the students. We found that the educators did not know the Polish commercial code despite the fact that at least one of the educators was a lawyer and the code has been translated into English, and that they assumed that the problems faced when privatizing a Dutch firm were the same as those faced by a Polish firm. Of course, this assumption was wrong. As a result, the conference continued but did not quite meet the expectations of the attenders or sponsors. Unfortunately, the educators thought they were very successful, because the Polish students did not object but remained courteous and attentive throughout. When we brought this problem to the attention of the educators, they simply defended their assumption rather than alter the program. Our conclusion was that the program was "packaged," including the hand-outs, the overhead projector slides, and the presentation itself, and to have made alterations that would customize the program to the specific needs of the students would have reduced the profit level.

Some American universities have developed programs in conjunction with Polish universities in order to enhance their reputation at home. On the other hand, many prestigious universities have developed relationships with Polish institutions as a direct outgrowth of their teaching and research programs, such as the University of Warsaw/University of Illinois venture. Professors of management have traveled to Poland in order to both teach Western ideas and to develop relationships with Eastern European colleagues, who are often funded by grants from their home institution or government.

Motivation of Polish Partners

For the Polish educator/partner this is an opportunity to start a new business venture in the business-training field. Many of the Polish partners in these new business-training ventures are new to business, and organization theory, and this connection with the West gives them instant credibility.

Virtually all institutions participating in management education and training programs have used the training business as a way to upgrade their facilities with new computers, office equipment, books, and educational software, which the government was unable to fund. In addition, this has been a way of adding experienced teachers to the staff at little or no cost. In early 1990, Polish educators were often offered the chance to travel to the West at no cost in order to upgrade their skills and knowledge. This incentive had, by 1993, become less and less important and less attractive. For example, an Assistant Professor of Law at the University of Warsaw was offered a three-week trip to Geneva for a meeting with the ILO, yet he declined because he would lose too much money while away, even though all expenses were paid and he would receive a stipend. Of real marketing value was the ability to attract tuition-paying participants to their programs by offering Western teachers and affiliations.

Problems of East–West Cooperation

While the self-interest motivations of both the Western and Polish participants have helped develop the market for and delivery of management education, the results of these efforts have been mixed. For one thing, there is an insufficient number of Polish managers, particularly senior managers who speak or adequately understand English, French, or German, which are the languages of instruction used by the Western educators. Furthermore, it has become very clear to the Poles that the universal language of business is English, so this self-selection of participants led, in 1992, to a declining number of applicants for education programs despite the expanding needs. A turnaround in demand in 1993 is expected.

Polish managers who are really participating in the new economic system have no time for further training, regardless of their individual need. While they often recognize that they are taking a short-term perspective, the fact remains that they are simply too busy to engage in training; they see the current rapidly developing market opportunities as too short-lived to interrupt their involvement in the business. This means, of course, that they are assuming an excessive amount of the management responsibility, which they could delegate if they had learned some effective approaches to delegation through the management education that they are too busy to take—a kind of vicious circle.

It has become quite clear that all too often there is a mismatch between assumptions of the Western educator about the students and the true knowledge and abilities of the Polish students, with the result that the educator teaches way below the ability of the Polish students. The reverse has also occasionally occurred—the teacher assumed that the students were far more advanced than they actually were. While no scientific data have been gathered on this phenomenon, anecdotal evidence is monumental.

In their haste and enthusiasm to get a program off the ground, the Polish institution has often created an overly heterogeneous class. This means that there are three general categories of students, all of whom influence the learning of each other: those for whom the material is beneath their level, with the result that they become bored and annoyed; those for whom the material is all new and very advanced and frightening; and those for whom the material is appropriate—often a distinct minority. For an experienced instructor, especially one who is familiar with Eastern Europe, this is a situation to which he or she can quickly adapt, but to the Western consultant who sees this as a new opportunity for profit, this is usually a very difficult problem, one often simply swept aside. Usually, this is the result of faulty or incomplete communication between the Polish organizer and the Western educator. Both parties are learning more about this problem as time goes by.

Like much of the rest of Poland's economy and society, education has undergone a turbulent period (which is not over) and many "half-baked" programs have disappeared. On the positive side, expectations of both the Polish and Western participants have become more realistic (Kasperson & Obloj, 1992). Western educators are now working much more closely with their Polish counterparts to deliver more well-tailored programs that address more specific needs; Western universities are learning more about the Polish education system and are able to target their activities so that they will do the most good and have the necessary resources; and Polish students are becoming better consumers of education products.

THREE DELIVERY SYSTEMS

Three categories of educational institutions, or delivery systems, have evolved in Poland and are portrayed in Fig. 1.

The Traditional Academic Institution

Currently, there is very high interest and demand from students, many of whom are shifting from technical fields and other social sciences into management. These institutions offer basic education for regular (traditional) students: five years of study leading to a degree. There are also a variety of programs for working students. At the completion of studies, the student receives a degree.

Some notable developments in this area are:

Figure 1
Emerging Education Systems in Poland

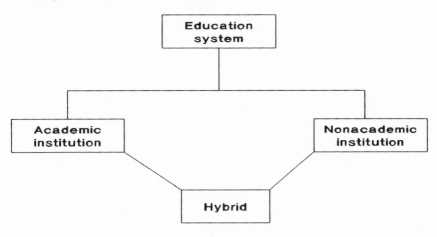

1. The School of Management at the University of Warsaw is aggressively modernizing its programs and facilities.
2. New schools and departments of management have emerged at other universities, economics schools, and polytechnics.
3. Modern training and development centers have emerged from the early experiments done with grants.
4. Because of unexpected and increasing demand for business studies, tuition is now being charged for special programs. The University of Warsaw, for example, had over 200 applicants for its special three-year degree program (academic year 1992–93), which has a tuition of 22 million zloty per year—about equal to the average Pole's salary for six months.

Most new schools are suffering from a severe shortage of qualified teachers and some faculty are teaching in areas in which they have no experience. These new schools of management depend on the existing teaching staff of the school, yet they are making every effort to offer a curriculum close to that offered by Western business schools. Some of the new schools are surviving simply on the basis of heavy support from Western universities through "twinning," in which teachers from the Western university come to the Polish institution.

The big change in academic institutions, however, is the creation of private universities, which are recognized by the Ministry of Education and able to grant degrees. They often specialize in specific areas, such as entrepreneurship. By mid-1993 there were several of these institutions in Warsaw, such as the Prywatna Wyzsza Szkoła Businessu i Administracji (the Private College of Business and Administration), with almost 1000 students and growing.

The Nonacademic Institution

These offer customized courses to a specific target audience, usually in a one-time meeting for which courses are constructed by selecting specific modules of one day or less. There are a wide variety of firms offering this type of education, most of which are small enterprises of five to ten people, and there has been a continual entry and departure of these firms in the education market. The curriculum is "issues driven" and concentrates on practical, "how-to" types of issues, such as taxes, banking, and new laws. It is specific and often technical, and the student usually receives a certificate of attendance.

The strongest of these institutions offer larger programs on subjects such as techniques of evaluating an enterprise, the process and procedures of liquidating a state-owned enterprise, training for members of supervisory boards (boards of directors), and evaluation of real property. These larger programs are usually the result of a combined effort by small management-training firms and strong institutions like the Agency for Industrial Development, the Ministry of Ownership Changes, and the Polish Chamber of Commerce.

While many early programs were disappointing and some potential participants now are skeptical about the quality of the nontraditional programs, new programs have been developed that are quite strong. An example is Szkoła Finansow i Zarządzania (School of Finance and Management), which delivers the programs of the Center for Privatization using teachers from Western Europe and the U.S.

The "Hybrid" Institution

These institutions have been founded by university faculty members as autonomous organizations tied to a university. They have impressive names and typically offer quality, medium-length programs, some of which can award an MBA. They are strongly supported by Western assistance, including lecturers, equipment, books, and academic software. One example is the International Postgraduate Management Center of the University of Warsaw, which is closely tied to the University School of Management.

The creation of these institutions is a response from teachers most closely related to the practice of management via both their academic discipline and consulting work. They often employ over ten full-time people and are continually trying to deal with a shortage of funding and a lack of qualified participants willing to pay the tuition. It appears that they may have reached a barrier to further growth, both financial and organizational. These institutions are becoming "regular" business schools, such as those found in the West, and are offering executive programs that are well-tailored to specific targets, as well as more traditional courses.

As of 1993, all three forms of management education were alive and thriving. Clearly, the dominant players are the traditional academic institutions, particularly those with a history of management education, and the specialized nonacademic programs. The number of institutions in total has become stable, with each addressing the needs of a particular segment of the market, either on the basis of geography, specialty, length of program, or age of participant. The hybrid, while seen as an exciting option in 1992 had by 1993 lost its glamour and gravitated to either the traditional university model or the professional-training model. One can measure the acceptance of each by examining the financial strengths, support from Western partners, growth of enrollment, recognition by the Ministry of Education, use by other Ministries, and stability of curriculum. On all counts, all are meeting the needs of the transformation in their own special way. In addition, the market for new, specialized short courses continues to expend, but only for those delivery systems that fully understand their target and mission.

CONCLUSIONS

Two fundamental questions emerge as a result of our review. First, is the pattern of management education that has developed in Poland reasonable for other postcommunist countries? Like Poland, most postcommunist countries have well-established educational institutions, but they had not previously been delivering free-market business knowledge. Therefore, there is a close similarity between the Polish case and other former communist countries. As shown in Fig. 1, new business knowledge will be delivered primarily by the three institutions: academic, nonacademic, and hybrid organizations. However, the role of each will vary from one country to another. It appears to us that many of the problems that have hampered management education in postcommunist Poland can be easily avoided with a little foresight. For example, so far the self-interest of educators has determined the kind of education provided and funding available. Policy makers can easily deal with this problem once they are aware of it.

Second, what can be learned from the Polish situation that is relevant to other postcommunist countries? We see three lessons that can be used to shape management education and development in these emerging free-market economies.

1. Build a new management education system based upon the market economy, but integrate it with previous programs appropriate for the new system, especially by providing management and marketing skills. The success of the transformation from command to market economy depends heavily upon the design and functioning of management education, as the Polish case illustrates. There may be some existing domestic programs from which the designers can benefit. In fact, for Poland, optimism for its economic future exists partly because its management education programs have been strong.

2. Recognize the problems that management must confront when the economic system shifts to a market-driven one. Cash flow, the legal context, and marketing all create new hurdles over which management must jump on the path through transformation.

3. Be prepared to have both domestic and Western educators and government representatives use education as a vehicle to enhance their own situation. This phenomenon also serves as a motivator to get things underway, so the "payoff" to participants must include more than simple altruistic patriotism. The point is that

one must recognize that blind faith in consultants, educators, and bureaucrats should be tempered.

The models of undergraduate education, MBA programs, Executive MBA programs, professional education, and consulting-based training that are found in the United States appear to be the broad categories of programs emerging in Poland. Accreditation, as a way of measuring and reinforcing quality, has yet to be organized, but the Ministry of Education is legitimizing some new private programs by granting them the power to award degrees.

The future appears to us to include a satisfactory supply of Polish educators, but a continuing linkage with Western universities, in the case of academic programs, has been developed in the past few years. As academic programs in other post-communist countries develop, they, too, will likely develop similar linkages. We question whether the later-developing programs will as easily find enthusiastic Western partners.

In summary, management education and training in Poland has substantially aided its transformation to a market economy. The present system has evolved through the transformation and can be best described as several different delivery methodologies that address different education-market needs. The system is becoming more stable over time, but it will continue to change until the transition to a market economy has stabilized and consistent and appropriate funding is available. Presently, the system is quickly adapting to the new era.

REFERENCES

Bennett, A. (1992). Schooling East Europe on business education. *The Wall Street Journal,* November 11: B1.

Chicago Tribune. (1991). "Business schools a growth industry in new Europe," March 10.

Financial Times. (1992). "Poland," April 28.

Gajl, N. (1988). *Reforms of Legal and Financial System of Public Enterprises in Poland and Other Socialist Countries.* Wrocław, Poland: Zakład Narodowy im. Ossolińskich—Wydawnictwo.

Kasperson, C.J. (1990). *A Review of Management Education in Poland.* Washington, DC: USIA.

——— & Obłój, K. (1992). Training Polish managers in a new economic era. *RFE/RL Research Report,* 1, 11: 64–67.

Lakińska, A., Kempisty, W. & Puszczewicz, B. (1992). *Institutions Involved in Management Training and Development in Poland: An Overview.* Warsaw: Task Force for Training & Human Resources.

Panevin, Y.L. & Van Fleet, D.D. (1993). *Managerial development and training in the U.S.S.R.* Manuscript.

Puffer, S.M. (1993). Education for management in a new economy. In Jones, A. (Ed.), *Education and Society in a New Russia.* Armonk, NY: M.E. Sharp.

Searing, J.E. (1990). Eastern Europe: Traps & opportunities. *Boardroom Reports,* December 5: 11.

U.S. Department of Commerce. (1992). *Eastern Europe Business Bulletin.* December.
Warsaw Voice. (1991). "Educational joint venture." September 1.
———. (1992). April 11: 1–8.
Zieleniewski, J. (1964). *Organizacja Zespołow Ludzkich: Wstep do Teorii Organizacji Kierowania.* Warsaw: PWN.

9

TeMAFL: Teaching Management as a Foreign Language

Some Observations and Reflections about Management Education in Central Europe

Arieh A. Ullmann

INTRODUCTION

Imagine having the task to teach a group of people how to ride and work with an elephant so that sitting on top of the animal they can log lumber in the jungles of Assam. These people have never seen an elephant, they have heard stories about this huge animal, some of them describing it as a ferocious beast, others as a powerful but gentle creature. There is one catch: You have no elephant at your disposal for your task.

This metaphor tries to capture the situation many Western instructors face who travel to Central Europe and to the CIS (Commonwealth of Independent States) to teach basic management know-how to the men and women who have been propelled into leadership positions in new enterprises, state-controlled firms, co-operatives, and government agencies. They try to the best of their abilities and experience to steer the organization through the shocks accompanying the transition to a new system. These managers are forced to learn a foreign language, the language of twentieth century market capitalism. This system, which so few of them had the opportunity to observe and study in situ, has been described to them in stark contrasts. Until recently, capitalism was officially declared a doomed system based on the exploitation of the masses by the few. Unofficially, capitalism was a wondrous engine that promised abundant goods and freedom of choice to everyone.

Although this chapter does not pretend to be the result of a rigorous scientific effort, it conveys impressions and experiences gathered during four 10-day visits over a nine-month period in late 1991 and the first half of 1992 in two medium-sized Hungarian cities. The purpose of these visits was twofold: to conduct seminars on strategic management for medium- and upper-level business executives, and work as a consultant to the leaders of the local government and the business community in one of the two cities as part of a U.S. government funded project to assist Hungary in the transition to a Western-style market economy.

HUNGARY: A SPECIAL CASE

Earlier Reforms

Unlike other Central European countries and the former Soviet Union, Hungary has a long tradition in economic liberalization that goes back to the late 1960s and continued until the demise of the communist regime (Bauer, 1991; Kornai, 1986). This tradition is evident in the reduced economic significance of the state compared to other Central European countries, which, however, is still far more prevalent than in Western economies (Table 1).

Reforms began in 1968, when state-owned firms were declared autonomous, which enabled them to formulate their short-term plans; the power to establish long-term plans remained, however, with the central planning authority. In the 1980s, the pace of the reform accelerated, beginning with the divestiture of large supply monopolies. In 1982, the legal basis for certain forms of small businesses was created. 1985 marked a major step forward towards liberalizing the economy. A privatization program was started that lead to the creation of over 10,000 new enterprises. These businesses formed the bulk of a newly established private sector whose function remained restricted to a secondary role (Bauer, 1991). New regulations mandated the election of top managers in state-owned firms by the employees, instead of being appointed by the higher authority. The state monopoly on foreign trade was gradually reduced, which increased the number of businesses with the right to trade in foreign currencies from 150 to over 2,000. A year later, bankruptcy legislation was enacted. In the same year, a first step was taken towards reforming the banking sector. A two-tiered banking system was created by spinning off the national bank's commercial business into three new major commercial banks and by creating a central bank after the Western model (*Neue Zürcher Zeitung*, 1992, no. 67). The reform also allowed the creation of new banks with foreign participation. In 1988, a new company law legalized private enterprises with up to 500 employees. In the same year, a comprehensive tax reform introduced a value-added tax, a personal income tax, and a corporate tax for private and public firms, which aligned Hungary more closely with its West European neighbors.

Table 1
Share of State Sector of Total Output

Czechoslovakia (1984)	97.0%
East Germany (1982)	96.5
Soviet Union (1985)	96.0
Poland (1985)	81.7
Hungary (1984)	65.2
West Germany (1982)	16.7
United States (1983)	1.3

Source: Audretsch (1991)

As a result of these reforms, which put it well ahead of the other former command economies, Hungary's economy displayed a mixture of command economy elements and market features. Kornai (1986) concluded that "the reformed system is a specific combination . . . of bureaucratic and market coordination" (p. 1699). However, the degree of bureaucratic intervention was much higher than in West European or North American economies—"there are millions of microinterventions in all facets of economic life; bureaucratic microregulation has continued to prevail [in the former state sector]" (p. 1700). These interventions had a significant impact on the firms' goal functions. For instance, while officially the firms were expected to act as profit maximizers, state-mandated prices were still widespread. Also, whether or not a company received credit from the state bank was not correlated with its past or expected profitability or credit worthiness. In addition to the official private sector an "informal" private sector similar to the underground economy in capitalist economies was an important factor in the economy. Kornai concluded that "there is somewhat less bureaucratic intervention and somewhat stronger influence of market forces [in the private sector] than in the state sector" (pp. 1703–1704).

Recent Transformation

Since the demise of the command system in 1989–1990, Hungary has continued to move towards a market economy. The process is now labeled "transformation" instead of "reform." In 1989, the new law on foreign investment unleashed a wave of joint ventures with foreign partners, which in 1991 reached 5,652, more than two times more than in the previous year (Tomlinson, 1992). In the same year, import controls were relaxed (Angell & VanSant, 1990; *Neue Zürcher Zeitung*, 1992, no. 67). In 1991, a second banking reform regulated ownership and tightened the regulations concerning reserves and capital structure to bring them in line with the recommendations of the Bank for International Settlements. Finally, a set of three laws solved the all important ownership problems by establishing a process to compensate individuals for loss of property experienced during the communist era (*Neue Zürcher Zeitung*, 1992, no. 112). In spite of the large number of state-owned enterprises that have been transformed into limited-share structures, the influence of the state remains high, since only about 10% of the companies formerly in state ownership are now privately owned, primarily by foreign investors (*Neue Zürcher Zeitung*, 1992, no. 58). The "active privatization process," i.e., the transfer of entire companies into private ownership, has proceeded slower than anticipated.

DETERMINANTS OF INDIVIDUAL BEHAVIOR

This chapter is based on two assumptions. The first is that previous experiences shape participants' reactions to stimuli. The second is an adaptation of the Sapir–Whorf hypothesis that language is not merely a device for reporting experience but also a way of defining experience for its speaker (Hoijer, 1974). The combined effects of the two are likely to lead to unintended effects in the instruction process.

Previous Experience Shapes Behavior

Managerial behavior is strongly influenced by the environment in which decision makers operate. This, in fact, is a restatement of the culture-specificity thesis of managerial practice (Limaye & Victor, 1991). The entire system of managerial incentives is based on the presumption that managers react to stimuli in their environment in pursuit of their own benefit (agency theory). Granick's classic work describing the "red executive" (Granick, 1961) gives a vivid account of the environment within which the communist executive operated. The research by Shiller et al. (1992) confirms that both in the West and the East situational factors determine behavior. By the same token, the Hungarian system of "indirect bureaucratic control" (Kornai, 1986) and the recent changes in the system have paramount consequences for managerial behavior (Melxner, 1991; Pearce, 1991). Kornai (1986, p. 1698) points out that:

Because of the thousands of bureaucratic interventions, the manager does not have full responsibility for performance. In case of failure he can argue, perhaps with good reason, that he made all crucial decisions only after consulting superiors. Furthermore, many of the problems are consequences of central interventions, arbitrarily set prices, and so on. Under such circumstances, the bureaucracy feels obliged to shelter the loss makers.

We posit that Hungarian managers' responses in courses on management topics will be conditioned by their lifetime experience in socialist enterprises (Pearce, 1991; Spender, 1992). This implies that Western instructors and consultants are likely to encounter behaviors by their students or clients that can only be understood in the context of Hungary's history and otherwise would seem puzzling if not irrational.

Language and Experience Interact

The Sapir–Whorf hypothesis of a causal interaction between language, culture, and experience claims that language organizes reality, guides mental activity, and shapes analysis of impressions. This statement has not remained unchallenged (Black, 1959). However, it seems that totalitarian regimes are strict followers of Sapir and Whorf. How else should one explain their efforts to redefine the meanings of terms such as "freedom," "democracy," "profit," and "value added" but as a deliberate strategy to shape their peoples' perceptions? Whorf and his disciples have developed their theory by comparing the languages of the Navaho and of other Indian tribes with European languages. Consequently, it is questionable whether their hypothesis can also be applied to the situation at hand relating (American) English to Hungarian. Yet, the history of Germany since the fall of the Berlin Wall in 1989 is a testimony to the cultural and linguistic estrangement can occur even within the same language due to the 40-year political and physical separation. This is all the more true for American–Hungarian interactions. The implication of the Sapir–Whorf thesis is that certain words will invoke different meanings for the Hungarians than what is understood by the Americans. Foreign instructors, caught unprepared, might not realize that their task is indeed much more complex, because in order to be successful they need act as transmitters of new meanings in addition to teaching management concepts and techniques.

Setting of the Management Simulation

The setting within which the following observations were made involved a week-long course on strategic management. The course consisted of two parts. First, participants were acquainted with key concepts of strategy in a seminar-style context. The second part consisted of a simulation exercise for which a Hungarian translation of Smith's *Manager* (Smith, 1987) was used. It stimulates competition in a consumer-product industry within a closed economy. Admission to the seminar was restricted to practicing managers at medium and upper levels with adequate knowledge about basic management concepts (accounting, marketing, human resource management, etc.). *Manager* is a simple total-management simulation which is primarily used in undergraduate introductory management courses in the United States. For each decision, 12 variables need to be considered, encompassing marketing (price, marketing effort, product R&D, market research), production (amount produced, process engineering, plant addition), finance (dividends, bank loans, stock, miscellaneous expenses), and a social-issue incident. Participants were grouped into teams of 3–4 persons who operated as a small company. All teams started off in an identical position. Throughout the entire seminar an interpreter provided simultaneous translation.

Observations of Managerial Behavior in the Simulation

Capacity Equals Demand. Many teams initially equated production capacity with demand. Thus, they assumed that they would sell all they produce, or, rather, that constraints existed at the supply end and not on the demand site. While this mistake also occasionally occurs in management courses taught at U.S. universities, it was harder to convey the difference to the Hungarians. Command economies are scarcity economies where all inputs into the production process are hard to secure. Since the plan directs the allocation of outputs, managers need not to be concerned about marketing.[1] Also, since plans are notoriously poor in assessing consumer demand and have traditionally neglected consumer goods in favor of industrial products, the market usually is cleared no matter how poor the quality. These circumstances also explain the observation that teams usually hoarded supplies without regard for the costs incurred, in spite of the fact that they had no reason to assume that supply was threatened in any way. Only after several decisions did inventory turnover approach more reasonable levels.

Fear of Debt. All firms started with $300,000 long term-debt with real annual interest at 16% and $786,000 in net worth. Initially, the environment was set to be quite favorable, with growing market demand and low price sensitivity. This allowed the less-efficient firms to pass on their costs to the consumer. The firms had 7,000 shares outstanding with the option to raise this number to 12,000. In most instances, players quickly seized upon this opportunity to repay long-term debt by issuing additional stock without regard to the implications on earnings-per-share and stock price. Discussions with the teams revealed that the decision to repay the loan was not based on cost–benefit calculations, but was a reflection of the prevailing environment in Hungary, with nominal interest rates ranging between 35 and 40%. In some instances, the relationship between earnings-per-share and stock price was not adequately understood.[2] This is hardly surprising given the nascent status of the Hungarian equities market. Furthermore, almost all participants revealed little confidence in the "sanity" of the simulated environment and expected sudden, unannounced jolts such as administrative decrees, supply shortages, rate and tax hikes, etc. Because of this, they felt it to be a wise move to avoid any long-term obligations almost at any cost.

Cash Hoarding. The simulation provides limited opportunities to invest excess cash. A successful firm may run into a situation where production engineering and marketing expenses can be covered with operating income. Thus the team is in a situation where substantial profits are being generated quarter after quarter, especially if it decides to keep production capacity constant when overall demand is stagnant or declining. After paying off their long-term debt, Hungarian teams did not select the options of increasing dividends and buying back stock in order to raise the value of their company. Instead, cash was hoarded at zero interest. During the debriefing sessions with the teams, it became clear that this behavior was related to three factors. First, insufficient understanding of the parameters influencing the value of a security played an important role. Second, the responsibility of the managers towards the owners of the company was not fully appreciated. Third, all participants felt it was important to have cash stashed away in case of an emergency. The argument that in such a case a short-term bank loan could be less expensive was met with skepticism. This reflected the current situation in Hungary in that participants mentioned that it was very difficult to obtain business loans and if so only at a very steep price.

Value of Information. The simulation allows teams to purchase market research such as an overall economic forecast, last quarter's sales in the entire industry, as well as important competitor intelligence (product price by company, average marketing, R&D, and engineering budgets). In the simulation, this information is significantly underpriced, with the most expensive market research variant costing less than 1% of quarterly sales. Additional information was provided at the end of each fiscal year in that the teams had to compile an annual report comprised of an annual income statement, balance sheet, and a brief letter to shareholders outlining major accomplishments and plans for the future. The annual reports of all teams were made available to everyone.

It soon became clear that the value of information is not well appreciated. Teams routinely underinvested in market research and made little use of it. Also, whereas in the U.S., participants would immediately pour over their competitors' annual reports, their Hungarian counterparts barely touched them. This observation can be explained by the fact that even under Hungary's relatively enlightened central planning regime the need for market research and competitive intelligence was relatively minor. In many sectors, competition is still weak resulting in a reduced need for this type of information. A third factor could be that just like her sister countries in the region, Hungary has a tradition of unreliable if not intentionally falsified statistical information (Hinteregger, 1992). A tradition of administered prices, a habit of keeping crucial information secret and of manipulating data when reporting to higher authorities has left its imprint on peoples' minds not to trust publicly available information. Because annual reports are in the public domain, these data could not possibly be correct, and thus can be safely disregarded. The alternate interpretation, that the participants did not know how to use the data, could be ruled out since the teams were given instructions and forms for condensing and interpreting the financial data. Also, by the time the first annual reports were made available, each team had had to interpret four of their own quarterly reports, which had the identical format.

The lack of understanding concerning the value of information was corroborated by the second sample of local government officials and leaders of local business organizations involved in local development. While these individuals repeatedly deplored the lack of reliable data for their work and were constantly searching for new data bases, they seemed to have very little use for whatever data they had available. One small business entrepreneur involved in computerized data collection and management had helped city hall in collecting data on the community. When it was pointed out to him that probably the same need existed in other communities and that his expertise could be expanded into a profitable business, he did not understand. Only after a 2-month visit to the United States did he comprehend the importance of up-to-date, accurate information for decision making.

Erratic Pricing. The Hungarian teams' marketing strategy seemed less coherent than that of U.S. teams. Most importantly, there seemed to be little consistency between the amount of resources invested in product R&D, resulting in a differentiation advantage, and the price charged to wholesalers. Furthermore, changes in prices were not clearly related to market-share position, strategy and/or the business cycle. In one instance, a team that had invested heavily in developing a highly differentiated product and, following textbook wisdom, priced its product at the higher end, dropped its price dramatically from one quarter to the next without a clear reason. When the author inquired about the thinking behind this change in strategy and pointed out that this move might negatively affect the product's image with final customers, the team members answered that they did not anticipate that the wholesalers would pass any of the savings on to the customers; therefore, the high-quality image of the product would not suffer. Their intention was to endear the firm with its distributors through high profit margins.

Static View of the Competitive Process. More so than their American counterparts, Hungarian participants had a hard time understanding the dynamic features of competition. The notion that a differentiation advantage could disappear and that consumer preferences might change, thereby reducing sales from one quarter to the next, needed to be learned during the simulation. Related to this was a lack of understanding of entrepreneurial risk. Participants had difficulty accepting an environment of incomplete information, where key relationships such as price, marketing, or innovation elasticity were unknown and had to be determined via trial and error. Again, this is a reflection of Hungary's recent past and of the fact that most participants were employees of (former) state-owned enterprises and industrial cooperatives.

Compartmentalized View of Competition as a Mechanism of Allocation. The Hungarians involved in economic development at the local level displayed a somewhat compartmentalized view of the prevalence of competition, which they perceived as being restricted to rivalry among firms. The notion that communities are in competition, too, for attracting businesses, was less obvious to them. In the past, competition had been downplayed in Hungary. Although the reform of 1968 opened certain sectors to competition, the influence of the bureaucracy has remained very strong. Typically, localities were not involved in location decisions for large plants, and the state took care of economic development to ensure adequate levels of employment. Therefore, there was no need for localities to actively search for new investment.

Social Responsiveness. The simulation contained one social-responsiveness variable. In each decision, the teams were confronted with an incident dealing with issues such as charitable donations, pollution control, supplier relationships, kickbacks, truthfulness in advertising, and several options from which to select. In order to ensure relevance, these incidents were adapted to the Hungarian situation. It was interesting to see that the teams had difficulty dealing with these questions on a fundamental level. Many of them had a hard time understanding why companies should be concerned with charity. In their view, this was the state's responsibility. Thus, coming from the opposite end of the spectrum in terms of their own experience where state-owned enterprises were deeply involved in the distribution of goods such as housing, food, and support of sports teams, their views were more akin to those of Milton Friedman (Friedman, 1962).

Implications for Pedagogy

The Teaching Objectives. The declared purpose of much of the teaching and consulting activity conducted by Westerners in Central Europe is to upgrade the skills of managers and public decision makers, given the changes in the political–economic structures in these countries. Since the late 1980s, hordes of Westerners have descended upon these countries emerging from communism, marketing and selling their skills. Indeed, cynical comments regarding the help of some forms of Western assistance can be heard in many places. A manager of a Big Six accounting firm observed: "When you are trying to shed a few people back in London, Budapest is an ideal place to send them" (Copeland, 1992).

Frequently, little emphasis is being placed on what should be learned, what the learners' initial knowledge is, and what the most appropriate method of delivery should be. The notion that certain terms could have different meanings, given the legacy of the socialist culture and environment, is rarely deliberated. The definition of learning "as a [planned] change in cognition, attitudes, or behavior" is ambiguous in several respects. Learning can concern declarative knowledge—concepts, facts, and figures that constitute the nodes of an associative network—or procedural knowledge—the effective application of knowledge, i.e., the linkages between the nodes (Gentry et al., 1992a). It is clear that at this point in history the task of teaching management in Central Europe, a heretofore foreign language, encompasses both elements: New concepts need to be learned, ranging from basic accounting to marketing, and old ones unlearned. Managers and business people need to have the "cultural literacy" to interact with Western counterparts. In addition, they must also be able to apply these concepts within their environment (Gentry et al., 1992b).

The Instructional Task. To clarify the instructional task, a modified version of Bloom et al.'s (1956) taxonomy is particularly useful for management education, given its orientation toward problem solving and decision making. It identifies five different levels of cognitive learning and appropriate assessment procedures for each (Table 2).

Table 2 makes clear that in order for teaching to be successful, ex ante clarification of the desired level of learning is critical. In view of the applied nature of management, learning should at least encompass levels 1 to 3. Effectiveness at higher levels is more difficult to achieve, not only because of the amount of practice required relative to the time constraint imposed on these courses, but also because at higher levels consideration of contextual factors gains in importance. This represents a great challenge to Western consultants. They will have a hard time providing tailored procedural knowledge, since they themselves usually have an incomplete understanding of the existing political, economic, and cultural environment in Central Europe. Thus, under optimal circumstances students and the consultant will learn from each other.

Since the issue at hand is Western assistance to Central Europe, clarification of

Table 2
Levels of Learning

Learning Objective	Description of the Learning	Assessment Process
1. Basic knowledge	Student recalls or recognizes information	Answer direct questions; tests
2. Comprehension	Student changes information into a different symbolic form	Ability to act on or process information by restating in his/her own terms
3. Intercultural understanding	Student differentiates between types of meanings and understands culture-specificity of terms	
4. Application	Student discovers relationships, generalizations, and skills	Application of knowledge to simulated problems
5. Analysis	Student solves problems in light of conscious knowledge of relationships between components and the principle that organizes the system	Identification of critical assumptions, alternatives, and constraints in a problem situation

Source: adapted and modified from Gentry and Burns (1981).

the terminology as well as the level of familiarity with fundamental concepts on which the more specialized management knowledge rests should also be determined beforehand. In view of the relatively benevolent nature of the previous regime in Hungary, which allowed exchange with the West on a limited basis ("Goulash Communism"), transmission difficulties are likely to be less than elsewhere in Central Europe and the CIS. To go back to the initial metaphor: It is essential to determine how accurate a picture of the elephant the participants have and what their perceptions embodied in language are before we teach them the commands and techniques to control the animal.

NOTES

1. A correlate to this is the finding that in October 1991 in a Rumanian university 800 students were enrolled in production/operations and only 25 in marketing.

2. In the original second version of the simulation, EPS does not affect stock price. The version used by the author was changed in this regard.

REFERENCES

Angell, K.J. & VanSant, J. (1990). *Investing in Human Capital: Hungary's Transition to a Market Economy.* Report Prepared for the U.S. Agency for International Development. Washington, DC: Development Alternatives.

Audretsch, D.B. (1991). Industrial Policy and International Competitiveness: The Case of

Eastern Europe. Discussion Paper FS IV 91-22, Science Center Berlin, Research Unit on Market Processes and Corporate Development.

Bauer, T. (1991). Experiences and prospects: The case of Hungary. In Giersch, H. (Ed.), *Towards a Market Economy in Central and Eastern Europe*. Berlin: Springer-Verlag.

Black, M. (1959). Linguistic relativity: The views of Benjamin Lee Whorf. *Philosophical Review*, 68: 228–238.

Bloom, B.S. (Ed.). (1956). *Taxonomy of Educational Objectives*. New York: David McKay.

Copeland, H. (1992). Consultants: Brain Gain or Boondoggle? *Budapest Weekly*, April 23.

Friedman, M. (1962). *Capitalism and Freedom*. Chicago: University of Chicago Press.

Gentry, J.W. & Burns, A.C. (1981). Operationalizing a test of a model of the use of simulation games and experiential exercises. *Developments in Business Simulation and Experiential Exercises*, 8: 48–52.

Gentry, J.W., Stoltman, J.J. & Mehlhoff, C.E. (1992a). How should we measure *experiential* learning? *Developments in Business Simulation & Experiential Exercises*, 19: 54–57.

———— (1992b). What is it that we want students to learn: Process or content? *Developments in Business Simulation & Experiential Exercises*, 19: 211.

Granick, D. (1961). *The Red Executive. A Study of Organization Man in Russian Industry*. Garden City: Anchor Books.

Hinteregger, G. (1992). Neugestaltung der Ost-West-Beziehungen. Informationsquellen und ihre Verlässlichkeit. *Neue Zürcher Zeitung*, international edition, no. 93, April 23, p. 18.

Hoijer, H. (1974). The Sapir–Whorf hypothesis. In Blount, B.G. (Ed.), *Language, Culture, and Society*, pp. 121–131. Cambridge, MA: Winthrop.

Kornai, J. (1986). The Hungarian reform process: Visions, hopes, and reality. *Journal of Economic Literature*, XXIV: 1687–1737.

Limaye, M.R. & Victor, D. A. (1991). Cross-cultural business communication research: State of the art and hypotheses for the 1990s. *The Journal of Business Communication*, 28: 3, 277–299.

Melxner, Z. (1991). A study of style. Results of a Dutch–Hungarian comparative survey on managerial features. *Invest in Hungary*, 6: 33–34.

———— "Ungarns Privatisierung von Ausländern dominiert." (1992). *Neue Zürcher Zeitung*, international edition, no. 58, March 11, p. 16.

———— "Härtere Gangart für Ungarns Finanzinstitute." (1992). *Neue Zürcher Zeitung*, international edition, no. 67, March 21, p. 21.

———— "Drittes ungarisches Entschädigungsgesetz." (1992). *Neue Zürcher Zeitung*, international edition, no. 112, May 16, p. 19.

Pearce, J.L. (1991). From socialism to capitalism: The effects of Hungarian human resources practices. *Academy of Management Executive*, 5: 4, 75–88.

Shiller, R.J., Boycko M., & Korobov, V. (1992). Hunting for Homo sovieticus: Sitiational versus attitudinal factors in economic behavior. *Brookings Papers on Economic Activity*, I: 127–194.

Smith, G.R. (1987). *Manager: A Simulation*, 2nd ed. Boston: Houghton Mifflin.

Spender, J.-C. (1992). Limits to learning from the West: How Western management advice may prove limited in Eastern Europe. *The International Executive*, 34: 5, 389–410.

Tomlinson, A.C. (1992). Hungary's "Little Guys" Think Big. *Wall Street Journal*, July 15, p. A13.

IV

PROCESSES FOR
TRANSFORMATION

10

Market Entry Strategies of German Firms and Industrial Transformation in Eastern Europe

Johann Engelhard and Stefan Eckert

THEORETICAL FRAME OF REFERENCE

It is clear that changes in the business environment of Eastern Europe have passed the threshold of change. According to the "fit" thesis, firms that align their operations to their business environment are supposed to perform better than those who do not (Venkatraman & Camillus, 1986). And since transformation in Eastern Europe induces revolutionary changes in the environment of foreign firms doing business there, the stimulus for foreign firms to react to changing circumstances appears to be very high (Macharzina & Engelhard, 1991). Thus, in the case of the operations of foreign firms in Eastern Europe, alignments in structure and strategy are expected in order to maintain an equilibrium between a firm and the environment. Since a firm's internationalization level is a component of its overall structure and a firm's internationalization behavior is a consequence of its strategy, radical changes in the environment are expected to affect both of them.

The concept of internationalization is interpreted in different ways by different authors. This process of "increasing involvement in international operations" (Welch & Luostarinen, 1988) is usually divided into several components that determine the level of internationalization of a firm. The number of components, however, varies according to the individual author (Luostarinen, 1979; Johanson & Vahlne, 1990). Nevertheless, the development of a firm's commitment to a certain foreign market is generally agreed to be a part of its internationalization behavior (Johanson & Wiedersheim-Paul, 1975; Johanson & Vahlne, 1977, 1990; Luostarinen, 1979).

According to the Nordic school of international management, a firm's foreign-market commitment increases in an incremental way. Firms increase exposure to foreign markets in "small steps" (Johanson & Wiedersheim-Paul, 1975; Johanson & Vahlne, 1977, 1990). Johanson and Wiedersheim-Paul (1975) identified a certain pattern of development ("the establishment chain") when analyzing Swedish firms. Since then, further proposals for the prescription of the development of a firm's international operations and involvement have become as numerous (e.g., Root, 1987; Buckley, 1982; Rugman et al., 1985; Cavusgil, 1980) as empirical studies regarding the patterns of a firm's international operations and involvement (e.g., Luostarinen, 1980; Hirvensalo, 1993; Turnbull, 1987; Millington & Bayliss, 1990). Our study concentrates on finding typical patterns of modes of market entry (called "internationalization paths") that firms exhibit when entering the markets of formerly socialist countries. Beyond the quest for typical patterns of internationalization, still other questions arise, such as how those sequences of market entry are influenced by the transformation of economic and political systems and whether or not certain patterns do influence the foreign-market performance of firms.

In order to gain insight into this subject, a research project was carried out in 1992 in the Department for European Management at the University of Bamberg, Germany.

RESEARCH DESIGN

For the purpose of the study, a questionnaire was developed and sent to 1417 companies all over (Western) Germany. In this questionnaire, German firms were questioned concerning their activities in certain Eastern European countries. Of the returned questionnaires, 268 answers could be used. (For further details about the firms analyzed in the sample see Engelhard & Eckert, 1994.) The Eastern European countries considered were Bulgaria (27 usable answers), Czechoslovakia (42), Hungary (78), Poland (39), Romania (26), and the former Soviet Union (56). (Since the secession of Slovakia from Czechoslovakia took place after the survey was conducted, this event is not considered in our analysis.)

As market-entry behavior was of special importance in our study, different modes of market entry had to be considered. Because there is no unanimous view about how to categorize modes of market entry (e.g., Toyne & Walters, 1989; Paliwoda, 1993), a differentiation that would be appropriate to the special circumstances in Eastern Europe had to be found.

Seven distinct modes were identified: indirect exporting, direct exportation without support by a firm-owned agency in the market (direct exporting "without own agency"), direct exportation supported by a firm-owned agency (direct exporting "with own agency"), licensing, subcontracting, joint venture, and a wholly owned subsidiary (Engelhard & Eckert, 1994).

To simplify, we assumed that the sequence of modes noted above also represented a chain of increasing risk exposure to the foreign market. This may not always be true, since the amount of risk exposure to a certain market also depends on many other components. Nevertheless, in general, it is accepted as a valuable approximation (see Langefeld-Wirth, 1990; Meissner & Gerber, 1980).

MARKET ENTRY IN EASTERN EUROPE

Pattern of Analysis

Since Eastern European countries in the past had established completely different economic and political systems compared to those in the industrial countries (Barsony, 1989), it is expected that Western firms will enter those markets in a careful way in order to limit risk exposure to a tolerable level (Johanson & Vahlne, 1977, 1990; Johanson & Wiedersheim-Paul, 1975).

To analyze the typical structure of market-entry sequences in Eastern Europe, firms were questioned concerning their operations in Eastern European markets between 1965 and 1992. The sequential order of modes of market entry of the German firms questioned are presented in Table 1. Modes of market entry are ranked according to their level of commitment. The numbers in the individual squares of the table display frequencies of changes from one mode of market entry to another. From the vertical reference of a specific square of the table we can identify how many firms have used a certain mode of market entry as a basis for a change to another, whereas the horizontal reference of an individual square displays information about the mode of market entry to which the firm switched.

Typical Mode of Entry

Looking at the results of our sample in Table 1, we discovered a typical pattern of market entry of German firms in Eastern Europe, at least on an aggregate level. Obviously, the first entry into Eastern European markets nearly always was some form of exporting. Most often, firms chose direct exporting "without own agency" as the mode of first entry. Thus, this mode serves as the initial position for the next step in the market. Firms that did direct exporting without an own agency most frequently established an agency of their own in the market afterwards. Again, this stage was primarily the starting point for starting a joint venture. And when firms changed their market operations after having established a joint venture, most frequently the joint venture was turned into a wholly owned subsidiary.

Therefore, the typical pattern German firms chose involves direct exportation without running an "own" agency in the market, followed by establishing an "own" agency in the market, afterwards starting a joint venture, and then converting it into a wholly owned subsidiary.

Entry Pattern According to Time Periods

Since the environment for the operations of firms in Eastern Europe has changed fundamentally over time, it will be even more interesting to analyze the market entry behavior of foreign firms differentiated by distinct periods of time and representing different eras of East–West relations.

For this, appropriate delimitations between different phases had to be found. In this context, we were using a differentiation primarily based on political aspects. Three phases of time, which were divided by two "critical events," were identified. The first period extends from 1965 to 1985, when Gorbachev became General Secretary of the Communist Party of the Soviet Union (Aslund, 1989). This phase can be described as typical of the cold-war era. From 1986 to 1989, the first opening of the Council for Material Economic Assistance (CMEA) countries could be felt, which was confirmed by an economic reopening of those countries

Table 1
Internationalization Paths of German Firms in Eastern Europe

to ↓ \ from →	No market activities	Indirect exporting	Direct exporting "without own agency"	Direct exporting "with own agency"	Licensing	Subcon-tracting	Joint Venture	Wholly owned subsidiary
No market activities	X	5	3	2	-	-	-	-
Indirect exporting	89	X	6	-	4	5	2	-
Direct exporting "without own agency"	129	35	X	3	2	2	-	-
Direct exporting "with own agency"	47	20	69	X	10	6	2	2
Licensing	19	11	20	11	X	3	-	1
Subcontracting	22	5	9	13	4	X	5	4
Joint Venture	11	8	18	30	7	10	X	6
Wholly owned subsidiary	14	6	17	19	10	9	18	X

(e.g., the liberalization of foreign investment legislation in all CMEA countries). Perestroika and glasnost induced some cultural convergence, but, nevertheless, a "wall of doubt" between East and West still existed. However, the removal of the Berlin wall in 1989 appeared as a "critical event" signalling that the cold war between East and West was definitely over.

Since the three phases are characterized by increasing cultural convergence between Eastern European countries and the West, the necessity of keeping to the incremental path of internationalization is expected to decline (Luostarinen, 1979). Tables 2, 3, and 4 demonstrate the internationalization behavior of the questioned German firms operating in Eastern European countries during the three time periods. Up to 1985 (see Table 2), export as mode of first market entry clearly dominated, whereas investment activities were hardly carried out. Furthermore, the internationalization path can be identified rather clearly, while the level of internationalization remains quite low due to the alien environment. Although the internationalization paths did not change from 1986 to 1988 (see Table 3), the stage of internationalization nevertheless rose during that time. As can be seen, many firms that had already operated in the region through exportation (especially when supported by their own agents in the market) established a joint venture in the market. But on the whole, investment activities were still scarce and almost always the consequence of a traditional strategy of market commitment in small steps. After 1989, however, the situation changed fundamentally (see Table 4). First, remarkably, the frequency of changes in market-entry modes rose dramatically. This is, on the one hand, due to a higher number of firms entering Eastern Europe, and on the other hand can be explained by the rising volatility of the environment, which required faster adaptations of foreign firms (Miller & Friesen, 1980). Second, while the typical path of incremental internationalization can still be identified, its clearness nevertheless vanishes and variations in internationalization paths grow stronger. Capital investments represented the core activities in this period. Whereas, on the one hand, more and more firms used investment operations as a mode of first entry, on the other hand, those firms that previously had been in Eastern European markets also raised their commitment levels to investment stages.

In summary, the market entry of German firms into Eastern Europe is characterized by a careful, incrementally increasing commitment. However, with the convergence of Eastern European and Western countries, this pattern of behavior is fading.

TRANSFORMATION STRATEGY AND MARKET ENTRY

Hungarian versus Polish Transformation Strategies

Another important aspect of the behavior of foreign firms in countries in transition refers to the question of whether or not the transformation strategy of Eastern European countries influences market-entry behavior.

To analyze this interrelationship, two countries were selected that had chosen

Table 2
Internationalization Paths of German Firms in Eastern Europe (1965–1985)

from / to	No market activities	Indirect exporting	Direct exporting "without own agency"	Direct exporting "with own agency"	Licensing	Subcon-tracting	Joint Venture	Wholly owned subsidiary
No market activities	X	1	1	-	-	-	-	-
Indirect exporting	70	X	2	-	1	2	-	-
Direct exporting "without own agency"	(103)	12	X	-	1	2	-	-
Direct exporting "with own agency"	32	7	20	X	3	1	1	-
Licensing	13	7	11	3	X	2	-	-
Subcontracting	14	1	2	3	1	X	-	-
Joint Venture	1	1	1	1	1	-	X	-
Wholly owned subsidiary	1	-	-	1	-	2	-	X

Table 3
Internationalization Paths of German Firms in Eastern Europe (1986–1988)

to \ from	No market activities	Indirect exporting	Direct exporting "without own agency"	Direct exporting "with own agency"	Licensing	Subcontracting	Joint Venture	Wholly owned subsidiary
No market activities	X	-	-	1	-	-	-	-
Indirect exporting	4	X	-	-	1	1	1	-
Direct exporting "without own agency"	11	8	X	-	-	-	-	-
Direct exporting "with own agency"	4	-	6	X	-	-	-	-
Licensing	2	1	2	-	X	-	-	-
Subcontracting	1	-	1	2	1	X	-	-
Joint Venture	2	2	4	8	1	1	X	1
Wholly owned subsidiary	1	-	2	-	1	-	-	X

159

Table 4
Internationalization Paths of German Firms in Eastern Europe (1989–1992)

from / to	No market activities	Indirect exporting	Direct exporting "without own agency"	Direct exporting "with own agency"	Licensing	Subcontracting	Joint Venture	Wholly owned subsidiary
No market activities	X	4	2	1	-	-	-	-
Indirect exporting	15	X	4	-	2	2	1	-
Direct exporting "without own agency"	15	15	X	3	1	-	-	-
Direct exporting "with own agency"	11	13	43	X	7	5	1	2
Licensing	4	3	7	8	X	1	-	1
Subcontracting	7	4	6	8	2	X	5	4
Joint Venture	8	5	13	21	5	9	X	5
Wholly owned subsidiary	12	6	15	18	9	7	18	X

contrasting strategies in transforming their economies: Hungary and Poland. While Hungary is well known to have pursued a strategy of "gradualism," Poland, which had failed to establish economic reforms earlier (Domsch et al., 1992), launched the Balcerowicz Program (Myant, 1993; Bak et al., 1991) at the beginning of 1990. This program included several components that were supposed to initiate the transformation of the Polish economy. Among the most important were the decontrol of nearly all prices, sharp cuts in public spending, and introduction of the internal convertibility of the zloty after a sharp devaluation (Myant, 1993; Winiecki, 1993).

Hungary, on the other hand, has a long tradition of market reforms (Lauter, 1990). Even as early as the beginning of the eighties, market prices were introduced to some extent and the foundation of small enterprises was fostered. In the following years, prices were increasingly liberalized and concessions for foreign trade were offered to a growing number of enterprises. In 1985, one-third of all prices in Hungary had already been decontrolled (Wesnitzer, 1993). Therefore, when the investment protection treaty with the Federal Republic of Germany was concluded in 1986, market elements were partly installed and the transformation of the economy had already begun (Engelhard & Eckert, 1993b).

In spite of Hungary's lead in transformation progress up to 1992, Poland, implementing market reforms in a rather abrupt manner, managed to catch up with Hungary (OECD, 1993; *Economist,* 1991), which preferred to change the economy in a gradual way *(Economist,* 1992).

Different Internationalization Behaviors

To examine the internationalization behavior of German firms in the Polish and Hungarian markets, several periods had to be distinguished in the two countries. Whereas in the case of Poland two periods were distinguished—the communist period (up to the end of 1989) and the transition period (from 1990 to 1992)—in Hungary three periods were considered: the communist period (up to the end of 1979), the pretransition period (from 1980 to the end of 1986), and the transition period (from 1987 to 1992). The results are presented in Tables 5 to 9.

Looking at Table 5, we see that the 39 German firms who responded regarding their activities in Poland exercised very careful market entry behavior before 1990. The dominant mode of first entry was direct exportation without an own agency. Capital investment activities were very rare. This situation did not essentially change after the implementation of the Balcerowicz Program. Export forms remained the dominant form of first market entry and the number of capital investments remained very small. When investment activities were carried out, they were always the consequence of former market activity and were never used as modes of first market entry. Furthermore, in the transition period from 1990 to 1992, no increasing dynamism in market entry behavior is to be seen. Thus, before and after the Polish shock therapy, German firms entered the Polish market very carefully in a step-by-step manner.

Table 5
Internationalization Paths of German Firms in Poland (1965–1989)

from / to	No market activities	Indirect exporting	Direct exporting "without own agency"	Direct exporting "with own agency"	Licensing	Subcontracting	Joint Venture	Wholly owned subsidiary
No market activities	X	-	-	-	-	-	-	-
Indirect exporting	10	X	1	-	-	-	-	-
Direct exporting "without own agency"	(13)	6	X	-	-	-	-	-
Direct exporting "with own agency"	8	1	3	X	1	-	-	-
Licensing	-	-	2	1	X	1	-	-
Subcontracting	3	-	-	3	-	X	-	-
Joint Venture	-	-	-	1	-	1	X	-
Wholly owned subsidiary	-	-	-	1	-	1	-	X

Table 6
Internationalization Paths of German Firms in Poland (1990–1992)

from → to ↓	No market activities	Indirect exporting	Direct exporting "without own agency"	Direct exporting "with own agency"	Licensing	Subcontracting	Joint Venture	Wholly owned subsidiary
No market activities	X	-	1	-	-	-	-	-
Indirect exporting	4	X	-	-	-	1	-	-
Direct exporting "without own agency"	5	1	X	-	-	-	-	-
Direct exporting "with own agency"	1	2	5	X	1	-	-	-
Licensing	-	-	1	1	X	-	-	-
Subcontracting	-	-	-	-	-	X	-	1
Joint Venture	-	-	-	1	-	-	X	-
Wholly owned subsidiary	-	-	2	2	-	1	1	X

163

In Hungary, however, there were basic differences in the internationalization behavior of German firms over time. The behavior of German firms in the communist period (up to the end of 1979, see Table 7) is similar to the Polish case. The dominant form of first entry during that time was direct exportation without an own agency, and few firms moved beyond that stage of internationalization. Furthermore, most of the firms just entered the market, but did not change their mode of market entry.

From 1980 to 1986 (see Table 8), export as the mode of first market entry still dominated, but, on the other hand, other forms of first market entry, including stronger cooperation between the Hungarian partner and the German firm, tended to confirm rising market commitment. On the whole, firms seem to have increased their internationalization level (e.g., via establishing agencies), and even some occasional investment activities are found. But the tendency to keep to a careful path of internationalization still remained.

However, after 1986 the market-entry patterns of German firms changed fundamentally. The establishment of wholly owned subsidiaries became the most common mode of first market entry. A strong tendency towards intensifying market commitment (especially capital-investment modes) from all levels of internationalization can be found. Furthermore, the number of changes in this period is much higher compared to the other periods.

Thus, the progress towards a market economy in Hungary in the middle of the eighties and signals that announced a stable environment as well as a stable transformation procedure, encouraged German firms to increase their commitment in the Hungarian market (Engelhard & Eckert, 1993b).

To summarize, Hungary's transition strategy—a stable and gradual transformation of the economy—attracted foreign firms much more strongly than Balcerowicz's Program, which produced a shock to the Polish economy. This would lead to the conclusion that a gradual transformation generally attracts foreign firms more strongly and thus more strongly supports the transfer of technology as well as management know-how. But this thesis is risky, since there are many other environmental components that influence market entry behavior as well (e.g., Pissula, 1992). For example, Poland's initial position in 1989, which was already shaped by hyperinflation, as well as Hungary's early start in implementing market elements into its economy, have to be considered. Nevertheless, transformation strategy seems to exert an influence on market-entry behavior of foreign firms. However, the intensity of this impact has to be analyzed through further research.

MARKET-ENTRY STRATEGY AND MARKET PERFORMANCE

Market-Performance Indicators

The final question to be considered is whether or not careful market-entry behavior (i.e., keeping to the typical path of internationalization) is more successful than a nonincremental way of penetrating the markets of countries in transition.

Table 7
Internationalization Paths of German Firms in Hungary (1965–1979)

from / to	No market activities	Indirect exporting	Direct exporting "without own agency"	Direct exporting "with own agency"	Licensing	Subcon-tracting	Joint Venture	Wholly owned subsidiary
No market activities	X	-	-	-	-	-	-	-
Indirect exporting	6	X	-	-	-	1	-	-
Direct exporting "without own agency"	(18)	-	X	-	1	-	-	-
Direct exporting "with own agency"	8	1	1	X	-	1	1	-
Licensing	3	1	-	-	X	-	-	-
Subcontracting	3	-	1	-	1	X	-	-
Joint Venture			1	-	-	-	X	-
Wholly owned subsidiary			-	-	-	-	-	X

Table 8
Internationalization Paths of German Firms in Hungary (1980–1986)

from / to	No market activities	Indirect exporting	Direct exporting "without own agency"	Direct exporting "with own agency"	Licensing	Subcontracting	Joint Venture	Wholly owned subsidiary
No market activities	X	-	-	-	-	-	-	-
Indirect exporting	5	X	-	-	-	-	-	-
Direct exporting "without own agency"	7	1	X	-	-	-	-	-
Direct exporting "with own agency"	-	1	6	X	-	-	-	-
Licensing	4	3	4	-	X	1	-	-
Subcontracting	4	1	1	-	-	X	-	-
Joint Venture	1	2	-	-	1	-	X	-
Wholly owned subsidiary	1	-	1	-	-	1	-	X

Table 9
Internationalization Paths of German Firms in Hungary (1987–1992)

to \ from	No market activities	Indirect exporting	Direct exporting "without own agency"	Direct exporting "with own agency"	Licensing	Subcontracting	Joint Venture	Wholly owned subsidiary
No market activities	X	1	-	1	-	-	-	-
Indirect exporting	2	X	1	-	1	1	1	-
Direct exporting "without own agency"	6	2	X	1	1	-	-	-
Direct exporting "with own agency"	7	1	(14)	X	2	3	-	1
Licensing	3	1	4	4	X	1	-	1
Subcontracting	5	2	1	3	2	X	2	2
Joint Venture	6	1	9	9	4	5	X	3
Wholly owned subsidiary	(10)	2	5	8	7	5	(12)	X

To examine this relationship, only performance valuations of investment modes were considered. To judge the performance of their present activities, firms were asked to assess them on a graduated scale, where 6 different rankings were available extending from 1 = "very successful" to 6 = "completely disappointing." (It is important to note that these valuations are very subjective in nature and thus depend to a high degree on the individual decision maker. Therefore, the term "market performance" in the context of this study refers to the performance that is perceived by the individual answering the questionnaire.)

Success Pattern

Examining the impact of the sequence of market-entry modes on joint venture performance all over Eastern Europe, we found that firms that chose the "typical path of market entry" identified previously perform better (median = 2) in the Eastern European markets than firms that have chosen other patterns of market entry (median = 3). However, the performance valuations of wholly owned sub-sidiaries do not confirm these results.

For further analysis, the dependence between patterns of foreign-market entry and foreign-market performance had to be differentiated on a country-specific basis. To compare the interrelationship, operations in Hungary and the former U.S.S.R. were selected. These two countries were chosen due to their extremely different environments. While Hungary is already in a relatively stable economic state and has already proceeded to transform its economy, the republics of the former Soviet Union have been shaken more strongly by post-CPE decay (see OECD, 1993) and, at least in 1992, only stood at the very brink of transition. (For a detailed prescription of the market-entry behavior of German firms in the former Soviet Union, see Engelhard & Eckert, 1993a).

When comparing the performance of market activities in these two areas, the fact is especially conspicuous that in the former Soviet Union there seems to be a stronger dependence of market performance on the internationalization path than in Hungary. Whereas, for example, firms that raised a joint venture without having been in the Soviet market before evaluate the performance of their ventures as quite bad (median = 5), firms that entered the Soviet market in a careful step-by-step way performed better (median = 3). In Hungary, on the contrary, firms that established a joint venture as a mode of first market entry performed better (median = 2.5) than firms that chose a more careful penetration of the market (median = 3). A similar situation is present in the performance valuation of wholly owned subsidiaries. Whereas subsidiaries that were the first entry of a firm into the Soviet market performed quite badly (median = 5) compared to those firms that chose more step-wise patterns of internationalization (median = 3), subsidiaries of German firms that were established as mode of first market entry in Hungary performed as good (median = 2) as those that were the consequence of other paths of market entry.

The path of market entry seems to have a positive impact on foreign-market performance when markets are very unstable. However, when market conditions become stable, the impact of the pattern of market entry on market performance vanishes. This would lead to the conclusion that while transformation lingers on, firms that choose a "careful" strategy and do not "leapfrog" steps in the typical internationalization sequence are better off than those who do not, and that their advantages fade when transformation proceeds. But, on the other hand, market performance is furthermore influenced by a countless number of other important elements. Therefore, our results can only reflect tendencies.

CONCLUSIONS

Firms are aware of changes in their environment and respond according to them. Thus, to foster the transfer of technology and management know-how by attracting foreign firms, policy makers in the Eastern European countries have to establish appropriate structures in the environment and transmit signals of the stability of market conditions in their countries. When those conditions are established, Western firms will leave their paths of careful market entry.

While transformation continues, a strategy of careful market entry seems to produce advantages compared to a strategy of foreign direct investment as a first market entry. After the transformation has exceeded a critical level, however, the gains of having chosen this strategy of small steps fade.

ACKNOWLEDGMENTS

The authors kindly acknowledge the helpful financial assistance of the Bavarian Ministry of Trade and Commerce during the execution of this research project.

REFERENCES AND SUGGESTED READINGS

Aslund, A. (1989). *Gorbachev's Struggle for Economic Reform.* London: Pinter Publishers.
Association pour la Compensation des Echanges Commerciaux. (1985). *Practical Guide to Countertrade.* Bodmin, Cornwall, UK: Robert Hartnoll.
Bak, H., Pysz, P. & Scharff, R. (Eds.). (1991). *Das Balcerowicz-Programm.* Erlangen: Deutsche Gesellschaft für zeitgeschichtliche Fragen.
Barsony, J. (1989). *Ökostroika.* Vienna: Orac.
Brabant, J.M. v. (1980). *Socialist Economic Integration.* Cambridge: Cambridge University Press.
Buckley, P.J. (1982). The role of exporting in the market servicing policies of multinational manufacturing enterprises. In Czinkota, M.R. & Tesar, G. (Eds.), *Export Management: An International Context,* pp. 174–192. New York: Praeger.
Cavusgil, T. (1980). On the internationalization process of firms. *European Research,* 8: 273–281.
Domsch, M., Bledowski, P., Bock, A., Hadler, A. & Lichtenberger, B. (1992). *Unternehmensführung in Polen—Ein Länderbericht.* Munich: Rainer Hampp.
Economist. (1991). Business in Eastern Europe (Special Survey). September 21.

————. (1992). Eastern Europe hesitates. May 16: 13–14.

Engelhard, J. & Eckert, S. (1993a). Internationalization paths and economic transition. In Kaynak, E. & Nieminen, J. (Eds.), *Managing East–West Business in Turbulent Times,* pp. 125–138. Turku: Raision Painopojat Oy.

————. (1993b). Markteintrittsstrategien deutscher Unternehmen in Ungarn, Ergebnisse einer empirischen Erhebung. In Engelhard, J. (Ed.), *Ungarn im neuen Europa.* Wiesbaden: Gabler.

————. (1994). *Markteintrittsstrategien deütscher Unternehmen in Osteuropäischen Ländern.* Bamberg: Betriebswirtschaftliche Beiträge (in preparation).

Handelsblatt. (1993). Das teure Abenteuer des ersten Joint Ventures. July 12: 8.

Hirvensalo, I. (1993). *Adaptation of Operation Strategies to Radical Changes in Target Markets.* Helsinki: Helsinki Kauppakorkeakoulun Julkaisuja.

Johanson, J. & Vahlne, J.-E. (1977). The internationalization process of the firm—a model of knowledge development and increasing foreign market commitments. *Journal of International Business Studies,* 8: 23–32.

————. (1990). The mechanism of internationalisation. *International Marketing Review,* 7(4): 1–24.

———— & Wiedersheim-Paul, F. (1975). The internationalization of the firm—four Swedish cases. *Journal of Management Studies,* 12: 305–322.

Langefeld-Wirth, K. (1990). Praxis der internationalen Joint Ventures. In Langefeld-Wirth, K. (Ed.), *Joint Ventures im internationalen Wirtschaftsverkehr,* pp. 16–218. Heidelberg: Recht und Wirtschaft.

Lauter, G.P. (1990). *The economic transformation of socialist economies and emerging business opportunities; the case of Hungary.* Paper presented at the 16th annual EIBA conference, Madrid.

Liuhto, K. (1993). From Russian roulette to managerial chess of the east—foreign experiences in successful enterprise management in Russia. In Kaynak, E. & Nieminen, J. (Eds.), *Managing East–West Business in Turbulent Times,* pp. 59–68. Turku: Raision Painopojat Oy.

Luostarinen, R. (1979). *Internationalization of the Firm.* Helsinki: Acta Academic Oeçonomica Helsingiensis.

Macharzina, K. & Engelhard, J. (1991). Paradigm shift in international business research: From partist and eclectic approaches to the GAINS paradigm. *Management International Review,* 31: 23–43.

Meissner, H.G. & Gerber, S. (1980). Die Auslandsinvestition als Entscheidungsproblem. *Betriebswirtschaftliche Forschung und Praxis,* 32: 217–228.

Miller, D. & Friesen, P.H. (1980). Momentum and revolution in organizational adaptation. *Academy of Management Journal,* 23: 591–614.

Millington, A.I. & Bayliss, B.T. (1990). The process of internationalisation: UK companies in the EC. *Management International Review,* 30: 151–161.

Myant, M. (1993). *Transforming Socialist Economies.* Aldershot: Edward Elgar.

OECD (1993). *OECD Wirtschaftsausblick.* Paris: OECD.

Paliwoda, S. (1993). *International Marketing,* 2nd ed. Jordan Hill: Butterworth-Heinemann.

Pissula, P. (1992). *Deutsch–Polnische Joint Ventures: Ergebnisse einer Befragung.* HWWA-Report Nr. 97. Hamburg: HWWA-Institut für Wirtschaftsforschung.

Root, F.R. (1987). *Entry Strategies for International Markets.* Lexington, MA: Lexington Books.

Rugman, A.R., Lecraw, D.J. & Booth, L.D. (1985). *International Business: Firm and Environment.* New York: McGraw-Hill.

Toyne, B. & Walters, P.G.P. (1989). *Global Marketing Management: A Strategic Perspective.* Boston: Allyn and Bacon.

Turnbull, P.W. (1987). A challenge to the stages theory of the internationalization process. In Reid, S. & Rosson, P. (Eds.), *Managing Export Entry and Expansion,* pp. 21–40. New York: Praeger.

Venkatraman, N. & Camillus, J.C. (1986). Exploring the Concept of "Fit" in Strategic Management. *Academy of Management Review,* 9: 513–525.

Wass von Czege, A. (1992). Sozialistische Betriebswirtschaftslehre (SBWL) und inter-systemare Wirtschaftsbeziehungen. In Schoppe, S.G. (Ed.), *Kompendium der Internationalen Betriebswirtschaftslehre,* 2nd ed., pp. 233–284. München: Oldenbourg.

Welch, L.S. & Luostarinen, R. (1988). Internationalization: Evolution of a concept. *Journal of General Management,* 14(2): 34–55.

Wesnitzer, M. (1993). *Markteintrittsstrategien in Osteuropa.* Wiesbaden: Gabler.

Winiecki, J. (1993). *Post-Soviet-Type Economies in Transition.* Aldershot: Avebury.

11

Problems of Corporate Finance in the Transition Period

The Case of Belarus

Martin K. Welge and Dirk Holtbrügge

INTRODUCTION

The transformation of the postcommunist economies into a market-based system affects most enterprises with respect to developing new sources of funds and establishing an efficient system of financial management. Although the number of possible sources of financing is growing rapidly, the availability of capital is still low. Moreover, enterprises are confronted with shortages in self-financing resulting from high rates of inflation, inefficient accounting principles, and qualification deficits.

In this chapter, the problems of raising capital and of financial management in former state-owned enterprises, with reference to the Belarussian economy, will be discussed. The various available sources of financing will be identified and the possibilities of Western assistance, based on specific questions arising in connection with shortcomings in corporate finance, will be shown.

THE FINANCING OF CAPITAL INVESTMENT IN THE FORMER SOVIET CENTRALLY PLANNED ECONOMY

The Traditional System

In the former centrally planned Soviet economy money played a minor and rather passive role. As a function of politically determined priorities, investment decisions and their financing were an integral part of the central allocation system. Consequently, virtually all enterprise investment was financed by transfers *(posobiya)* from the state budget, to which most profits were remitted. Until the reforms of the mid-1960s, long-term bank credits did not exist. Even after that, the distinction between credits and budgetary transfers remained blurred, given the soft terms of the former and the frequency with which arrears were not collected. Moreover, private savings played a minor role in financial investments because private and enterprise banking were separated.

In addition to centralized investments, short-term credits granted by the Soviet State Bank (Gosbank) were used to compensate for certain deviations from the plan, which could have been practically any expenditures that seemed legitimate and did not conflict with it. Certain types of investments could also be financed by that part of retained profits allocated to the amortization fund, the development of production fund, and the social-welfare fund. It was, however, always cheaper for enterprises to borrow rather than use their own resources because interest rates on short-term credits were very low (International Monetary Fund et al., 1991; Nove, 1967, pp. 155–245).[1]

First Reforms

The first attempts to reform the system of enterprise financing, to overcome the "soft budget constraint" (Kornai, 1980), and to make users of capital responsible for its effective allocation were made during the era of Perestroika. By the Law on State Enterprises, promulgated on July 1, 1987, state enterprises were committed to profit-and-loss accounting *(khosrazchet)* and self-financing *(samofinansirovanie)*. At the end of 1989, approximately 8.5% of Soviet enterprises had to finance all expenditures out of revenues, including wages, replacement of fixed capital, and net investment. The majority of enterprises were guaranteed basic funds for investment and wages with only additional funds to be financed out of profits (Filtzer, 1991).

Parallel to reforms in the industrial sector, the traditional banking system was modified by transferring all commercial activities from Gosbank to noncompeting, specialized state-owned banks: the Promstroibank (Building Industry Bank), Agroprombank (Agriculture and Industry Bank), Zhilsotsbank (Bank for Housing and Social Development), Sberbank (Savings Bank), and Vneshekonombank (Bank for Foreign Economic Relations). At the same time, the state bank monopoly was abolished and independent cooperative and commercial banks that were free to extend additional loans on their own initiative and risk were permitted (Babicheva, 1990). Although their number rapidly increased to more than 1500 by September 1991, their qualitative importance remained insignificant (Martyanov & Damanov, 1991; Schrettl, 1991).

Due to the halfheartedness of Gorbachev's economic policy, characterized by a dysfunctional mixture of centrally planned and market elements, the reforms undertaken did not produce the expected results. Stuck in the middle between plan and market enterprise, managers were neither afraid of political nor of market forces and, therefore, were not motivated to use their financial resources effectively. Especially in large-scale enterprises, the transfer to self-financing occurred merely on paper, without any reorganization of production, investment, or accounting. On the contrary, the growing amount of budgetary transfers, the number of nonrepaid credits, and the enormous state budget deficit indicated that the financial discipline of enterprises steadily decreased.

THE TRANSITION TO A MARKET ECONOMY IN BELARUS
AND ITS IMPACT ON CORPORATE FINANCE

After the disintegration of the Soviet Union and the formation of the Commonwealth of Independent States (CIS) in late 1991, Belarus, the former Byelorussian Socialist Soviet Republic, as well as the other 15 newly proclaimed independent states, began to develop their own institutional framework to guide their economy's transitions from a centrally planned to a market-based system. Due to cultural and economic reasons, however, a more gradual and less radical transformation, compared to that undertaken by the Russian Federation, is preferred (Holtbrügge 1993).[2]

A major element of this market-oriented transformation is a significant reduction of the scope and availability of budgetary transfers and "automatic," low-interest bank loans to state enterprises and private companies.[3] According to the Law on Enterprises in the Republic of Belarus of December 14, 1990, enterprises are fully responsible for compliance with credit contracts and payment discipline. Those enterprises that repeatedly do not fulfill their payment obligations may no longer be financed by budgetary transfers and are declared bankrupt.

At the same time, the collapsing economic relations between the republics of the former Soviet Union and the significant decline of the population's purchasing power caused a diminishing demand for their products, while expenses rose due to increasing corporation taxes and dividend expectations of shareholders. As a result, even successful and market-oriented enterprises experienced substantial difficulties in financing their operations. Since announced budgetary transfers are to be reduced significantly, Belarussian enterprises are, for the first time, confronted with the necessity to develop new sources of finance in order to meet their financial requirements and to establish an efficient system of internal financial management.

SOURCES OF FINANCE

Equity Finance

The first and most promising alternative for long-term financing is privatization *(privatizaciya)*—transformation of state enterprises into joint-stock companies *(akcionernye obshchestva)* and the raising of ownership capital by issuing shares *(cennye bumagi)*. Compared to the Russian Federation and most other former Soviet republics, in Belarus the preconditions for privatization are more favorable, due to the size of the country, its rather diversified and modern industry, and clear ownership structures. The Law on Privatization, however, which was passed on January 19, 1993, states that 50% of the shares of state enterprises are not supposed to be sold through public offering (as in the United Kingdom or in France) or by auctions (as in Hungary and Poland) but by the distribution of privatization vouchers *(vauchery)* to citizens (as in the Russian Federation or the former Czechoslovakia). Depending on age and number of working years, all residents are entitled to receive a certain number of vouchers, which they can change (within a certain time) for shares of enterprises that are to be privatized. While the free distribution of shares to the whole population is aimed at achieving a relatively equitable, massive, and fast privatization process, the possibilities of raising ownership capital through the issue of shares are limited, since the amount of fee-charging privatization will be relatively low (Aslund, 1991; Milanovic, 1991).

At present, the speed of privatization in Belarus is still very slow. As of January 1, 1993, only 57 state enterprises with a total stocks worth 1,004.8 million rubles had been privatized. Twenty-six of them were leased, 14 purchased by work collectives, six transferred into joint-stock companies, one sold to an exclusive owner, and one sold by auction (*Belorusskii delovoi vestnik,* 1993). As a result, the stock exchange *(birzha cennych bumag),* which was established in the Belarussian capital, Minsk, in 1992, is of no great importance, whereas in the Russian Federation "the current drive for registering more and more new stock exchanges and firms of brokers resembles the Klondike gold rush at the beginning of the century" (Romanova, 1991, p. 42).[4] In 1992, only 115 transactions with a total volume of 189.3 million rubles were carried out (Tichonov, 1992). The main problems in developing the Belarussian stock market are shortcomings in the information, evaluation, and clearing systems, the lack of basic infrastructure (banks, brokers, and stock exchanges), and the totally overloaded telecommunications network (Kozlov & Semin, 1993). Moreover, many companies are unwilling to issue their stocks for free trading because of incoherent regulations (Romanova, 1991, p. 42).

Issue of Bonds

Although enterprises are principally allowed to finance their development by the issue of bonds *(obligacii),* this source of finance has not played any significant role until recently, because enterprises are basically confronted with the same problems that occur with the issue of shares.

Commercial Credits

The financing of investment through commercial credits is considerably limited by shortcomings of the Belarussian capital market and the lack of a highly developed legal and institutional framework. As in the first years of economic reforms in Poland, attention was paid on problems of privatization, while the need to restructure the banking system and to create a real capital market was ignored. Although the establishment of a two-tier banking system was outlined in December 1990 in the Law on Banks and Banking and the Law on the National Bank, monetary and credit policy in 1991 continued to operate as it used to do under central planning, with extensive interference in decision making. Up to the end of 1991, for example, interest rates were set in consultation with Gosbank on a

Union-wide basis and were at the same level in Belarus as in the rest of the former Soviet Union. Moreover, the banking sector is still dominated by the government-controlled descendants of the former all-Union specialized banks, accounting for 67% of lending (International Monetary Fund, 1992, p. 35).

The 30 newly established universal commercial banks, of which Belbiznesbank, Priorbank, Commercial Bank Belarus, Westbank and Poiskbank are of greatest importance (see Table 1), operate more competitively than the former specialized banks. These banks are typically incorporated as limited-liability companies with enterprises, collectives, and government bodies as shareholders. Twelve commercial banks have been given the right to participate in the limited foreign-exchange market, where they can buy and sell foreign currency at market rates in order to service their clients' export and import activities. Commercial banks, however, face a number of legal restrictions, i.e., the maximum amount of risk for one borrower cannot exceed half of the bank stock and the total amount of large credits shall not exceed eight times the bank stock. Moreover, the vague rules on bankruptcy and the obsolete accounting system make it virtually impossible to assess the credibility of both newly founded and old companies (Schrettl, 1991).

Belarussian companies, in principle, may also obtain foreign-currency credits *(inostrannye krediti)* from abroad. Since Belarus is the only CIS-member country without foreign debt, this might become a very significant potential source of financing in the future.[5] The Belarussian State Ministry for Economic Planning (Gosekonomplan), however, strictly controls this form of financing by issuing licenses. According to a decree of Gosekonomplan of December 22, 1992, licenses are provided only for certain priority spheres of investment that are outlined in the economic program of the government. Moreover, applicants must prove the profitability of the investment through a feasibility study *(techniko-ekonomiches-*

Table 1
Activities of Belarussian Banks in 1992

Name	Number of branches	Resources (millions of rubles)	Credits (millions of rubles)
Agroprombank	125	368,037	105,511
Promstroibank	42	281,668	107,766
Sberbank	159	65,987	16,212
Belbisnesbank	22	121,389	39,075
Priorbank	20	38,760	9,747
Belarus	11	16,417	10,095
Westbank	6	11,960	7,827
Poiskbank	6	9,021	3,894
Dukat	7	6,552	2,016
Brestkombank	6	2,418	1,479

Source: Weißrußland & Unternehmen 1993.

koe obosnovanie) and clearly specify the expected foreign-currency reflux (*Delo,* 1993). Until May 1993, five credits of German, Austrian, Italian, and Spanish banks, with a total volume of approximately US $69 million, have been licensed (*Finansovie izvestiya,* 1993).

Leasing

The legal framework for leasing arrangements (*arenda*) was introduced in 1988 by the former Soviet government and extended by the Law on Leasing of the Republic of Belarus on December 12, 1990. With the help of these leasing arrangements, enterprises, enterprise subdivisions, or work collectives may lease assets such as land, machines, or even whole factories from their parent organization—ministries, enterprises, or production associations. Originally planned as a surrogate for large-scale privatization of state enterprises, leasing is now becoming an important source of financing for those enterprises not able to purchase assets due to financial restrictions and the shortcomings of the capital market. However, lessees are facing a number of structural and financial difficulties. Beyond that, leasing charges to lessors are generally exorbitantly high and in some cases have merely replaced part of the old profit taxes, which ministries have used to subsidize loss-making enterprises (Filtzer, 1991, pp. 994–995).

Foreign Investment

The highest expectations of Belarussian companies to overcome their financial problems are possibly connected with the opportunity to attract foreign investors. The inflow of foreign direct investment (*inostrannie investitsii*) is regulated by the liberal Law on Foreign Investments on the Territory of the Republic of Belarus, which the parliament passed on November 14, 1991. According to this law, foreign enterprises are permitted to purchase shares in projects that were started but not completed because of financial difficulties. Another possibility is the formation of enterprises, either fully owned or created jointly with Belarussian legal entities and persons. The minimum contribution of a foreign investor to ownership capital is US $20,000, which may be made in hard currency or in rubles, either obtained as a result of currency exchange in banks of the republic or from economic activities. In addition, foreign investors are allowed to participate in privatization of state enterprises. In contrast to the investment law in the Russian Federation, however, shares of operating enterprises must first be offered to the workers of the enterprise and then to the company itself before they can be purchased by foreign investors.

In 1992, the number of joint ventures (*sovmestnye prepriyatiya*) increased from 283 to 716, of which 313 were created jointly with Polish, 116 with German, and 62 with American companies. Two of the most prominent joint ventures are Belwest (with the participation of the German Salamander Import-Export GmbH) in Vitebsk and Belpak (with the participation of PepsiCo) in Mogilev (Batsanova, 1992). In addition to these, 116 fully owned subsidiaries of foreign companies were established. The actual amount of foreign direct investment of approximately US $384 million is, however, still very low compared to the enormous financial needs of the country.

Foreign-Currency Loans and Grants of International Organizations

In order to support the difficult transition process in Belarus and the other republics of the former Soviet Union, Western countries have launched various aid programs, of which those of the EBRD and TACIS are most important (Holt-brügge, 1992). The European Bank for Reconstruction and Development (EBRD) was established in April 1991 with a capital of ECU 10 billion. Its main objective is to promote productive and competitive investment in the countries of Central and Eastern Europe. The EBRD offers various kinds of finance—loans with a maximum of 10 years for equity, guarantees, and underwriting. Loans to commercial enterprises do not require government guarantees, but a full commercial return will be sought, with interest rates reflecting the risks attached to the projects. The EBRD finances a maximum of 35% of the total cost of projects and does not directly finance loans of less than ECU 5 million.

Although at least 60% of funding in Belarus is to be directed either to private-sector enterprises or to state-owned enterprises that implement a program to achieve private ownership and control, mainly public-sector projects are financed. During his visit to Belarus in February 1993, for example the former EBRD president Jacques Attali and the Belarussian government agreed on financing approximately 20 public-sector projects, including the reconstruction of the railway station in Brest, the modernization of the electricity and telecommunications network, and the construction of a motorway between Warsaw and Moscow; the only commercial project, however, was an ECU 50 million loan to the Belarussian Automobile Factory, BelAZ (*Belorusskii rynok,* 1993).

The Technical Assistance to the Commonwealth of Independent States (TACIS) program is funded by the European Community budget and managed by the European Commission. Funds, however, are made available only as nonreimbursable grants to finance projects and reconstruction program in certain priority areas and not as loans for commercial activities. In 1992, a total of ECU 14.63 million was made available to Belarus, of which ECU 7.23 million were planned as a support for enterprises, i.e., for privatization, the establishment of small- and medium-sized enterprises, military conversion, and financial services.

FINANCIAL MANAGEMENT

High Inflation

Perhaps the greatest obstacle to efficient financial management is the high rate of inflation, which reached approximately 1,100% in 1992 (Holtbrügge, 1993). This hyperinflation makes it nearly impossible to forecast future financial flows and to evaluate the consequences of various investment and financing decisions.

As a consequence, the financial-planning horizon of most enterprises is extremely short. It is even graver that enterprises have no incentives to undertake large capital expenditures; instead, they prefer to invest less, seek investments with shorter payback-periods, and use production technologies that are less capital-intensive (Filtzer, 1991, p. 999).

Obsolete Accounting Procedures

Another reason for inefficient financial management is obsolete accounting procedures. Since most enterprises calculate on the basis of past-oriented, distorted prices rather than on market prices, future earnings, expenditures, and residual financial requirements are nearly impossible to predict. Moreover, the qualifications of financial personnel are very low, since nearly all investment and finance decisions had formerly been removed from the enterprises' sphere of influence. Consequently, the dependence of corporate discretion on profit and liquidity, or differences between earnings and cash flow, are not considered. Also, accounting axioms, current-position ratios, or methods of simultaneous investment and financial planning are totally unknown.

Lack of Financial Information

As a consequence, financial decisions in most enterprises depend on vague estimates rather than on sound financial analysis and control. This causes a lot of difficulties in the attraction of both shareholders and commercial creditors, since creditworthiness and profitability are very difficult to assess. Foreign investors and creditors, in particular, expect exact, reliable, and quantitative financial programs and feasibility studies before investment decisions will be made. Otherwise, the inflow of foreign capital will remain insignificant. The TACIS program, for example, was used to less than 20% of its potential in 1992, simply because most proposals did not meet the required standards.

Taking into account the deficits in internal financial management and external shortcomings in the capital market, the importance of efficient corporate finance becomes evident. Until recently, however, not even one large-scale enterprise has been declared bankrupt. Enterprise managers are obviously able to force government to extend budgetary transfers in the form of tax relief or other hidden subsidies. The transition to market principles, therefore, mainly affects newly established entrepreneurial companies, which are neither able to exert political pressure on government official nor to rely on clearly defined and accepted legal and economic principles.

CRITERIA AND FORMS OF WESTERN ASSISTANCE

As long as the preconditions for an effective use of investment capital are not created by the Belarussian government, Western financial assistance will only delay rather than facilitate the transition process. Commercial banks, especially, must become totally independent, entrepreneurs *(preprinimately)* must no longer be discriminated against, and credit decisions must depend on economic rather than political criteria.

Taking the enormous financial needs of Belarussian enterprises into consideration, Western assistance should only be of qualitative and not of quantitative importance. Foreign credits should therefore be used to assist entrepreneurs rather than to subsidize obsolete large-scale enterprises. Furthermore, a greater demand-orientation and better coordination of financial assistance is needed. For this reason, the German Reconstruction Loan Corporation (Kreditanstalt für Wiederaufbau) opened a coordination office in Minsk in March 1993.

Another important form of Western assistance is training of financial executives and bankers. Like the publication of textbooks and case studies, however, these training programs should be jointly designed, realized, and evaluated with local economists and experts, and be of long-term duration.

Finally, the most promising form of Western assistance is the promotion of foreign investment by establishing hard currency pools or insurance funds. The case of the EBRD, which in 1992 spent more money on its office equipment, travel, and salaries than for supporting the Central and Eastern European Countries, demonstrates that foreign investors are more efficient catalysts of change than inexperienced and bureaucratic governmental institutions.

NOTES

1. For the three decades prior to the reforms of 1987–88, the interest rate on short-term credits was fixed at 0.5%.
2. In Belarus, the preconditions for the transformation from a centrally planned to a market economy are significantly better than in most of the other former Soviet republics. Since Belarussian industry was nearly totally destroyed during World War II and rebuilt in the 1950s and 1960s, it is relatively modern, productive, and diversified. Because of this advantage, the Belarussian economy generated one of the highest living standards in the former Soviet Union in recent years (Sagers, 1985). The country, however, faces the enormous burden of overcoming the awful aftermath of the Chernobyl disaster.
3. The share of budgetary transfers to enterprises in total expenditures was outlined to decrease from 29.5% in 1990 to 20.9% in 1992 (International Monetary Fund, 1992, p. 64).
4. The first stock exchange in the former Soviet Union was established in Kharkov (Ukraine), in September 1990, that is, nearly two years earlier (Romanova, 1991, p. 42).
5. In July 1992, the Russian Federation took over the Belarussian share of the former Soviet Union's foreign debt of US $3.4 billion. Concurrently, Belarus conveyed all its foreign assets and real estate to the Russian Federation and guaranteed the free exchange of all Russian goods and services throughout its territory.

REFERENCES

Aslund, A. (1991). Principles of privatization. In Csaba, L. (Ed.), *Systemic Change and Stabilization in Eastern Europe,* pp. 17–31. Aldershot: Dartmouth.

Babicheva, Y. (1990). Commercial banks: A game without rules. *Business in the USSR,* 1(7–8): 36–40.

Batsanova, G. (1992). PepsiCo's message in a bottle. *Deloyie Lyudi,* 3(7–8): 20.

Belorusskii delovoi vestnik. (1993). Privatizaciya—i neeffektivno, i nespravedlivo. January: 4.

Belorusskii rynok. (1993). Evropeiskii bank udovletvoren. February (4): 1–2.

Delo. 1993. Kak poluchit' inostrannii kredit? 1–2: 42.

Filtzer, D. A. (1991). The contradictions of the marketless market: Self-financing in the Soviet industrial enterprise, 1986–90. *Soviet Studies,* 43(6): 989–1009.

Finansovie izvestiya. 1993. May 29–June 4: 5.

Holtbrügge, D. (1992). Westliche Hilfe ist kein Zauberelexier. Möglichkeiten der Unterstützung des Systemtransfers in der UdSSR durch die westlichen Industrieländer. *Osteuropa,* 42(1): 41–55.

Holtbrügge, D. (1993). Im Schneckentempo ins Unbestimmte. Stand und Perspektiven der Wirtschaftsreformen in Belarus. *Osteuropa,* 43(9): 839–852.

International Monetary Fund. (1992). *Economic review Belarus.* Washington, DC: Author.

International Monetary Fund et al. (1991). *A Study of the Soviet Economy.* Washington, DC: Author.

Kornai, J. (1980). *Economics of Shortage.* Amsterdam: North-Holland.

Kozlov, A. & Semin, A. (1993). Aktsiya prodana. Chto dal'she? O problemach razvitiya infrastruktury rynka cennych bumag. *Ekonomicheskaya gazeta,* 30: 11.

Martyanov, V. & Domanov, N. (1991). Commercial banks: At the cutting edge of reform. *Business in the USSR,* 2(10): 44–47.

Milanovic, B. (1991). Privatisation in post-communist societies. *Communist Economies and Economic Transformation,* 3(1): 5–39.

Nove, A. (1967). *The Soviet Economic System.* London: George Allen & Unwin.

Romanova, A. (1991). Shares market: Stake your claims now. *Business in the USSR,* 2(1): 42–43.

Sagers, M. J. (1985). The Soviet periphery: Economic development of Belorussia. *Soviet Economy,* 1(3): 261–284.

Schrettl, W. (1991). Structural conditions for a stable monetary régime and efficient allocation of investment: Soviet country study. In Blommestein, H. & Marrese, M. (Eds.), *Transformation of Planned Economies: Property Rights Reform and Macroeconomic Stability,* pp. 109–126. Paris: OECD.

Tichonov, R. (1992). Belarusskie birzhi: smert' poodinoshke ili ob-edinenie. *Dobry veshar,* October 6.

Weißrußland & Unternehmen. (1993). Gesamtüberblick der belorussischen Banken. 4–5: 27.

12

Technological Management
for Transformation

Ulrich Dörrie

TECHNOLOGY IN THE SOCIALIST ECONOMY

History

In the West, technology as part of the system of productive factors has for a very long time been considered to be independent of the prevailing political system, be it market-oriented (capitalist) or plan-determined (communist) (Gutenberg, 1971). The communist states have, on the other hand, always alleged the existence of a specific socialist production system (with the worker at the center of technology) as well as socialist products (goods of optimum use to the consumer rather than of maximum profitability to the supplier). Consequently, technology had a defining and enforcing role, for example:

- Pacemaker technologies (innovations of international significance, such as microelectronics, new materials, robot systems)
- Innovation (centers of excellence in firms and industries)
- Ministries of technology (from traditional sectors like heavy industry to modern fields like electronics)
- Scientific technology centers (for process- rather than product-oriented technologies, such as the Institute for Welding in Moscow, with a staff of more than 3,000 scientists and researchers)

Technological progress of any kind (fulfillment of production plans, individual achievements) was always part of the daily news in all media. Unique feats like the first satellite ("Sputnik") and the first pictures of the dark side of the moon could not be used enough for propaganda purposes. Special incentive systems were introduced as "material incentives" to innovation and rationalization in order to attain continuous improvement of productivity. As early as the 1930s, a Russian miner, A. G. Stachanow, increased his shift output to 1,300% by effectively using modern equipment. Through this feat he became the prototype of the ideal worker in an advanced socialist system.

Discrepancies between ideal and reality were usually ignored. There were a few reforms but they only cured some of the symptoms and were often only of a temporary nature. Thus, in the 1960s the New Economic System of Planning and Directing (NÖSPL) was introduced in the German Democratic Republic (GDR). This system called for orientation on world market standards and gave industrial enterprises *(Kombinate)* a greater degree of independence of the central planning institutions. Being, however, essentially formal, it could not compensate for the existing overorganization and the lack of market proximity.

In spite of the shortcomings of the socialist economy, a politically and economically stable situation persisted until well into the 1980s within the communist bloc and also in its relations with the rest of the world, especially the Western industrial states. The Soviet Union as the unquestioned leading power in the Socialist Bloc supplied the other COMECON states mainly with raw materials and energy, but also some high-tech products such as nuclear power plants, aircraft, and weapon systems at preferential prices, in return receiving industrial goods (ships, machinery, facilities, and high-tech components). Inside the communist bloc, orders from the Soviet Union always had absolute priority in planning and execution.

A similarly well-established division of work prevailed in the communist states' relations with the Western countries, especially the United States and the European Community. Western Europe received raw materials, oil, and natural gas (paid for, in part, by the construction of the necessary pipelines), and supplied mainly industrial goods, especially machinery. In times of economic sluggishness in the West, often more than 50% of all the exported machinery went to the communist countries.

But for reasons, the analysis of which would go beyond the scope of this chapter, the system did not work—either politically or economically. Towards the end of the last decade, the state of comparative stability was deteriorating with increasing speed to one of disintegration, chaos, and, finally, total collapse. People in the communist states had to realize that their standard of living, instead of getting higher, was continually going down, not only relative to the West but absolutely. The never-ending struggle for everyday items and the lengthening of the queues in front of the shops led to frustration, loss of morale, and disbelief in socialist ideals. Short supply of practically everything, lack of motivation, and growing pessimism developed into a self-accelerating process of deterioration and disintegration in every field, not only within each state but also in their relations with each other, resulting in delays and defaults in delivery, extreme price increases, mutual blaming and fault-finding, and general distrust and suspicion. (It is said that former East German Head of State Erich Honecker, presenting President Gorbachev with the first 1-megabit chip developed and built in the GDR by Carl Zeiss, Jena, made the snide remark, "This one works!," alluding, of course, to unsuccessful efforts in this field by Russian scientists.)

Suffering from the aftermath of the Afghanistan war, the Soviet Union was no longer able to control its sphere of power. In Poland, workers organized Solidarnosc, the first nonconformistic labor union in the Eastern Bloc, exposing the flaws and errors of the economic and political system and not only demanding profound changes, but also calling for the over throw of this system. Hungary resumed its historical connections with Austria (which has neutral status, being part of neither NATO nor the Warsaw Pact). This allowed for free transfer of goods and finally of people. The Iron Curtain had its first hole. Only a couple of months later it came down completely, with the collapse of that most notorious communist structure, the Berlin Wall. The process of disintegration continued at breathtaking speed. The communist parties dissolved, as did the Warsaw Pact. The Baltic states gained independence. Apart from Ukraine, Belorussia, Russia, and Kazakhstan there are now 21 republics and 11 autonomous districts in the territory of the former Soviet Union. Czechoslovakia has separated into two republics and minorities are seeking independence everywhere.

Conditions for Transformation

Transformation of national economies into free-market systems, which had been made the prerequisite for assistance from the West, necessitates comprehensive social and political changes, some of which have a direct influence on technology management, including:

- Liberalization of economic relations, especially trade and capital transfer
- Rigorous cutback of subsidies
- Transfer of firms and industries to private ownership
- Encouragement of foreign investments
- Reduction of public spending and budget deficits
- Currency devaluation

The decision to transform the economy meant accepting the necessity of passing through a "valley of tears" (see Fig. 1), resulting from the fact that the newly developing private companies need time to compensate for production losses in the formerly state-controlled sectors (Holz et al., 1992).

Only in the former GDR, the "valley of tears" was and is being filled up almost entirely by material, personal, and financial assistance from West Germany, in compliance with the so-called "Pact of Solidarity for German Reunification." Almost all of 13,000 state-owned companies have by now been transferred to private ownership (a small percentage had to be closed down) by the "Treuhand," a fiduciary association established for the purpose of denationalizing East German companies.

Despite the fact that the former Soviet Union and its successors have received more than $50 billion from Germany in recompense for the withdrawal of the Soviet Armed Forces from East Germany, the valley will be especially long and deep in the former USSR. It is expected that the GNP, after decreasing by 10% in 1991 and 18% in 1992, will again diminish by 8% in 1993, coupled with a further increase in foreign debt.

Figure 1
The Process of Transformation ("Valley of Tears" Model)

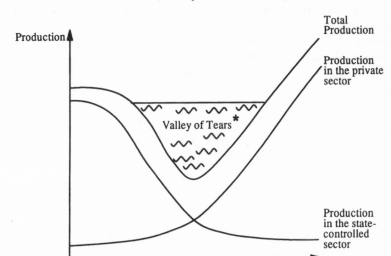

* Depth and duration depending on Western assistance

Poland and the Czech Republic have already increased their GNP by 1% and Hungary by 3%. These countries seem to have passed the bottom of the valley.

State of Technology at the Beginning of the Transformation Phase

All fields of technology were in very poor condition everywhere in the Communist Bloc. From the industrial point of view, this applied to product technology (except weapons), process technology, and the technological environment. Products were outdated, obsolete, not supplied in accordance with demand, and of uniformly bad quality. Failure rates were and still are extremely high. (According to the leading German automobile club, the ADAC, the only two cars exported to the West in considerable quantities by former communist countries, the Russian "Lada Samara" and the Czech "Skoda Favorit," are way at the top of the breakdown statistics.) Most products are hardware-oriented; they contain little software and less intelligence. There are, of course, some high-tech products like high-performance industrial lasers, but these are produced at extremely high cost.

The industrial enterprises themselves are in even worse condition. Due to the permanent necessity of deficiency organization, the industrial enterprises were bloated horizontally and vertically. All of them had their own, often extensive, facilities for plant and machine engineering and construction, service and maintenance, energy production and supply, as well as social facilities like day-care centers, medical services, and shops. Some modern production facilities were indeed imported from Western countries, especially from West Germany, but they were few and far between. Much more common was machinery dating from before the Second World War. When the Bata family recently returned to their shoe factory in Czechoslovakia, time seemed to have stood still for 50 years—the workers were still using the same machines in the same buildings.

The wasteful and careless use of material and energy resulted in enormous pollution. The concrete industry, for example, still operates practically without any environmental protection. The situation in the related technological infrastructure is no better. The fact that there has not been any substantial maintenance of the logistic infrastructure necessitates low speed limits and long detours. In Siberia the most important transport routes are frozen rivers used as roadways in the winter; in the summer there is only air freight. The communication network, especially the telephone system, is superannuated and does not come up to international standards (until recently, there was no telephone directory for Moscow). The Chernobyl catastrophe demonstrated to the world the disastrous condition of the safety standards of Soviet nuclear power plants.

TECHNOLOGICAL MANAGEMENT IN THE PROCESS OF TRANSFORMATION

In the following sections, the transformation of a formerly government-owned company is seen from an entrepreneurial point of view, under circumstances typical for the former communist bloc. Necessary differentiations will be made later. It must be pointed out, however, that the currently dominant attitude of western inventors, who mean to take advantage of the lower wages and salaries in the East, is not of strategic significance (Porter, 1991). As an integral part of a company's decision-making system, technological management must provide (apart from every-day quick-response activities):

- Long-term definition and realization of strategies of extension—development and integration of new products and processes within the company results in innovation management
- Medium-term intensification of resource utilization within the framework of the existing production program, resulting in rationalization management.

In the former state-controlled companies, there had been positions on the board of directors for R&D and production. Due to the classical nature of the administrative system, contact between the two departments was possible only on the upper-management level. Future-oriented structures for a step-by-step way to strategic management of technological functions (Adler et al., 1992) have to guarantee, by employing project managers, that all departments involved are systematically integrated in team structures at an early stage of the innovation and rationalization process. In this way, an optimum combination of efficiency and effectiveness will be achieved (Pfeiffer & Weiss, 1992). In spite of the crushing multiplicity and intensity of pressing technical problems in former COMECON companies, technological management must be long-term oriented. The former practice of curing only the symptoms cannot secure competitive advantages.

Megatrends for Innovation Management

Within the framework of strategic technology management the following mega-trends (Naisbitt, 1984; Pümpin, 1989) are of increasing importance.

Quality. Quality is becoming the absolute yardstick for product and process technology. There can no longer be excuses for "seconds." All organizational auxiliaries will be an integral part of quality management. Quality standards may even be determined by individual customers (e.g., Marks & Spencer sets standards for the apparel industry).

Time. All aspects of the time factor have to be observed:

* Timeliness and punctuality (e.g., just-in-time delivery)
* Acceleration and velocity (e.g., quick-response programs for multistage processes, minimization of processing time up to stockless value chains)
* Permanence and sustainability (durability of agreements, no return to the former leisurely pace of production)

Environment and Ecology. A better-informed public is rapidly becoming aware of environmental problems. Therefore, companies must adopt the most environment-compatible technologies, repurchase guarantees must be given, and products must be recyclable. Economical use of material and energy will greatly enhance the acceptance of new products.

Individualization. The change from seller to buyer markets will take place in the Eastern countries. In close relation to this stands the growing significance of the service sector, which provides those extra qualities that products are increasingly expected to possess.

Formation of Systems. Type and size of economic systems are subject to change:

* Integration and separation. As large industrial units collapse or are dissolved, new systems come into being, based on cooperation in the field of products, process, region, and customers. Hard- and software competencies have to be coordinated; policies (e.g., "only one face to the customer") have to be put into practice.

- Internationalization, nationalization, and regionalization. Between the two poles—"global player" and "local player"—many positions are possible. Products of greater technical complexity call for more global playing.

Substitution of Classical Technologies. Classical technical products and machines of an insular nature, with nonstandard interfaces, that are mass- and single-purpose oriented, will be replaced by:

- Chemical–biological technologies (e.g., medical treatment)
- Molecular technologies (e.g., implantation techniques)
- Electronic technologies (e.g., robotics)
- Adaptive mechanical technologies (e.g., low-weight machines)

The process of miniaturization will cover everything from miniplants to microchips.

Total Flexibility. A high measure of horizontal and vertical (or rather a combination of both, i.e., lateral) flexibility will be necessary, thus permitting quick adaptation to new challenges.

Life-Cycle Concept. Not only products but also all other (technological) phenomena in an enterprise have a life cycle consisting of four phases. The first is an observation phase (weak signals are received and orientations, drifts, and tendencies established). This is followed by a maturation phase (from project selection via R&D to engineering and production planning). The next is a market or utilization phase (the innovation is first used increasingly, then constantly, then decreasingly). The fourth stage is a discharge phase (end of production and service, recycling). The life-cycle concept and the fact that the market phase is shortening while the other (cost-intensive) phases are getting longer is generally accepted for products, and thinking in phase is becoming more frequent in other fields, too (Höft, 1992). But, in many cases, industry has not realized that the life cycles of technologies are also getting shorter, so that more efficient technologies are ever faster replacing the obsolete ones. To wait and see can cost the future.

Let us consider a producer of hard-metal tools (e.g., drills) in Poland: today it gets a great number of orders from the automobile industry in the West. Nevertheless, its strategic position is just as threatened as that of its Western competitors, compared to whom he has a clear cost advantage. The strategic threats are:

1. Decrease of automobile production
2. New tool materials, like ceramics
3. New materials in automobile construction (e.g., plastics)
4. Near-net-shape production

5. New processing methods (e.g., laser drilling)
6. Different connecting techniques (e.g., gluing)

"Overtaking without catching up" (the impressive but never realized motto of former East German head of state Walter Ulbricht for the Sixth Party Convention in 1963) is the only chance to overcome the menace of new technologies. For an industrial enterprise, this means to be the first to introduce innovative product technologies and the first to use innovative process technologies.

Activity-Net Analysis

In general, the production process and the economy are represented as a multi-section value chain or as a pipeline from nature to final consumer. In order to illustrate not only the horizontal but also the vertical and lateral relations between individual enterprises, the extensive interlinkage of the productive systems can be shown as an activity net on a "globe of economy," with nature and consumption forming the two poles (see Fig. 2).

Position and extension of an enterprise are subject to alterations (e.g., extension of the system border of the enterprise in Fig. 2), depending on competition and risks/opportunities in adjoining fields. There may even be threats from far-away industries (e.g., the polyester industry poses a threat to the steel industry in the construction business by substituting fibers for steel reinforcement bands).

In the globe of economy model the "northern" or nature region is dominated by enterprises from the former Soviet Union. Enormous natural resources in agriculture and mining can be extracted and processed. For this, too, there are new technologies, especially for processing (e.g., new techniques of ore dressing).

The equatorial zone of the globe is occupied mostly by companies from Eastern Europe, requiring large numbers of personnel. Labor costs in these countries are comparatively low, and workers and engineers are highly skilled and motivated. On the other hand, the establishment of a future-oriented industrial production system faces difficulties in former East Germany, which is now part of the German economy. Due to political agreements, wages and salaries have now reached about 80% of the West German level, one of the highest in the world. In Russia, a construction worker today is paid 40 cents per working hour; his colleague in Poland and in the Czech Republic earns 1.5 dollars, whereas a worker in Eastern Germany gets 10 dollars and more per hour. In Central Europe there are hardly any natural resources. Therefore, on the globe of economy it is mainly the region around the south pole, the final step to consumption, where these East German companies must be located. Only in this field can the necessary, extremely high per-capita output be achieved, in combination with either very high investments or highly efficient supply systems (e.g., in close cooperation with companies in eastern Europe).

The Activity-Net Analysis investigates structure and relations within and between individual positions on the globe in a five-factor system (see Fig. 3). The

Figure 2
Activity-Net "Globe of Economy" Model

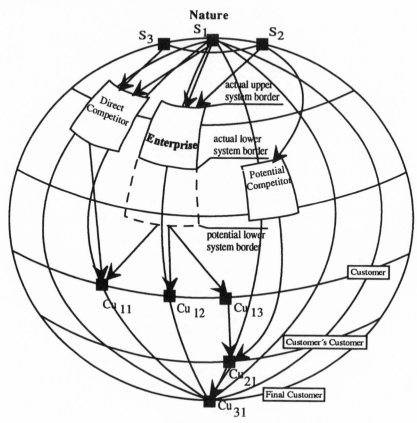

Nature

S_3 S_1 S_2

actual upper system border

Direct Competitor

Enterprise

actual lower system border

Potential Competitor

potential lower system border

Customer

Cu_{11} Cu_{12} Cu_{13}

Customer's Customer

Cu_{21}

Final Customer

Cu_{31}

Consumption

Legend:	
$Cu_{11}, Cu_{12}, Cu_{13}$	= Customers of Enterprise
Cu_{21}	= Customer's customer
Cu_{31}	= Final customer, i.e. consumption
S_1, S_2, S_3	= Suppliers of Enterprise

factors are Input (I), Personnel (P), Organization (Org), Technology (T), and Output (O).

In Eastern Bloc industrial companies, the physical and communication relations often took place in the "market place": goods were physically offered by the producer and taken away by the buyer. In contrast, Western industries have

Figure 3
Development of Enterprise Interactions

1. Marketplace Interfaces

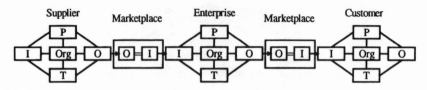

2. Input-Output Interfaces

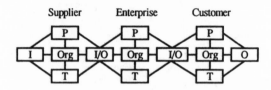

3. Structural Interfaces

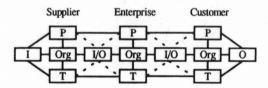

reached at least stage two of the integration process: there is substantial bargaining at the system border, with an ambivalent input/output relation and mutual profit determining sale and purchase.

Network orientation does not, however, stop at this point—it is fast developing in the direction of structural integration. Direct communication between the elements of the socio-technical systems not only saves time but also permits the substitution of feedback systems (i.e., passive learning) by feed-forward systems (active learning). When a market-oriented system is introduced in a former communist country, the potential of network-oriented systems must be taken into account and put to use.

Technological Perspectives in Industries

On the basis of megatrends and activity-net analyses, tendencies of the technological development of the most important industries in the former communist bloc can be formulated. In the field of product technology there are chances that companies may recover on their own (see Fig. 4). But in process technology the chances are that they be kept stable or improved only with help from the West. The reasons for this are obsolescence of machines and facilities (resulting in very high capital requirements, and lack of personnel knowledge and know-how).

Figure 4 also shows which regions offer locational advantages for different industries, which size is typical for each, how quickly adaptations can become effective, and the degree of necessity of denationalization. These can, of course, only be preliminary orientations, based on average conditions.

Investment for Transformation

Independent of the type of investment intended (replacement, rationalization, or innovation investments) integration of the new technologies into the existing industrial system must be guaranteed by observing the following criteria (Pfeiffer, 1965):

1. Technical level of the new solution in comparison with existing solutions (e.g., quality, quantity, reliability, maintainability, complexity)
2. Degree of conformity with the existing socio-technical system
   * structural compatibility (technical, e.g., linkability and component reliability; personnel, e.g., specific existing know-how, acceptance)
   * functional compatibility (input–availability; output–applicability)
   * process compatibility (reliability, multishift operation)
3. Potential market (customers' acceptance of the new technology)
4. Financial suitability (initial investment, installation costs, learning costs, supplier's terms policy)
5. Time suitability (time of delivery, speedy service)
6. Rival offers (same technology/different supplier, equivalent technology)
7. Confidence (reliability, sustainability)

In the process of decision making for the investment the informational basis changes more and more to soft facts instead of pseudo exact hard facts (Wildemann 1987).

Technology-Oriented Models of Cooperation

Without cooperation with Western partners, successive improvement of the standard of living through transformation to a market-oriented system cannot be achieved. In addition to financial aid (e.g., $800 million for the Skoda company and $400 million for the oil industry in Russia), used by the customer for buying equipment, the following types of technological cooperation are possible:

Figure 4
Technological Perspectives in Industries

Industry	Product Technology	Process Technology	Predominant Region	Typical Company Size	Evidence of Results	Necessity of Denationalization
Mining, oil	⇒	↗	1,2	l	t,s	-
Construction	⇗	↗	1,2,3	m,l	t	(x)
Chemical, Plastics	↗	↗	1	l	t,s	(x)
Timber, Paper	⇒	↗	1	l	t	(x)
Mechanical Engineering	→	→	1,2	m	t	x
Vehicles, Shipbuilding	→	→	3,1,2	l	t	(x)
Air- & Spacecraft	⇒	→	1	l	t,s	-
Furniture	⇒	↗	2,1	m	o,t	x
Electrical Engineering	⇒	→	3,2,1	m	o,t	x
Precision Mechanics, Optics	⇒	→	3,1	m	o,t	x
Office Equipment, Data Processing	→	→	3,2	m	t	x
Musical Instruments, Toys	⇒	→	2,3	s	o,t	x
Ceramics, Glass	⇒	→	2,3	m,s	o,t	x
Textile, Apparel	⇒	↗	2,3	m	o,t	x
Food	⇒	↗	1,2,3	l,m	o,t	(x)
Services, Logistics	↗	↗	1,2,3	m,s	o,t	(x)

Legend:

⇗	Increasing Chances	↗	Increasing if Aided by Western Technology
⇒	Stable Chances	→	Stable if Aided by Western Technology
1	Former Soviet Union	l	Large
2	Eastern Europe	m	Medium
3	Former East Germany	s	Small
o	Operational (Weeks)	x	Yes
t	Tactical (Months)	(x)	Indifferent
s	Strategic (Years)	-	No

1. Acquisition of companies—in all former communist states foreign investors are by now allowed to purchase part interest sometimes majority interests, and even entire companies)

2. Systems transfer (shifting of entire firms or parts thereof to the Eastern countries)

3. Element transfer (machinery and material transfer to Eastern companies operating as workbench extensions); personnel transfer for transmitting knowledge and know-how

4. Information transfer (support for gaining know-how; direct ordering by blueprint)

The success of cooperation will increase with the number of link-pins existing between partners (Lawrence & Vlachoutricos 1993). There have been connections of many years' standing with large-scale enterprises, especially in the Soviet Union, where transformation often means conversion (i.e., transition from military to civil products). The future of these large enterprises lies between total dissolution and unqualified continuance of the existing situation.

The private sector, too, can be divided into transformed, formerly private small businesses and new privately owned companies.

Today it is the extreme wage advantage that makes engagement in the East attractive to Western investors. European entrepreneurs speak of the "Far East next door." Gradually, however, a new network is beginning to form. It is long-term oriented, in accordance with a correctly interpreted market economy where mutual profit, not the mere fulfillment of basic needs, determines economic relations.

REFERENCES

Adler, P.S., McDonald, D.W. & MacDonald, F. (1992). Strategic management of technological functions. *Sloan Management Review,* 33(2): 19–37.

Gutenberg, E. (1971). *Grundlagen der Betriebswirtschaftslehre, Band 1, Die Produktion* (18th ed.). Berlin: Springer-Verlag.

Höft, U. (1992). *Lebenszykluskonzepte.* Berlin. E. Schmidt.

Holz, D.-U., Hülsbömer, A. & Schilling, G. (1992). Dauer und Schwere des Zerfalls bestimmen die sozialen Kosten des Transfers in Osteuropa. *Blick durch die Wirtschaft.* December 29: 2.

Lawrence, P. & Vlachoutricos, C. 1993. Joint ventures in Russia: Put the locals in charge. *Harvard Business Review,* 74(1): 44–54.

Naisbitt, J. (1984). *Megatrends.* London: Futura.

Pfeiffer, W. (1965). *Absatzpolitik bei Investitionsgütern der Einzelfertigung.* Stuttgart: Poeschel.

Pfeiffer, W. & Weiss, E. (1992). *Lean Management.* Berlin: E. Schmidt.

Porter, M. E. (1991). *The Competitive Advantage of Nations.* New York: Free Press.

Pümpin, C. (1989). *Das Dynamik-Prinzip.* Düsseldorf: ECON.

Wildemann, H. (1987). *Strategische Investitionsplanung.* Wiesbaden: Gabler.

V

ILLUSTRATIVE CASES

13

Private-Sector Development in Poland

Cases from Service Industries

Tomasz Mroczkowski, James Sood, Maciej Grabowski, and Przemyslaw Kulawczuk

INTRODUCTION

When communism collapsed in Eastern Europe, many Western observers predicted that it would take years before a capitalist private sector could develop there. After all, communism was supposed to have extinguished the entrepreneurial spirit and all understanding of market forces. Fortunately, history has proved these predictions to be false, and East-Central Europe in the past three years has seen an explosion of entrepreneurial activity.

While state-owned companies are declining rapidly, new private companies are growing at about 25% annually and are in fact keeping the East-Central European economies afloat. Poland is at the forefront of this process; private enterprise now accounts for half of the economy and more than 55% of its workers are employed in private companies (*Economic Trends,* 1993). It is important to understand this phenomenon of private-sector redevelopment after communism. Did it just suddenly explode or did it evolve gradually? What was the importance of government policy? What can be done to sustain further growth of private companies?

The cases presented in this paper give us important insights to these questions. The companies are selected from the services sector, where privatization has occurred most deeply and rapidly. Nearly 90% of retail and wholesale trade, over 75% of construction, and over half of the transportation services in Poland are now privately owned. The services sector had been traditionally the most neglected part of the socialist economy. Poor distribution leading to constant shortages of goods was a symbol of communism's failures. Today the streets of Warsaw, Prague, and Budapest have many attractive shops and restaurants, all thanks to the entrepreneurial activity in the services sector. The present appearance of the cities and villages of these countries, after decades of drabness, is a remarkable testimony to the change that has occurred. Gdansk, the city from which our entrepreneurs in this study come, was the seat of the Solidary movement. But it has always been a busy international port open to the world, and so it is at the forefront of innovation today. It is one of the places in Poland where new economic activity is at its busiest and most exciting.

The cases were developed as part of a wider study of the state of the private sector in Poland, undertaken under the auspices of the Polish Chamber of Commerce. The stories of the companies show us some universal aspects of entrepreneurship. One of these aspects is the critical importance of the "restless activity" of the entrepreneur. The cases document how these individuals were able to identify and seize the opportunities resulting from the fundamental change in the economic system. Less obviously, they show that liberalization of the economy in the twilight years of communism was in fact a gradual and evolutionary process. Certain forms of limited private business were permitted in the mid 1980s, and this became an important preparatory phase for later growth. Many of the entrepreneurs took advantage of these early opportunities and used them to build for the moment of full liberalization in 1989. The ever-changing circumstances tested their ability to adapt and survive in what was becoming a market economy in just a short time. It is a market economy that is developing from a systems transformation of a historically unprecedented character.

CASE ONE: ELKOR COMPANY LTD.—JAROSLAW GAWRYLUK, MANAGING DIRECTOR

Foundation and Business

In 1985 a group of persons composed mainly of graduates of The Gdansk Polytechnic established the Elkor Cooperative. The founders intended to raise capital through filling orders for ship repair and anticorrosion-protection services, and then invest the capital in electronic equipment manufacturing. At that time any other legal form of establishing a firm was impossible and associations of private capital had not been reinstated as yet in Polish economic practice. As demand for ship maintenance, painting, and anticorrosion-protection services was strong, the idea of raising capital in this way proved to be successful. In the second half of the 1980s, the Elkor Cooperative was already widely known in Poland as the only domestic manufacturer of digital town clocks and small telephone exchanges. The success allowed the cooperative to expand its sales revenue and number of employees.

However, the changes in the Polish economy led to the conclusion that dynamic growth of the firm would be impossible without stronger management. Moreover, the legal form of a cooperative, whose members have an equal vote irrespective of their capital input, neither facilitates the making of strategic decisions nor provides a proper and sufficient motivation for persons directly involved in management. That is why the persons most strongly involved in Elkor (17 in all) decided to set up a limited liability company without liquidating the Elkor Cooperative. Using the name under which they had been working for several years with a good reputation, the partnership soon assumed a strong position in the market, offering a similar range of services and products as the Elkor Cooperative.

Other employees of the cooperative gradually moved to the partnership and its capital increased rapidly.

Organization and Competitiveness

In 1990, the large-partnership form of Elkor, which was already involved in many different undertakings, became unmanageable. It was decided to set up several new partnerships, each of them dealing with a specific type of activity such as production of electronic telephone exchanges, ship-maintenance services, and foreign trace. At that time the company employed about 500 persons. The new structure resembles to some extent a holding company; however, the new form of operation has imparted a greater dynamic to its activity.

Elkor was steadily expanding its share of the market for maintenance and painting services ordered by the shipyards of Gdansk and Gdynia, and then of Szczecin. Perceiving the main weakness of both state-owned and private competitors as the lack of high-quality equipment, Director Gawryluk decided to purchase necessary equipment that would allow Elkor to compete successfully with other domestic firms and other repair shipyards in the Baltic Basin. To this end, he first purchased two compressors produced by the Atlas Company in Sweden and two more from Ingersoll Rand Co. in the United States. One more similar machine was leased from a private firm. At the present time, negotiations are underway for leasing more compressors of similar standards. As a result of undercapitalization of state-owned enterprises and a continuing capital weakness of other competitors, Elkor holds a very strong position on the market and obtains a large part of all orders made by the repair shipyards. Its position is equally strong in the ship-building yards, but their scale of operations is larger and hence the position of Elkor in this market is not as strong as in the repair shipyards. Presently, Elkor employs 60 persons providing its services in Gdansk, Gdynia, and Szczecin. Director Gawryluk intends to enter the Ukrainian port of Odessa, and possibly to offer the firm's spare production capacities to Western Europe, and more specifically to Southern Italy. The future of this part of the company looks good because of lower labor costs in Poland. This allows Elkor to make competitive offers for repair services to domestic and foreign shipowners. Nonetheless, the size of orders depends on the number of ships being repaired or built and, thus, indirectly on the situation in world trade.

Difficulties Hampering Growth

The growth of the partnership, however, may be temporarily hampered by difficulties facing the other operations. The most recent example is a problem encountered in sales of digital telephone exchanges, which required substantial outlays of capital to launch their production. Following the required certification of the exchanges before sales could be made in Poland, the firm now faces difficult competition, which it considers unfair. Namely, the Korean government guarantees very low interest credits to the foreign customers of Samsung, a Korean company, for export sales of telecommunication equipment. This posed a serious competitive threat to Elkor. Today Elkor is the only manufacturer of digital exchanges in Poland, but it faces a shortage of orders caused by actions such as this and the well-known deficit of the Polish central budget, which finances public investments in the field of telecommunications. This lack of funding is even more frustrating, since improving the Polish telecommunications industry is a high government priority.

The main problem hampering the growth of the Elkor Co. is the lack of availability and high cost of credit. It is quite obvious to Director Gawryluk that his firm would be expanding faster if credit were more easily available. The problem lies more in actually obtaining credit than in having the required collateral. Another problem is the extensive delays in payments from customers, causing the firm to have liquidity problems periodically. Meanwhile, banks, with their credit offers limited by credit quotas, cannot provide sufficient capital. This frequently forces Director Gawryluk to delay paying part of the wages to the employees.

It should be pointed out that payments arrears exert a very unfavorable impact not only on the current financial standing of the firm but also on the strategic decisions concerning its growth. Consequently, this is a very important problem to be solved by Elkor, as well as by many other Polish companies. The situation is further aggravated by difficulties encountered in recruiting and retaining properly qualified and responsible workers. Many workers are usually absent from work on the day after collecting their wages, drink alcohol at work, and in general do not take a serious interest in their efforts. It is also sometimes difficult to control the intermediate-level personnel. The nature of services provided and their range cell for a flat organizational structure. As a result, appropriate supervision becomes a critical issue.

CASE TWO: PRZEDSIEBIORSTWO BUDOWLANE CONSTRUCTION COMPANY—KAZIMIERZ WILK, PROPRIETOR/MANAGING DIRECTOR

Problems of Establishment

In 1985, Kazimierz Wilk established his firm as a proprietorship. Today, he employs 16 persons and conducts building operations as a principal contractor in the local market. Mr. Wilk started the business at a time that was not very easy for private firms. Although the national economic decision makers were not fully convinced at that time about the economic effectiveness of state-owned enterprises, the central government programs were oriented to the public sector, with very little attention being devoted to private firms. Kazimierz Wilk is a graduate of The Gdansk Technical University with a specialization in civil engineering. Nevertheless, he had to hide his university diploma when seeking permission for setting up his own firm in 1985 because revealing this fact could have become an insurmountable obstacle for registering his firm (the government regulated the employment of college graduates). Coming from outside the Gdansk Region and being connected with the area only through university studies and sport achievements (throwing the javelin) made his start rather difficult, as informal connections in the economy of shortages were very important.

Development Phase

Initially, Kazimierz Wilk employed only a few persons and did not possess any equipment of great value. At that time he was ready to accept any order. Small orders were placed mainly by individual investors building their own houses. The employees hired by him proved to the most important assets of his firm, and the same persons still work for him. The first orders and the survival of the difficult initial period, led to a new situation in which Wilk started shaping the image of his firm and its growth strategy more systematically. Generally, he built his strategies on three assumptions, which he has been following until today with some adjustments to changing conditions.

First, he assumed that promotion through advertising of building services is not fully effective in Poland. As a result of a relatively large number of competitive construction companies, mainly private but also municipal and state-owned ones, a good reputation was mainly what ensured business. Performing construction work reliably and punctually and guaranteeing high quality standards played a much more important role in securing orders. It should be noted that such a strategy was uncommon at the time, when the demand for building services was high, and one could hardly expect that it would become important. The strategy adopted by K. Wilk helped him obtain orders from his established customers or from new customers recommended by them.

Second, Wilk concentrated his efforts on upgrading the level of services by directing his firm to perform more complex building operations. An example of this is rebuilding the roofs of historic houses in Gdansk. Thirdly, the principle that experienced employees would be charged with a wider range of responsibilities was adopted. Simultaneously, clear and strict rules of procedure were applied towards unreliable and undisciplined employees. The ultimate result is a stable group of workers on whom Wilk can rely. Thus, he can focus his efforts on negotiations with customers and acquiring new orders and does not need to be personally involved in time-consuming supervision of construction work. It must be added here that the labor turnover among the employees has been quite small, because of the high loyalty of team members.

Policy and Problems

Wilk has never taken any credits, believing that the interest rate is excessively high and could expose his firm to major financial difficulties. Yet he believes that the firm's growth is constrained by the difficult access to credit. Today, the firm has sufficient fixed assets to use as collateral to obtain credit, should the interest rate drop.

The adopted development strategy of the firm has secured its good position in the market, which has been confirmed by numerous orders, including many prestigious projects. This has contributed to a satisfactory financial standing at a time when most state-owned competitors have withdrawn from the market and the number of large competitors is limited. That does not imply that the firm has not experienced any failures or that it does not have any difficulties at present.

The most spectacular difficulty was when the firm was a subcontractor for a cooperative. Although Wilk's firm had completed its services for the cooperative, which had received the payment from the primary customer, the cooperative did not pay Wilk's firm for the subcontractor's work. Two court trials, both won by Wilk, did not lead to payment of the sums due, because the cooperative did not have any liquid assets. This illustrates how the present legal procedures encourages abuses and create major constraints on economic activity.

Today, the firm acts as the principal contractor of investment projects employing subcontractors. It also operates, just as it did in the second half of the 1980s, as a subcontractor for other firms. Its owner points out that the last few years have witnessed a marked shift of orders from the public sector (schools, hospitals, municipal investments) and from state-owned companies to private investors. Among more significant projects executed by the firm are the main office of the Solidarnosc-Chase Bank in Gdansk, renovation work for the Polish-American Press Society, and the reconstruction of the roof of the Town Hall in the Old Town of Gdansk. The firm has 16 permanent employees at present and it would like to acquire more equipment but finds it difficult to purchase machines that would be suitable for small and medium firms in the Polish market.

Wilk does not perceive any need for changing the structure of his firm. It relies on a few team leaders responsible for particular projects. With the present low demand for building services, there is no need for a promotion campaign or aggressive marketing. The adopted strategy seems to be successful for the time being.

Human Resource Challenges

The most important development issue is that of properly qualified workers and of remunerating them in accordance with the law. Wilk stresses that it is difficult to find highly qualified employees, particularly those with a good attitude toward their work. One reason for this is the small difference between unemployment benefits and wages, and, a second reason is that the very high social security taxes restrict possibilities of raising the wages paid to the employees. Moreover, a more recent phenomenon in the labor market is the hiring of Russian workers by other construction companies without the required permits. Hence, there is a need for changes in the unemployment benefits policies and the reduction of wage taxation by social security fees. It could be added that the present situation creates a black market in labor and postpones the necessary changes in employee attitudes toward work.

Financial Constraints

Temporary liquidity problems exist because of the long time needed by commercial banks to make money transfers. The firm's growth possibilities are also restricted by the previously mentioned delays in payment for its services. Meanwhile, excessively expensive credit limits the growth opportunities of the firm. Since possibilities of purchasing equipment from abroad are limited, the firm is forced to use obsolete equipment.

CASE THREE: PRIVATE CITRUS WHOLESALE CO. —JAROSLAW POLOCZANSKI, PROPRIETOR/MANAGING DIRECTOR

Start of the Business

The owner/manager started wholesale trade in citrus fruit and bananas in mid-1990, when he first imported a truck-load of bananas from Vienna. Today he is one of the largest fruit wholesalers in Northern Poland, with his own ripening rooms and distribution system. Mr. Poloczanski began his professional career as a team leader in a corporate set up by his friends in the mid-1980s. At the beginning of 1990, the economic changes occurring in Poland placed a new challenge before him. The pent-up demand for goods inaccessible on the market for long years, an absence of strong competition, and the possibility of large profits induced him to change his professional activity. The importing of fruit, especially bananas, was an accident and not a carefully planned choice. In early 1990, he met a banana wholesaler from Vienna. This was a turning point, even though at that time he had no idea about the transport, storage, and ripening of bananas. He started his business with a few thousand dollars from family savings and obtained his first contract in June, 1990.

Poloczanski realized soon that in this business the most important thing was efficient and reliable transportation and appropriate storage facilities. When the first cargo of bananas was brought in, he owed the success of his operation to the favorable weather and a bit of luck. The next time around he rented refrigerated trucks. Relatively soon, he changed his supplier from Vienna to wholesalers from Antwerp and Rotterdam, which are the main ports for importing fruit in Europe. Considering that the volume of trade in bananas had increased to 15–20 thousand boxes a month, the elimination of one middleman brought substantial savings.

Initial Problems

The truck transportation based on contracts made with commercial carriers proved to involve greater difficulties than expected. Namely, the trucks hired from state-owned companies were unreliable with regards to punctuality of deliveries and maintenance of required temperature and humidity. Consequently, Poloczanski had to use the services of foreign carriers, but even they could not guarantee delivery times to destination points in Poland, blaming delays on protracted border-crossing formalities. The long waiting lines for customs control and clearance of cargos had a negative impact on the operations, as the transport of fruit requires speedy deliveries under proper conditions. Finally, he embarked upon a new system, which meant that he had to be at the border each time his goods were entering Poland. His presence at the border would speed up the formalities, while his partner was responsible for contacts with customers, smaller wholesalers, and retailers. In order to maintain constant contact with his firm in Poland and with suppliers, he installed a telephone in his car.

The company did not initially own its facilities, but rented them from a company called Banan Gdanski, a state owned warehouse in the port of Gdansk. However, they did not have appropriate ripening equipment. Hence, apart from renting the premises, the company invested in ripening equipment for this warehouse. Another problem was the lack of experience of the retailers in handling fruit, which could reflect negatively on prices and demand. Bananas, which had been unavailable on the Polish market for many years, call for special care in transport and storage that posed a major problem for retailers and small wholesalers. It was solved by arranging a few training sessions for these customers.

Problems of Expansion

With the turnover stabilized at the level of 15–20 thousand boxes a month in mid-1991 and with a network of customers in different parts of Poland, it was decided to invest in warehouses and ripening rooms. The company was aware of the risks involved—only the most effective suppliers with a well-organized distribution network and contracts made directly with producers could remain in the market. That prediction was soon confirmed and small and medium-sized importers began to drop out of the market. In the meantime, the company established contacts with other major importers and adopted informal forms of financial assistance in case of liquidity shortages. The most important decision in 1991 was building ten cold-storage rooms in Gdansk. This project has allowed the company to become independent of rented premises.

One of the principles followed by the firm was granting 30-day credit to customers. In the case of regular customers, this payment period was extended further. As a result, in January 1992, regular customers owed the company about 100 million zloty, while other one-time customers owed 700 million zloty. That is why the firm was forced to initiate legal proceedings to get back at least a part of overdue amounts.

The biggest problem for the firm's growth is the absence of stable rules for managing a business, which makes it impossible to plan any operations, even for the intermediate term. The firm is affected most adversely by changes in custom tariffs, taxes, currency-exchange rates, and so on.

Moreover, very difficult access to bank credits, especially the presently pro-hibitive interest rates, hamper the growth of even very dynamic firms. Up to this time, the company has not tried to take credit fearing that it would mean the end of the firm, because of the difficulty in meeting the high repayment costs.

In order to run a successful fruit import business, it is necessary to have access to current and reliable market information. Such information is not easily acces-sible in Poland and, hence, established international traders have the stronger bargaining position when concluding contracts with a Polish partner. Another problem is difficult access to names and addresses of other fruit suppliers, because Poland lies outside the network of information concerning these issues.

CASE FOUR: HURTOWNIA ELEKTROTECHNICZNA— MICHAEL GORSKI, MANAGING DIRECTOR

The Beginning

Michael Gorski set up his firm with a colleague in 1985. The firm dealt with installing electric wiring systems in new buildings. During that period in Poland, a craftsman could have his own company, but the number of employees he was permitted to have was severely limited. Gorski was well prepared for this venture because of experience gained during his earlier work as an inspector in the Power-Engineering Plant and because of his technical university education.

The new firm gradually built its market, obtaining the first orders from a power-engineering plant and later from other companies. Its operations included laying cable networks, lightening-rod installations, changing internal electrical lines, and other similar projects. Its activity involved a very large input of labor but a very small input of capital. Accepting orders for labor-intensive electrical services, the firm had to recruit hard-working employees. That task was facilitated by the firm's location in Gniewin, a rural area with an abundant labor force, about 70 km south of Gdansk. Hence, its first employees came from villages. The newly established firm did not possess its own building, and tools and materials were stored in an industrial trailer. One of the biggest obstacles encountered by the firm during that period was purchases of needed supplies, and the company solved this problem by going from one local shop to another or by buying them from state-owned companies. Another problem was that some employees lacked self-discipline and a motivation to work. The fact that the state sector was willing to employ anyone made labor discipline more difficult to maintain.

Initial Problems

Although the firm was receiving regular orders, many state-owned companies were most unwilling to place orders with private firms. Socialized units providing similar services were in a stronger position because of the state's financial support. Also, there was a general conviction that private firms were "thieves" because of the distorted ideology of the socialist state.

Because of the lack of acceptance as a private firm, the partnership had to join a crafts cooperative. At that time, cooperatives were treated as socialized units. Actually, the change was only minimal, although it did help overcome the resistance of customers placing orders for electrical installation work. At that time the firm employed three or four persons.

The two partners eventually decided to go separate ways because of a disagreement over their respective contributions to the work. It was agreed that the two would operate separate firms that would cooperate with each other in building electrical substations. Gorski was to do the installation and the other partner was to build the casings. They are still cooperating in this manner.

Change of Profile

The area in which the services were sold was shifting towards Gdansk, which forced Gorski to dismiss the rural employees and to replace them with local employees. In his opinion, the latter did not differ much from their predecessors. The company also began to gradually change in its profile of activity. Whereas electrical-installation services had dominated previously, now the building of electrical substations started to increase. This was of a great technical significance, because previously most work was done on customers' premises and now much of the work was performed in the workshop. Almost all of the substation work was for large state-owned companies such as electric utilities.

Quite specific changes took place in the electrical installation market in 1989. Customers were suffering from lack of financial resources, but their orders were rather large and increasing. The intense financial difficulties of customers were resulting in long delays in payments to contractors. High inflation caused cost calculations and estimates to be grossly inaccurate after contracts were awarded. Unfortunately, valorization clauses were not used at that time. Moreover, any delay in payments would result in further losses. Under such conditions, further provision of installation services required substantial financial resources, which the company did not possess. The novel situation called for adaptation. The payments difficulties were gradually eased by abandoning the part of installation services with long implementation cycles and switching to the construction of electrical substations. The company also decided to contract debt with a crafts cooperative.

The behavior of firms experiencing delays in customer payments was quite interesting. Despite delays, which often lasted many months, small firms did not advance any claims through courts and neither did they charge any penalty interest. The reason was quite simple; small firms offering electrical installations had a relatively small number of customers. Advancing claims through courts or demanding interest for delayed payments was synonymous with self-elimination of the firm from the market. Small firms could hardly afford this and, consequently, they continued to cooperate with unreliable customers as long as they could.

In spring 1989, as a result of the demand for electrical substations, the company erected a new workshop. The workshop was designed as quite a large building in order to accommodate future growth. Up to then the company had been renting premises in several different places; now operations could be conducted at one place.

Because of his interest in small business issues, Gorski became one of the cofounders of the Private Entrepreneurs Club in Gdansk. Initially, it was conceived as an organization posing a challenge for the craft chambers, which were controlled under the old regime by a specific nomenclature. These craft chambers acted as a control institution in relation to private entrepreneurs grouped within them. Controlled by obedient functionaries of the socialist state, they only added to the petrification of private business. The opening of the independent Club of Private Entrepreneurs, with Michael Gorski as its first chairman, undermined the local system that was linked with the declining regime. The Club, which soon had over one hundred members, became the major business association in the area.

Wholesale Operations

The reorientation of the firm's profile of activity was connected by withdrawing from a part of its electrical installation services business in favor of production of electrical substations. It took place in 1989 and proved to be insufficient. A sudden collapse of the investment market in 1990 also affected the production of electrical substations. Payment difficulties among customers intensified, and delays in payments would sometimes reach several months. Because of the rapid expansion of private trade, the company decided to open a wholesale center for electrical materials and equipment in November, 1990.

The warehouse from which wholesale operations were to be carried out was leased from a state-owned construction company, which, as a result of recession, could not fully utilize its premises. The first items to be sold were company inventories. Later on, more products were obtained from state-owned companies that also had big inventories. A network of suppliers was gradually developed, based mainly on large state-owned companies. The biggest problem facing the wholesale center was the financing of purchases, which had to be paid for almost exclusively with cash. Meanwhile, the number of customers was growing gradually but steadily. Promotion consisted of advertisements in the local newspaper and the direct mailing of advertising leaflets. The leading principle of the advertising campaign was providing simultaneous information about the firm's wholesale and production operations, which allowed savings in outlays on advertising. The main wholesale customers were craftsmen, small firms, state-owned companies, and retail stores. Owing to the growth of the wholesale center, the firm regained financial stability.

New Perspectives

An expression of the "restless activity" of the entrepreneur was Gorski's embarking upon a new product development with two other firms. The new product was a floor heating system that was then not offered in Poland. His contribution will be the automatic control process for the heating system. Another interesting undertaking was the launching of the sales and assembly of automatic installation switches. These new venture attempts have not proved to be spectacular financial successes, but they reflect the entrepreneurial nature and developmental character of the firm.

In spite of high inflation rates and the collapse of the market for electrical installations, company turnover has increased to 2,800 million zlotys and employment has reached 16 workers. The development of the firm shows a general trend; many manufacturing and service firms sought survival in trade. To survive as a producer of goods and a supplier of services it was necessary to search constantly for new production and service opportunities.

CASE FIVE: PLAN ARCHITECTS AND DEVELOPERS CO., LTD.—JACEK MISSIMA, MANAGING DIRECTOR

The Partnership

Plan was established in May, 1988 by two architects, Jacek Missima and Marek Jancelewicz, with U.S. $90 capital. The firm offers architectural and town planning services and all aspects of investment development. After three years, the company employs 19 people and has carried out contracts for a number of significant clients within a 200 km radius of Gdynia. Plan has achieved a strong position in the marketplace through employing active marketing methods and winning prestigious prizes in important competitions. Just four years ago, both founders had a very limited idea of finance, marketing, and management.

The idea of setting up a business evolved during discussions between the two friends, who are both graduates of the Gdansk Technical University. At that time, they worked in a design practice, under the auspices of an architects' cooperative. They decided to follow their own path because they were convinced that the firm was inefficient due to excessive bureaucratic administration. As Jancelewicz states, "the key to our decision was our eagerness to run our own business."

At that time, the registration of the first postwar private limited liability companies took place, based on the regulations of the Commercial Code of 1934. These new firms constituted a novelty in the Polish economy of the day. However, even relatively simple registration procedures, after 50 years of interruption, posed serious problems for attorneys. This happened in the case of Plan. The partners asked an attorney for help and also, not trusting their own managerial abilities, they offered a share of their new company to another person, who was to be the manager responsible for marketing. The attorney became a shareholder because the architects did not have sufficient funds to finance the efforts required for the registration of the company. The share held by the manager was to bind him closer to the firm, and serve as a reward for work, since at the beginning the company did not have the funds to offer him an adequate salary. This manager did not live up to expectations and eventually left the firm.

Business and Clients

Initially, Plan was created with the aim of providing standard architectural services, which enjoyed a relatively high demand at the time. A project of remodeling an attic in the village of Choczewo was its first contract. Today, Plan is carrying out the design for the Granary Island project in Gdansk. This venture is as important to the city of Gdansk as Docklands is for the city of London.

Jacek Missima, who gained his professional experience working for a Parish Council, directed Plan's activities towards the public sector, including schools, fire brigades, and the army. The circle of clients was expanding. This turned out to be very important in 1991, because in that year public institutions, among them the army, lost their ability to pay, and bad debts to Plan reached quite high proportions. The main clients of Plan are: city councils—35%, the army and fire brigades—25%, state companies—15%, private individuals—15%, and private firms—10%. Taking advantage of the lack of firms offering complex building and investment services in the Polish market, the firm decided to widen its scope of activities by introducing these additional services into their business. In addition to the services initially offered, Plan now offers town planning and interior design.

Government agencies and state-owned companies were the first to suffer from the financial crisis, caused largely by a severe recession. Such a situation was difficult to foresee, because these clients were considered the most reliable payers. Overdue payments, usually of between 3–4 months, reached a total of 120 million zlotys. The army offered to pay part, but excluded the penalty interest levied against the delayed payment of the total, or as an alternative offered to pay the total at an undisclosed date in the future (delayed payment penalties are 0.2% per day). The widening of their circle of clients substantially assisted the company in these worsening market conditions.

Expansion Strategies

Another strategy adopted was to design projects and then to search for investors afterwards. This happened in a case of an 18th century palace, which at present remains in the possession of the State Treasury, and is gradually becoming ruined due to the lack of finance for its care and renovation. The firm made a comprehensive plan of utilizing the palace and its adjoining area, which included plans for the creation of a golf course and a hotel. The project was written up in English and, in accordance with Western requirements, incorporated the projected costs of development. The company managed to attract interest in Great Britain; however, discussions are still continuing. Another direction explored by Plan for market expansion is the creation of demand for town planning services among city council officials. Up until now the Polish town planning system was subject to extreme centralization and excessive detail. Town planning is now a local responsibility, but the older city architects are not sufficiently trained or experienced to undertake their new roles. Missima realized that this also reached beyond the abilities of Plan and decided to set up an association with other professionals under the name of

"The Gdansk Architects Group." The Group organized a seminar on town planning lasting several days for chosen officers and members of the councils from the Gdansk region, with lecturers from Harvard University. Looking at the communist legacy of architectural deserts within postwar Polish cities, the firm realizes that a change in the attitude towards town planning is necessary for the proper development of Polish cities. The change of deep-rooted attitudes and behavior of professionals requires time. In the meantime, the Group is one of the main coauthors of a new concept for regulations governing town planning.

Plan uses long-term strategies for its development in unstable conditions of economic transformation. Additionally, Plan's eventual aim is to offer a service that so far has been completely absent in the Polish market: Plan aims to become a development company offering a full financial-service package, architectural and construction services, market research, and the sale of the property to investors. At present, Plan is working on a complex of living quarters, offices, and services infrastructure with full restaurant and recreational facilities for a group of private investors who want to transfer their existing businesses into modern premises. This complex will require two hectares of land, including a building to house a private bank founded by the project's investors.

Organization and Personnel

Plan was very flexible in its employment policy. When it was faced with an increased amount of work, it employed additional people on a contract basis. The structure of the firm is tailored to current projects, and every project is headed by its own manager. External relations, such as discussions with clients, stipulating contract conditions, etc., remain in the hands of the two partners. Plan has sought the cooperation of specialist designers in particular areas, such as designing ventilation systems, and uses their services in difficult and important projects. The careful selection of full-time employees leads to its success even in the current difficult economic climate. However, having large amounts of debts outstanding is its principal problem. Trusted employees often receive only a part of their monthly salary; the balance is paid when Plan collects some of its outstanding dues. Of course, this situation is only possible with the full acceptance and understanding of the management decisions by a committed workforce.

THE CHALLENGES OF SUSTAINED GROWTH

Need for Flexibility

The case studies illustrate the challenges that emerging companies face in an environment where the economic, political, legal, and social systems are undergoing fundamental transformations. As their markets change, the entrepreneurs have to devise new strategies and be able to reorient their activities as Mr. Gorkin was doing with his floor heating system project. They have to increasingly take into account competition from both national and international firms, as in the case of Elkor's Korean competitors.

Many small businesses in Poland failed to overcome the problems posed by high inflation coupled with high interest rates, falling demand, and a recession on a scale reminiscent of the great depression of the 1930s. The companies described in this paper have survived, yet their stories show the common problems that Polish business must overcome if the private sector is to continue its impressive trajectory of growth.

Problems of Finance

Perhaps the most difficult of these problems has to do with financing. It is evident from these cases that the start-up capital for the companies came from the savings of the entrepreneurs, families, and friends, and not from bank loans. Moreover, persistently high interest rates prevent the companies from subsequent borrowing, even though their expansion needs call for additional investment. The financial stability of several of the companies is being jeopardized by systemic delays in payments due from customers or cooperating firms. As the case of Mr. Wilk's company illustrates, the difficulties in executing claims through the legal system are such that most managers have no use for this recourse. Indeed as Jaroslaw Poloczanski, the fruit importer and wholesaler, points out, entrepreneurs have to operate in a system where the relevant legal and regulatory "rules of the game" are unstable. This, together with the lack of a developed financial system, creates the most significant barriers to future growth of private businesses.

Strategies of Motivation

The cases also point out that the work ethic in Poland has not completely recovered from the era of full employment policies and artificial labor shortages induced by state-owned companies under communism. The years of indifference toward work during the socialist period have conditioned employees not to be concerned with their productivity, quality of products, customer service, or reliable behavior and performance. Because of the difficulty in disciplining or dismissing employees under the present labor code, Polish entrepreneurs have quickly recognized the importance of dealing with this problem.

One motivational approach is to reward the better employees with wage increases. As Mr. Wilk states, however, it is difficult to increase wages substantially for two reasons. The first is that the large majority of companies cannot raise the prices of their products or services to cover the higher costs because demand would drop sharply. The second barrier to high wages is the additional cost of 1.65 times the wage increase because of the 65% national insurance tax. Thus, substantial wage increases usually mean prohibitive expense and lower sales.

Another approach to resolving this difficulty is to contract with selected individuals for the performance of specified tasks instead of hiring employees to do the work. One advantage of this is that the individual is responsible for the payment of the wage and national insurance taxes. In addition, unsatisfactory workers can be dismissed easily. Despite the obvious long-term adverse consequences for both employers and employees, this practice is being used more frequently in a number of countries, including the United States.

Professionalizing Management

The need to professionalize management in the Polish private sector is evident. For instance, in an ideal world, new entrepreneurs in Poland would be able to obtain training and guidance in fundamental responsibilities such as planning, organizing, staffing, directing, and motivating, as well as the functional skills of accounting, finance, marketing, and production/operations. In the real world of present day Poland, however, this is unlikely to happen in most cases. Not only can these small companies not afford the cost of the training or for the managers to take the time off from work, but after 50 years of communism and war, there are few people qualified to provide the guidance, training, and business education.

Thus, the new entrepreneurs and managers will have to learn the skills to meet their responsibilities on an experiential basis. There is one important argument to support this approach, however—there are no proven operational systems for building enterprises within an economy that is being transformed from a planned to a market basis. Rapid "learning by doing" appears to be another common thread in the five cases. Perhaps one of the lessons to be drawn from these case studies is that thriving on change (and sometimes chaos) appears to be a key characteristic of the entrepreneur.

Institutional Development

Private enterprise in Poland is also becoming better organized. Like Michael Gorski, who founded the Gdansk Club of Private Entrepreneurs, other Polish business people have formed and joined chambers of commerce or business associations. These organizations are beginning to make their voices heard in the community as well as by government officials at all levels.

The difficult process of transforming institutional and legal structures must continue for the private sector to be able to assume increasing responsibility for the economy. The sooner the private sector becomes a recognized partner of the government in the reforming countries of Eastern Europe, the sooner these nations will become true democracies with stable economies. Helping bring about the political as well as economic maturation of the private sector has become an important priority for the people of Poland as well as supportive and concerned Western countries.

REFERENCES

Central Planning Office (1992). *The Economy, Basic Tendencies of 1992.* Warsaw: Author.

Economic Trends. (1993). Warsaw: Polish Statistical Office, Gus.

Polish Private Enterprises: Analysis and Policy Recommendations. (1992). Warsaw: Polish Chamber of Commerce.

14

Transforming Management in Central Europe

William R. Pendergast

THE TRIPLE REVOLUTION

The companies in East and Central Europe that survive and prosper over the next 5–10 years will merit recognition as heroes of modern enterprise. These companies face a "triple revolution" that includes: 1) the modernizing of archaic internal operations, 2) the systemic transformation of local economies from central planning to free markets, and 3) the accelerating contemporaneous changes in global management practices and industry structures that define the benchmark criteria for their eventual success. In the face of these unprecedented challenges, there can be no a priori specification of prospective winners and losers among existing enterprises. The only certain observation is that it will require an effort of great intensity and that only truly excellent local firms will succeed.

This chapter advances conclusions about the major challenges facing these firms. In particular, it focuses on the skills of modern management that require attention and on the cultural patterns of management behavior that are important to the transformation of Central and East European enterprises. The observations presented here are based on meetings over a two-year period with top and middle management of numerous companies in the Czech and Slovak Republics and on the written results of over 30 case studies prepared by faculty at the Czechoslovak Management Center (CMC) and by Western collaborators.[1] Although the research base is limited to the Czech and Slovak Republics, many of the conclusions agree with those by other authors who have examined firms elsewhere in the Central and East European region (Abell, 1992; Grayson, 1993).

MANAGEMENT TRANSFORMATION

Central European firms require a wholesale transformation of their internal management structures, skills, and practices. This implies a radical revolution in the prevailing management paradigm rather than an incremental process of successive approximation of existing models. The point of departure for these firms is one of antiquated management methods and systems, low-quality products, obsolete technology, and insufficient capital investment.

- Company management was centralized, dependent on ministerial directives, and emphasized administration or "running things." The typical form of company organization was functional.

- The system rewarded physical volume of production required by the central five-year plan rather than product quality or financial measures of performance. This was true even in transportation enterprises such as airlines (Olson & Matesova, 1992). In a production-oriented system, obtaining supply inputs was the major operational problem. This led to a "dictatorship of suppliers" in which the purchasing function assumed predominant importance (Pearce & Cakrt, 1992). It also induced defensive vertical integration of firms and an accumulation of inventory. The very low (negative) prevailing interest rates under the socialist system alleviated problems in financing large inventories of inputs.

- Companies had no experience of competition. Many firms had monopoly positions within their domestic marketplace and these markets were protected from external competition by inconvertible currencies. Sklo Union, for example, dominated the Czechoslovak market for flat-glass production with a market share that ranged between 85–100% (Matesova & Spiro, 1992).

- Products were obsolete, low in quality, and undifferentiated. Czechoslovak Airlines (CSA), for example, did not offer first-class service on its flights as that would imply social stratification. Even when the physical attributes of products were of high quality, there was little attention paid to the "enhanced" product of intangible attributes, such as delivery, service, or information. Some companies maintained parallel production of high-quality products for export to the West and standard- (low-) quality products for domestic and East European markets (Matesova & Spiro, 1992). These separate standards of quality extended from the product itself to packaging.

- Output was allocated administratively rather than "marketed." Companies had no information about demand for their product or service or on the profile of their client base (Olson & Matesova, 1992). Exports were distributed internationally by monopolistic state trading firms.

- Enterprises became highly diversified. Companies with similar product lines were consolidated for administrative convenience into wide-ranging state-owned conglomerates. Since 1989, many such conglomerates were changed into independent, state-owned joint-stock companies that were subsequently privatized.

- Companies were overstaffed and undercapitalized, with consequent low labor productivity. At a major Slovak steel company, for example, steel output per employee was half that at similar enterprises in the United States (Leanna, 1992). At one Czech firm, annual sales per employee was $11,000 per year while annual sales per employee at its Western joint venture partner was nearly 20 times greater (Pearce & Cakrt 1992: 5).

Systemic Economic Transition

Companies in East and Central Europe have experienced a succession of disturbances in their macroeconomic environment. In Czechoslovakia and many other Central European countries, these changes included price liberalization, currency devaluation, loss of export markets, privatization, liquidity crisis, import liberalization, and high interest rates.

Price Liberalization. In January 1991, price liberalization freed approximately 80% of Czechoslovak prices and led to dramatic increases in both input and consumer prices. The effects of currency devaluation in 1990 and the removal of state subsidies had created strong upward pressure on prices. Consequently, in Czechoslovakia by June 1991, consumer prices had increased 60% since the beginning of the year. This forced companies to make business decisions based on unreliable information about prospective costs and to determine their own product prices without established guidelines or customary practices for pricing in a market economy. Since state wages remained regulated, it also eroded the purchasing power of consumers and led to a decline in domestic demand.

The liberalization of prices also placed on the management agenda the question of techniques for establishing prices for products and services. Pricing in a market economy requires a perspective and skills that are undeveloped in Central Europe. Previous practice was based on simple cost-plus pricing. Financial goals in general were not paramount for socialist enterprises. Targets were posed in terms of physical units of output, such as number of products (Olson & Matesova, 1992). Establishing and adjusting market prices in a transitional economy with rapidly rising costs and insufficient information is a major issue for enterprise management.

Currency Devaluation. Currency devaluation resulted in import-price escalation. The Czechoslovak Crown was devalued during the Fall 1990, losing half its value in several months. This raised the cost of many foreign input prices and contributed to the burst of inflation associated with price liberalization. It reduced domestic purchasing power and aggravated a production decline resulting from the loss of foreign markets.

Trading Patterns. The dissolution of established trading patterns within the former COMECON economic area led to the loss of important export markets. In Fall 1989, for example, 63% of Czechoslovakia's foreign trade was with COMECON partners. The loss of these markets, the increase in domestic competition by foreign firms, and a severe contraction of domestic demand led to a slump in industrial production of 25–35% by October 1991. The secession of Slovakia compounded these problems for Czech and Slovak firms. One-third of Czech exports customarily went to Slovakia. In February 1993, trade between the two countries fell by 60% from its 1992 level. In the first month after the currency split, Slovakia developed a large trade deficit with the Czech Republic. The new border between the two countries and the requirement of VAT collection created distribution problems for firms in both countries.

Privatization. The privatization process required management attention and disrupted accustomed commercial relationships and procedures without creating a substitute infrastructure of transparent new laws, practices, or policies. Instead, existing institutions, power structures, and practices collapsed after 1989, leaving a vacuum. For example, the distribution trade throughout Czechoslovakia collapsed during 1991 as wholesale enterprises failed. Manufacturers were unprepared to deal directly with the hundreds of newly privatized small retail enterprises (Matesova, 1992c). One Slovak candy manufacturer saw the number of its customers rise from 90 to 2500, requiring a tremendous increase in administrative and sales support (Galik, 1992b). This was equally true of companies that faced the imperative of foreign trade for the first time without state trading intermediaries.

The privatization process and its many delays also created a sense of management uncertainty and insecurity. This resulted in a reluctance to undertake new ventures. There was little incentive to initiate new activities before the question of ownership was resolved, and many managers put their job security before risky new ventures (Matesova, 1992a).

Liquidity Crisis. A severe liquidity crisis arose, due to high interest rates, the collapse of internal demand, and the loss of East European markets. This created problems of cash-flow management and debt collection. Czechoslovak industries customarily held sizable inventories of input factors as a hedge against supply shortages. They financed these inventories by low-interest loans that carried no requirement for repayment of principal. Beginning in 1990, banks increased interest rates on loans to 23% and required principal repayment (Matesova, 1992b). At the same time, the decline in both domestic and foreign markets led to bloated inventories of final products. Rapidly growing entrepreneurial companies like TIPA encountered cash-flow problems due to the investment requirements of rapid expansion (Jirasek & Mracek, 1992).

In 1991, intercompany debt in Czechoslovakia represented nearly 20% of GNP (Frydman et al., 1993: 41,48). Besides the problem of financing inventories, many companies were unable to pay their bills because of their own unpaid receivables. In February 1993, for example, the Poldi Steel Works at Kladno outside Prague halted production when the Czech Energy Works (CEZ) reduced power to the factory due to unpaid electricity bills. Poldi's inability to pay its bills resulted from its own unpaid receivables from other large Czech companies such as Skoda Plzen and CKD Praha (*CTK Daily News and Press Survey,* 1993). The secession of Slovakia in January 1993 made the payments situation even worse. Some Slovak firms defaulted on payments to Czech companies, leading them to discontinue exports.

Managing this "vicious circle of debt" is one of the major problems for enterprises. Companies have responded when possible by the creation of mutual clearing systems, requirements for advance payment in cash, and letters of credit or bank declarations. With the advent of a new bankruptcy law in Spring 1993, companies will need to address their inadequate financial structures by such measures as asset sales or foreign investments.

Import Liberalization. Import liberalization brought an influx of high-quality Western products as well as low-cost imports from the Far East. Domestic consumers were attracted by the novelty and quality of these new products, and in some cases low-cost imports had a price advantage over local products.

Interest Rates. Interest rates increased from negative levels during the socialist regime to levels that currently range between 14 and 20%. This creates a financial drain and inhibits investment.

Throughout much of the region, these economic disruptions have been complicated by political uncertainties such as the separation of the Czech and Slovak Republics and the turmoil in Yugoslavia and the CIS states. Managing in such turbulent conditions would require skill even by managers accustomed to the uncertainties of a market economy. In Central and Eastern Europe, however, the prevailing economic environment had been artificially stable. The government and the Party mandated low inflation, full employment, no competition, and strict control of prices, rents, interest rates, and currency (Nath & Jirasek, 1992). Managers in this region had no experience with the necessity of environmental monitoring and adaptive response.

Despite its uncertainties, this situation also carries opportunities for Central European firms. First, the fact that change has become a worldwide norm legitimizes and necessitates the transformations that these enterprises require as they enter world markets. Second, skillful Central European companies may "leapfrog" transitional stages of development and avoid simply replicating obsolescent practices. Third, the state of flux and uncertainty creates an opportunity to engage as a participant in the definition of new ways of doing business. Finally, specific economic advantages such as low wages and undervalued currencies provide at least a temporary boost to export opportunities.

Global Management Change

A time of turbulence and uncertainty is transforming management structures and practices throughout the world. The competitive structure of major industries such as computers, automobiles, and consumer electronics is undergoing radical change. Once-dominant players such as IBM are no longer predictable leaders within their industry. Major Japanese firms in the consumer electronics and automotive industries also find their profits plunging and their leadership challenged in many markets. The very definition of many industries is changing. The computer industry, for example, is no longer a hardware-dominated sector, since software and networking have emerged as the leading factors.

The management of companies is undergoing change as they adjust to momentous shifts in their competitive and operational environments. Layoffs and downsizing have accompanied the flattening and narrowing of organizational structures. Asea Brown Boveri (ABB), for example, has slashed its central staffs and created a decentralized association of quasiautonomous operating units. BMW, Audi, and Mercedes are moving investments abroad for the first time to escape high local taxes and costs of production. In the United States, Sears

Roebuck closed an era with the termination of its mail-order catalogue, under pressure from specialized niche players in the catalogue and off-price sector. In a major transfer of industrial power, IBM, once the largest American company, missed the technological revolution within the computer industry.

Consideration of several trends in contemporary management of global firms suggests that they threaten to create an accelerating gap between the emerging management practices of world-class companies and the conventional existing practices of Central European firms:

- Corporate downsizing is reducing employment and flattening organizational structures, leading to intense demands on remaining employees and requirements for new skills.

- New product development processes are being redesigned to anticipate client needs, avoid expensive redesigns, and promote continuous innovation.

- Widespread "benchmarking" and other techniques of organizational learning and continuous improvement are leading to advances in efficiency, productivity, and quality.

- Just-in-time inventory processes are reducing the financial cost of inventory stocks and increasing productive efficiency.

- Teamwork and cross-functional activity are becoming standard elements of corporate development programs.

- Companies are making dramatic progress in the reduction of production-cycle time.

- Employee empowerment programs have become an indispensable part of quality management programs.

- Mass customization of products and services is replacing standardized mass production in many industries.

- The "virtual corporation" implies a lean organizational structure and an ability to broker projects that assemble the best available expertise.

This worldwide upheaval in corporate management creates both dangers and opportunities for firms in Central Europe that seek to make the transition from socialism to a market economy. For these companies, the management challenge to simply adopt modern competitive management structures and processes on a par with those of average Western and Japanese firms is great. The task is complicated by the enormous acceleration of change in world-class firms and their industries. This creates a moving target in the very standards of excellence that will determine which companies succeed and which ones fail.

THE NEED FOR TRANSFORMATION OF CENTRAL EUROPEAN MANAGEMENT

Transformation begins with an accurate perception of the existing situation—what "is." Research at the Czechoslovak Management Center has investigated more than 30 local firms. The results point clearly to the need for a thorough revamping of entire companies in order to approximate common management practices in the West, much less to emulate benchmark standards in world industry. An inventory of the current situation highlights some of the obvious areas that are badly in need of reformation. These fall into two categories: 1) the organization and skills of modern management, and 2) the attitudes, culture, or mentality that are the driving force of private enterprise.

Ultimately, the role of management as a profession must be acknowledged. Conventionally, managers throughout the region have been viewed as administrators with little autonomous decision-making ability or authority. In many cases, they were caught in the middle between directives emanating from higher ministerial authority and the intrusive role of works councils at the factory level.

Management Organization and Skills

Organizational Architecture. Companies throughout Central Europe require an entirely new organizational architecture and supporting internal operating systems. This requirement arises from the need for a more transparent structure to attract foreign investment, the implications of the privatization process for enterprise governance, and the need to adopt competitive forms of organization. In particular, this process requires the establishment of new approaches to corporate governance, the divestiture of uneconomic activities, workforce reductions, and decentralized organizational structures.

Corporate Governance. Enterprise governance in the past was based on strict control by relevant ministries; self-management groups and workers' councils at the plant level had a large role (Abell, 1992). Hierarchical control placed the top manager and deputies in the subordinate role of administration. The Ministry issued directives that top managers passed to deputies for implementation, leaving the manager in the role of "watchdog" or "enforcer" (Nath & Jirasek, 1992).

Managers and directors of newly privatized companies need to work out a new architecture of corporate governance and establish appropriate relationships between company management, governing board, shareholders, and other stakeholders. The composition and responsibilities of the governing board must be defined and supported by such practices as independent audit. Directors themselves must acquire the necessary skills for effective oversight. In particular, they must avoid the temptation to engage in micromanagement and adversarial relations with corporate management.

Divestiture. The process of restructuring enterprises will require divestiture of numerous uneconomic or nonproductive activities. During the socialist era, firms developed a wide panoply of products for administrative convenience and engaged in a defensive form of vertical integration to ensure sources of supply and of subcontracted services. At the same time, they developed a network of social services that ranged from health care and schooling to recreation. In 1991, for example, Spolana Neratovice owned 2169 apartments for employees, catering services and canteens, health care facilities, five recreation facilities with 517 beds, fitness centers, kindergartens, and training facilities (Sauer, 1992).

Companies were also subject to the extraneous demands of political authorities. In one example, local political authorities in Czechoslovakia required a chemical-equipment manufacturer to grow and harvest hay on its adjoining meadows. The company had to plant the hay and dispatch employees with scythes to harvest it (Pearce & Cakrt, 1992). In these circumstances, it is no surprise that many managers acquired a deep cynicism about the value and meaning of work and of the integrity of the enterprise.

Ironically, whereas large conglomerates face the necessity of divestiture, some new start-up entrepreneurial firms have pursued a deliberate strategy of opportunistic and experimental diversification to reduce their dependence on a single, narrow sector during a period of uncertainty and turbulence. This was true of many small retail stores that often carried a bizarre assortment of products. Trial and error seemed to be their guiding philosophy. One entrepreneurial company began operations with business activities in such diverse areas as travel services, fruit farming, shoe production, telecommunications, security systems, construction, frozen food, and investment finance (Jirasek & Mracek, 1992). The CEO of this firm commented: "If we wanted to survive, we had to diversify." This company has grown in two years from its original nine founders to over 500 employees. The management of such start-up enterprises is a major issue for the entire Central European region, which has historically lacked the small and medium-sized firms that are important for innovation and job creation.

Workforce Reductions. Divestiture must extend to the workforce, since companies commonly served the social function of employment. Official unemployment under socialism was zero, and political authorities intended to keep it that way. The low wage structure for workers created little economic incentive for companies to reduce employment levels. In addition, high levels of employment conveyed political influence for companies. In many cases, large companies are the only employer within a geographic area. Combined with the very low mobility of labor because of housing shortages and other considerations, this created a situation in which companies carried an employment obligation. This sense of social responsibility is reflected in the fact that, although industrial production fell by 25–35% in 1991, layoffs have generally been much less (Nath & Jirasek, 1992). In some cases, though, companies have reduced employment significantly. To some extent, these reductions were voluntary, as employees in state firms with regulated wages departed for better situations.

Workforce reduction is one of the greatest management challenges of transformation. Besides the question of numbers, there exist no criteria for evaluation, retention, or dismissal of personnel. Past employment practice was based on neither seniority nor merit, and prior to 1989 there was a universal right to work in Czechoslovakia (Leanna, 1992). The regional economic and political impact of workforce reduction will pose problems for both enterprise managers and political authorities.

The combination of overemployment, low labor productivity, and rapidly rising salaries threatens to undermine the temporary cost advantages of Central European countries. In former East Germany wages have already reached 70% of West German levels, while productivity per worker lags at 45% (*Wall Street Journal*, 1993). In view of the difficulties of wage containment, it will require significant workforce reductions for companies to retain their competitiveness.

Decentralization. At the enterprise level, companies are creating new organizational structures and reporting relationships. The standard form of company organization in the past was functional and commonly centered around manufacturing plants. There was little, if any, decentralized divisional management by product or line-of-business. This inhibited the development of initiative and responsibility at the divisional level and deprived companies of a major training ground for the development of general-management personnel. One of the imperatives of organizational transformation is decentralization of the organizational structure and the decision-making process. Sklo Union, for example, determined that a divisional structure is appropriate for its product mix (Matesova & Spiro, 1992).

Functional Management Skills. Companies must establish a more complex and differentiated internal architecture. They require the development and internal integration of entirely new organizational units such as accounting, finance, marketing, and human-resources management. This requires new technical skills in many functional areas, but it also requires an appreciation for the ways in which these activities fit together and interrelate in the management of a modern enterprise. Companies must develop techniques for the cross-functional integration of activities, and much more effective vertical and horizontal communication systems.

One of the recurrent problems for companies in Central Europe is to establish the appropriate organizational structure to accommodate new functional departments. In many cases, for example, new marketing or quality control departments find themselves situated too low in the organizational hierarchy to have an impact on top management decision making (Gluckaufova & Tadikamalla, 1992; Tesar & Pribova, 1992).

Accounting. Deficiencies in the field of accounting lie not so much in the absence of quantitative records as in their presentation and use for management decision making. In fact, most Central European organizations drown in antiquated and unnecessary record-keeping. Accounting records have been available on an aggregate basis, but without distinctions according to product lines or departments that permit an evaluation of the profitability of activities. There has been no distinction between fixed and variable costs that permit an assessment of profitability at different activity levels. The financial Vice President of a major chemical company acknowledged: "a number of supervisors and managers could not give reliable information about the unit cost of the materials they consume, man-hours spent in their departments, and about the overhead costs" (Sauer 1992). In the area of financial accounting as well, the absence of outside shareholders relieved firms of the necessity to issue transparent financial statements.

Human-Resource Management. The role of human-resource departments previously was spread between the administration of social benefits, recordkeeping, and political activities. The close association of personnel departments with the Community Party resulted in their being discredited after the fall of Communism. This was compounded by the rather thin set of functions that had been the domain of Personnel. In many companies, for example, compensation and benefits fell in the domain of the Economic Department (Pearce & Cakrt, 1992).

Compensation systems bore no relationship to performance evaluation or to the creation of incentives. A prevailing philosophy of "economic egalitarianism" led to level salary structures. Consequently, personnel in similar positions were paid identical salaries and top management received very low multiples of salaries of the average worker (commonly a 2:1 or 3:1 ratio and no more than 6 or 7:1) (Nath & Jirasek, 1992). Since promotions brought little ostensible economic reward, employees found other ways to exploit their positions.

The management-selection process was dominated by the Communist Party. All managers of significant rank were required to belong to the Party, and the regional Party Committee approved all company promotions (Pearce & Cakrt, 1992). This led to the frequent recruitment of mediocre managers who occupied positions of privilege that were not deserved (Nath & Jirasek, 1992). In this situation, managers spent their energies preserving their jobs rather than on performance maximization.

Following 1989, the entire management group in many companies was changed at least once, resulting in a loss of strategic continuity and in inexperienced newcomers in top management positions. One Slovak consumer electronics firm had its top management replaced three times between 1989 and 1992 (Galik, 1992a).

One of the greatest needs of companies is to develop systems of personnel evaluation and aptitude assessment for the new and different roles that are created within the enterprises. Companies have little idea who their "best" people are. Even less do they have a notion of which employees are best suited for the novel functions of marketing, accounting, public relations, etc. They need to develop ways to place people in appropriate positions and to establish paths for career development.

Marketing. Marketing is an area in which Central and East European firms are devoid of experience, both domestically and internationally. Prior to 1989, the very word "marketing" was proscribed in Czechoslovakia. Within the domestic market, output was administratively allocated. Internationally, export-trading firms monopolized international sales. As a result, companies were divorced from the consumers of their products and had no reason to develop the organizational structure or skills common to contemporary market enterprises.

In 1990, Czechoslovak firms were freed from their dependence on state-owned trading companies. Some companies have made dramatic export progress. Spolana Neratovice, for example, saw its chemical exports increase from 22.5% of total sales in 1990 to 50% in 1992, with most exports going to Western markets (Sauer, 1992). While most of Spolana's foreign sales continue through the Chemapol foreign-trade company, it has begun to sell some products directly and has increased it sales staff.

Marketing professionals in East and Central Europe have particular requirements that set the immediate agenda for the development of marketing education and practice. Many firms have established a formal marketing activity for the first time during the past eighteen months. The multiplication in the number of corporate players through privatization, new-enterprise creation, and foreign competition gives special urgency to the adoption of appropriate and effective marketing practices.

The special needs that require particular attention include:

1. The "marketing mentality" of customer-orientation and market research
2. Integration of marketing into the development of competitive strategy
3. Sales-force organization and management
4. Structuring and managing organizational interfaces within the firm between the marketing department and other functional activities
5. A special prominence of industrial marketing within the existing economic structure of countries like Czechoslovakia
6. An unusual role for marketing in the creation of markets that have been inhibited by inefficient distribution systems
7. The necessity of foreign-market development to replace lost markets with traditional trading partners
8. A complete overhaul and development of communications technology and infrastructure to permit some of the most common Western approaches to marketing (Pendergast, 1992).

Quality Management. Although quantitative techniques of quality management are known throughout Central and Eastern Europe, the structure of industry-set quality standards at minimal levels. Domestic monopolies were typical in most industries and foreign trade within the socialist bloc was based on barter. Most exports like lumber and steel were commodity products that did not require high levels of technology. The capital-intensive orientation of economic activity and low productivity created a domestic economy of scarcity. Under these conditions, neither planners nor enterprises were concerned with raising the quality of output or making advances in research, development, and technology (Gluckaufova & Tadikamalla, 1992).

Consequently, despite government efforts in Czechoslovakia to establish a state office for standardization and the creation of various rules, regulations, and quality-control departments within companies, these remained largely ineffective. Production evaluations introduced in 1968 and benchmarking comparisons produced positive results, as did the introduction of technical testing centers. The problem at companies, however, was not the absence of technical know-how about quality control, it was the absence of management skills to put it into practice. At

Spolana Neratovice, for example, the former organizational structure did not empower the quality-control department to properly implement change (Gluckaufova & Tadikamalla, 1992). Since 1990, the quality-control manager reports directly to the company director.

Quality in the services industry is an entirely new field that will be of especially great importance. In general, the economic structure of Eastern economies has been dominated by heavy industry. The services sector will inevitably expand as these economies take a more diversified form.

The Culture of Modern Management

The greatest transformational challenge for Central European industry pertains to the mentality or culture of management. Individuals do not respond behaviorally to acquired skills or techniques, such as those used in functional management occupations. These are merely utilitarian devices. People respond adaptively to their operational environment of organizational structures, policies, and culture. The transformation of management culture in Central European firms must emphasize two critical aspects of the managerial mentality. The first is the importance of systemic or holistic thinking about the nature of the modern business enterprise. The second is the nature of companies as voluntary associations of individuals where people pursue the achievement of individual and collective goals.

Systemic (Holistic) Thinking. The modern enterprise is a complex "open system" that exists both in time and in space. The spatial dimension includes the internal physiology of the organization as well as its relationship with its external environment. The temporal dimension emphasizes the nature of the firm as an autonomous, goal-oriented organization that must visualize and then actualize its own future through strategic activity.

Interfunctional Management. The internal complexity of organizational structure in the differentiated, modern enterprise requires an emphasis on the lateral interdependence of functional business units. Organizations that include such disparate activities as production, accounting, information systems, marketing, finance, and human-resources management must develop formal and informal coordination devices that blend the constituent parts into an interactive whole. The effectiveness of these devices rests upon the ability of management to adopt and infuse throughout the organization a spirit of cohesion and mutual interdependence. New product development, for example, requires the participative and simultaneous involvement of individuals from research and development, engineering, production, marketing, and finance. Marketing departments must recognize that their strategies and sales techniques have a direct effect on the production department. Companies in Central Europe must overcome their poor existing vertical and horizontal communications that inhibit this sort of lateral integration.

The External Environment. The company also exists in an interactive relationship with its external environment. Socialist enterprises, by contrast, operated in disregard for their physical environment, responded to hierarchical directives instead of market signals, and existed in a macroeconomic environment that was maintained at artificially stable levels. In this situation, they became closed entities driven by internal programs for production activity.

The multiple environments of the market enterprise include the macroeconomic policy environment established and maintained by government, the marketplace for the company's products or services, the universe of competitors, and the community at large. The company must find appropriate ways to identify and relate to these multiple environments. This requires both sensitivity to external changes and the development of internal capabilities for environmental scanning and observation and the incorporation of this information into decision making. Most important, the company must view the external environment as the ultimate source of cues for modifications in corporate activity. This external or market orientation requires a complete reversal in the accustomed thinking of management that has responded to hierarchical directives.

Management must acknowledge that the firm is no longer internally driven by hierarchical commands that set priorities on physical volume of output. The firm in a market economy operates in an environment that defines the parameters for company behavior. Firms get their marching orders about product line, prices, quality, and service from the burgeoning marketplace of consumers who possess the resources and alternatives to take their business elsewhere. Companies must adjust continually to the changing macroeconomic framework of money supply, interest rates, and labor markets established by governing authorities. External competition by local and foreign firms requires vigilance and adjustment in both strategy and operations. Companies have responsibilities to their local communities and to their physical environment as well as to internal stakeholders such as employees and shareholders. The management of enterprises in a market economy must formulate its actions while facing both inwards and outwards to accommodate these diverse requirements.

The Strategic Dimension. Companies in a market economy exist in time as well as in space. The temporal dimension requires strategic thinking. The activity of strategic management is alien to the heritage of socialist enterprises. Companies themselves were excluded from participation in strategic decisions handed down by government ministries. Moreover, managers in these firms come typically from engineering or technical backgrounds that were suitable for the character of these companies as production platforms for the implementation of central plans. Such managers prefer to work at operational activities. The Dutch vice president of the managing board of a large Czech textile firm commented: "The first task was to develop managers, not doers. . . . Everybody wanted to work on the operational level. Strategic work was not respected, appreciated, and rewarded enough, as strategic decisions . . . were not considered work" (Matesova, 1992b). This heritage of hierarchical direction and of technical personnel is compounded by the immediate challenge of short-term survival that confronts these firms and distracts them from long-term thinking.

Management must develop the ability to view the firm as a self-directed entity that must visualize alternative future scenarios and chose among them. This requires more than the technical analysis of industry structures and company capabilities. Most importantly, it requires the creative visualization of alternative futures and the adoption of specific policies to increase the probability of preferred outcomes. It also requires the agility and flexibility to adjust to unexpected changes in the terrain. The habit of strategic thinking may be the true revolution that is required for management to transform enterprises in Central and Eastern Europe. Deprived of technical and hierarchical directives that leave only only imple-mentation and operational issues for resolution, management must accept the responsibility for the freedom to select, while facing the risk of future failure, the destination as well as the course for their enterprises.

The Social Contract. The greatest operational implication of a market econ-omy is plentiful supply and consequent freedom of choice. Companies and individuals have alternatives, and the freedom to choose, in a competitive mar-ketplace of goods, services, capital, and labor. Individuals choose employment in particular firms to achieve both individual and collective goals. Employment becomes more than a lifetime activity that provides subsistence income and security for the external pursuit of satisfactions but that conveys little intrinsic self-realization. In a market economy the business enterprise represents a vol-untary association of individuals who choose participation to achieve multiple objectives. The implications of this character of free enterprise are profound. It requires a wholesale transformation in the management and leadership of busi-ness. Ultimately, it affects the entire moral and behavioral climate of organiza-tions.

In effect, this new form of private enterprise as a voluntary association of individuals both engenders, and requires for its own success, the personal qualities of commitment, responsibility, risk, decision making, and creativity that were negated by socialist forms of organization. It implies a vast change, for example, in the relationship between the organization and the individual. It becomes a mandate for top management of a firm to engender commitment to the enterprise by employees who might otherwise exercise their option to leave. This entails the development of an identification by the individual with the organization, its success, and its failure. People who are committed to an enterprise and identify with it acquire a sense of responsibility and personal engagement in its operations. This entails a concern for improvement, for the analysis of problems, and the identification of solutions. It brings forth a productive wellspring of creativity and concern for continuous improvement in both products and processes. This in-volvement of the individual in the enterprise generates a sense of accountability and a willingness to experiment and take risks on behalf of the organization. It brings forth a disposition for teamwork and communication throughout the organizational network. These qualities atrophied in socialist organizations.

TRANSFORMATION MANAGEMENT

The perspectives outlined above make the case that a thorough transformation of enterprises and their management is required for the survival and success of companies throughout East and Central Europe. The nub of the challenge lies in the fact that not only enterprises but also their management requires transformation in order to achieve enduring results. Only enlightened management can effectively transform an enterprise. The process of transformation thereby emerges as a classic puzzle of the chicken and the egg.

A few fortunate companies will benefit from spontaneous transformational leadership. These leaders will engage in the simultaneous transformation of their enterprises and of the skills and culture of management cadres. It is important, however, to acknowledge that these leaders face inordinately difficult challenges in the scope of changes that they must make and in the relative paucity of resources at their disposal.

In other cases, both the impetus and the resources may come through the channel of foreign partners. Corporate transformation is a resource-intensive process. Many Czech and Slovak firms are attracted to joint ventures precisely because they can bring a combination of capital, new products, distribution rights, technology, and training. They must beware, however, of the likelihood that foreign partners may be interested primarily in acquiring local market knowledge and access (Deloitte Touche Tohmatsu, 1992).

The management of these divergent goals of joint-venture partners is a major challenge for Eastern and Central European firms. One Czech manufacturer of small home appliances, for example, hoped to benefit from its joint venture with a large West European electronics firm by learning about new product development processes, quality control practices, and Western marketing techniques and requirements. The West European partner, by contrast, seemed interested primarily in a captive, low-cost base of contract manufacturing and access to local markets for its own competing products. This situation resulted, naturally, in frustration and potential threats to the Czech partner (Tesar & Pribova, 1992).

It is important, finally, to recognize that the time frame for substantial corporate turnarounds in the West has required several years. This observation provides a perspective that necessarily moderates expectations and enhances the significance of even modest steps forward in Eastern and Central Europe.

NOTES

1. Approximately half of these case studies are from Fogel (1992). The other half are the product of a research project on Enterprise Behavior and Economic Reforms: A Comparative Study in Central and Eastern Europe undertaken by researchers at the World Bank,

the London School of Economics, the Portuguese Catholic University, and The Czechoslovak Management Center.

REFERENCES

Abell, D.F. (1992). *Turnaround in Eastern Europe: In-depth Studies.* New York: United Nations Development Programme.

CTK Daily News and Press Survey (1993). February 10, 8.

DeLoitte Touche Tohmatsu International. (1992). *Successfully Managing Investments in Eastern Europe.*

Fogel, D. (1992). Managing in Emerging Market Economies: Cases from Central and Eastern Europe and the CIS. Boulder, CO: Westview.

Frydman, R., Rajsaczynski, A., Earle, J., et al. (1993). *The Privatization Process in Central Europe.* London: Central European University.

Galik, R. (1992a). *Industry case study: Czech and Slovak Federal Republic—consumer electronics.* Unpublished case for the World Bank project on Enterprise Behavior and Economic Reform, Czechoslovak Management Center.

Gluckaufova, D. & Tadikamalla, P.R. (1992). Total quality management in Czechoslovakia. In Fogel, D. (Ed.), *Managing in Emerging Market Economies: Cases from Central and Eastern Europe and the CIS.* Boulder, CO: Westview.

Grayson, L.E. (Ed.). (1993). *Cases in Management in Eastern and Central Europe and Russia.* International Institute of Applied Systems Analysis and the Darden Graduate School of Business.

Jirasek, J. & Mracek, I. (1992). *Industry case study. Czechoslovakia: Footwear/food.* Unpublished case for the World Bank project on Enterprise Behavior and Economic Reform, Czechoslovak Management Center.

Leanna, C.R. (1992). Downsizing at the Slovakia steel company. In Fogel, D. (Ed.), *Managing in Emerging Market Economies: Cases from Central and Eastern Europe and the CIS.* Boulder, CO: Westview.

Matesova, J. (1992a). *Industry case study. Czechoslovakia: Investment engineering.* Unpublished case for the World Bank project on Enterprise Behavior and Economic Reform, Czechoslovak Management Center.

Matesova, J. (1992b). *Industry case study. Czechoslovakia: Textile/cloth.* Unpublished case for the World Bank project on Enterprise Behavior and Economic Reform, Czechoslovak Management Center.

Matesova, J. (1992c). *Industry case study. Czechoslovakia: Textile/garments.* Unpublished case for the World Bank project on Enterprise Behavior and Economic Reform, Czechoslovak Management Center.

Matesova, J. & Spiro, M. (1992). Glavunion—the privatization option. In Fogel, D. (Ed.), *Managing in Emerging Market Economies: Cases from Central and Eastern Europe and the CIS.* Boulder, CO: Westview.

Nath, R. & Jirasek, J. (1992). Transformation management in Czechoslovakia. In Fogel, D. (Ed.), *Managing in Emerging Market Economies: Cases from Central and Eastern Europe and the CIS.* Boulder, CO: Westview.

Olson J.E. & Matesova, J. (1992). Czechoslovak Airlines—pricing in a market environment. In Fogel, D. (Ed.), *Managing in Emerging Market Economies: Cases from Central and Eastern Europe and the CIS.* Boulder, CO: Westview.

Pearce J. & Cakrt, M. (1992). Ferox manufactured products: part A and part B. In Fogel, D. (Ed.), *Managing in Emerging Market Economies: Cases from Central and Eastern Europe and the CIS*. Boulder, CO: Westview.

Pendergast, W.R. (1992). The new Czechoslovak marketing profession. In Tesar, G. (Ed.), *Management Education and Training: An Eastern European Dilemma*. Melbourne, FL: Robert E. Krieger.

Sauer, M. (1992). *Industry case study. Czechoslovakia: Heavy chemistry*. Unpublished case for the World Bank project on Enterprise Behavior and Economic Reform, Czechoslovak Management Center.

Tesar, G. & Pribova, M. (1992). Electro-products Limited. In Fogel, D. (Ed.), *Managing in Emerging Market Economies: Cases from Central and Eastern Europe and the CIS*. Boulder, CO: Westview.

Epilogue

Evidence of Corporate Transformation in Postcommunist Countries: Towards a Theory of Transformation Management

Brij Nino Kumar

The authors of this volume were invited to contribute chapters dealing with management issues and problems that have become relevant to enterprises in postcommunist countries (PCCs) as they attempt to cope with the shift to a market economy. Never before in economic history has the environmental framework of organizations undergone such radical change as a consequence of the breakdown of an inherently inefficient economic system as in the PCCs. Of course, the most marked characteristic of this dramatic process is that it has happened without force and war; it has been a peaceful revolution. But, a revolution it is all the same, leaving no walk of life untouched, least of all productive enterprises, which, after an initial phase, themselves become important agents of change.

For management scholars of all fields of specialization, this phenomenon poses a great challenge to study the economic problems associated with the process. We have called this process organizational or corporate transformation and the managerial activities and institutions involved in accomplishing it "transformation management." This volume analyzes its various aspects and problems.

PROBLEM OF DEFINITION

Except for the general statement of the problem as given above, the authors of the book were not exposed to any kind of guidelines as to what corporate transformation or transformation management might and should include. The reasons for this are twofold. First, it is difficult to delineate a definition of these phenomena that would be generally accepted, and second, no editor can and should restrict authors to a minutely defined framework at the risk of limiting the scope of analysis.

This academic freedom, on the other hand, poses the difficulty that each author has a somewhat different understanding of the terms, which makes it difficult to arrive at general conclusions. This problem becomes more serious when, as in our case, demarcation of closely related concepts is fuzzy. We are especially concerned with the differences between corporate transformation and planned change, between corporate transformation and organizational development, as well as organizational learning. A full consensus among scholars of organization theory cannot be reached at this time. What, however, can be expected is the agreement that corporate transformation is not just different in degree but also in kind from other business changes. We agree with Kilmann et al. (1988) that otherwise "there would be little justification for adding one more academic term to the already jargon-filled social sciences" (p. 2).

SOME BASIC CHARACTERISTICS

Looking through the literature (Kilmann et al. 1988; Davis 1982), it seems justified to consider corporate transformation as a new phenomenon. Although not necessarily first introduced in connection with the revolution in Eastern Europe, it has gained in importance and profile ever since. Never before in economic history have organizations questioned and thrown overboard their very purpose, structure, strategy, and culture. In this process in the PCCs, many former state-owned enterprises have succumbed to the ordeals of radical change; others have been severely damaged and are on the verge of collapse. As this development continues, it becomes apparent that only those enterprises can survive that are capable of transformation.

Looking at the evidence of this process in the PCCs, the concept of transformation compares with related models as follows:

• Comparison to planned change: Corporate transformation is ad hoc and even erratic, following discontinuities in the sociopolitical environment ("discontinuity management").

• Comparison with organizational development and learning: Corporate transformation is typically not applied to isolated parts of the enterprise, with little awareness and support on the part of top management (Kilmann et al. 1988), but rather in a systemic manner, encompassing all elements within the organization and the relationships between them, thus affecting a complete and radical renewal ("turn-around management").

Based on these elements, the findings of the authors of this book identify the following key issues and tasks of transformation management in the PCCs. These are summarized according to themes developed by Kilmann et al. (1988):

1. Transformation management is a response to environmental and technical changes.
2. Transformation management is a new model for organizing for the future.
3. Transformation management is concerned with dissatisfaction with the old and belief in the new.

4. Transformation management is a qualitatively different way of perceiving, thinking, and behavior.

5. Transformation management is expected to spread throughout the organization.

6. Transformation management is driven by line management.

7. Transformation management is orchestrated by internal and external experts.

8. Transformation management is transitory.

The following sections briefly examine how these identified key issues of transformation management were referred to and explored in the chapters of this volume. This will put the chapters on a common theoretical basis and simultaneously move us towards a unified theory of transformation management.

TRANSFORMATION MANAGEMENT IN PCCs

Response to Environmental Change

There is strong evidence in most chapters of this volume that forces in the sociopolitical environment provide the impetus for transformation. This relationship forms the core of Chapter 1, by Savitt, on privatization of former state-owned enterprises, where change is initiated solely by radical changes in the environment. Another example of how firms respond to environmental pressure is Chapter 4, by Deskovicz, which shows how corporate governance in Slovenia changed due to interest groups that emerged when the centrally controlled socialistic order gave way to a market-oriented economy. Chapters 8 and 9, by Kasperson and Dobrzynski and Ullmann, show how corporations in transformation have to respond to environmental forces from a human-resources perspective. Pendergast, in Chapter 14, explores through case analyses how managerial functions like compensation practices respond to what he calls the "triple revolution."

Model for the Future

Transformation management in the PCCs can perhaps be viewed as most revolutionary with regard to changes in society. The former state-owned enterprises have radically broken away from the old structures and are envisioning a new reality that is fundamentally different from the previous state. Top management has a relatively easy job of converting organization members to their vision of the future, since the whole society has departed from the old system and is thirsting for a new way of life.

Breaking out of the old ways and formulating new blueprints for action are dealt with in the chapters of Part Two. The breakup of combines and the design of new organization structures, as shown in Chapter 5, by Gaitanides and Bredenbreuker, is an example of how transformation management can be considered as a model for the future. For Reineke (Chapter 6), creating a "third" culture through merging

of Eastern and Western enterprises is a vision that is an important part of the
process.

Responding to the Dissatisfaction with the Old

The collapse of the socialist system and subsequent political developments like
the unification of Germany and the dissolving of the superpower Soviet Union
basically have their roots in the enduring dissatisfaction of the masses of people
with their economic condition. In the state-owned enterprises in all former PCCs,
widespread discontent and lack of motivation have been noticeable for a long time.
Deficits in leadership skills (Albach, 1992) have contributed to the fading morale
and subsequently to the poor performance.

In Chapter 2, Kozdroj and Van Fleet look into this aspect of discontent and
dissatisfaction in Polish organizations. They criticize the manager's role and
management practice and identify the tasks of transformation management in this
respect. Similarly, Tullar (Chapter 3) shows the problems in Russian organizations
leading to discontent and low morale of workers. The task of transformation
management is also to convince top management that change is viable. The author
makes suggestions within the frame of American–Russian joint ventures.

Transformation Management is a Qualitatively Different Way

There is no doubt of the fact that the PCCs and the state-owned enterprises need
contextual renewal. A change in the state of affairs by degrees is not the answer
to the pressing problems provoked basically by the former socialistic system. In
fact, as Davis (1982) puts it, transformation is a shift of context, itself understood
as "assumptions through which all experience is filtered." The major task of
transformation management is therefore to bring the context of state-owned enterprises into question; only by doing that can renewal be expected. To this effect,
the chapter by Pendergast and the case studies presented by Mroczkowski et al.
(Chapter 13) reveal that it is necessary for organization members to perceive and
handle problems in ways that are diametrical to the standard procedures in the
PCCs. It becomes essential to act on "zero-base" concepts, the type Hammer
(1990) recommends in "process reengineering models," and even to think in
paradoxical terms, as suggested by Quinn and Cameron (1988). Domsch and
Ladwig (Chapter 7) present a model that can assist in designing transformation
development training concepts meant to recondition thinking and behavior so that
they are congenial to initiating and implementing such renewal and contextual
shifts.

Transformation Management throughout the Organization

Corporate transformation in terms of basic renewal and "turn-around" management alone suggests that transformation management must be systemic, i.e.,

spread throughout the organization. As pointed out earlier, this differs from organizational development that is restricted to certain areas. This is very much true of former state-owned corporations, where, as Gaitanides and Bredenbreuker show in Chapter 5, the entire organization and its environment are influenced by the socialistic context, and reorganization must be implemented throughout if it is to be effective.

This does not mean that transformation must be implemented to the same degree everywhere. This is pointed out by Welge and Holtbrügge in Chapter 11, who show how financial sourcing and financial management must be adapted to the new contextual framework. The chapter by Dörrie (Chapter 12) recognizes that different functional areas like technology management in former state-owned enterprises might have different capacities for learning and change. It appears that in connection with technology and innovation, absorption of new paradigms will be quicker, due to the lesser influence of context in this area. On the other hand, transformation management can also be unsuccessful in some areas if the expectations are too high, as demonstrated in the case studies by Mroczkowski et al.

Transformation Management and Line Management

Revolutionary change and turn-around, as being experienced in former socialist countries, reshape the entire organization—corporate transformation is systemic. This phenomenon implies shifts in overall structure, process, strategy, and people. In order that this radical change does not end in chaos, it has to be effectively channeled by responsible line-management sufficiently qualified and competent to handle the connected problems. The following issues seem to be especially important in the context of the PCCs.

Achieving Synergies. As suggested by Gaitanides and Bredenbreuker (Chapter 5), interlinking change and the pay-offs between different business and functional areas is a major task. Former state-owned enterprises face two major shortcomings in tackling this problem: 1) deficits in organizational infrastructure, e.g., lack of coordinating mechanisms and underdeveloped communication and information systems; and 2) lack of thinking in terms of functional interdependencies among Eastern managers.

Overcoming Resistance to Change. Change in organizations invariably provokes resistance, due to anxiety regarding the new state or commitment of members to the status quo. This phenomenon is accentuated in organizations in the PCCs due to the mass unemployment following the breakdown of socialism. The case studies by Pendergast make it quite clear that line management in former state-owned enterprises requires a very sensitive hand in overcoming legitimate anxieties while introducing new concepts. Convincing diehards (former Communist cadre) of the advantages of the new system is not easy. Whereas in East Germany these people were simply replaced by managers from West German companies, the other PCCs do not have such possibilities of easy substitution and have to bear with former staff due to the dearth of competent new personnel. Lack of sensitive line management has nurtured antireform movements in many former state-owned enterprises, as several cases in Eastern Europe, especially in Russia, have shown.

Motivating Organization Members. This task of line management is closely connected with overcoming resistance to change when it comes to convincing and winning organization members over to the new system. As shown in Chapters 8–10, this job is even more formidable in PCCs because employees are not accustomed and trained to take the initiative on their own. In view of such history, incorporating adequate motivational structures, for instance by designing appropriate incentive systems or fostering functional leadership styles, becomes a major task for line management.

Transformation Management and Outside Experts

In change theory, the role of outside experts ("change agents") in initiating and implementing change is well recognized (Bennis et al., 1961). Their position differs from that of line management in the organization primarily in acceptance and competency. In transforming corporations in PCCs this role has been played very effectively by foreign companies, which have been buying and also entering into cooperative agreements without equity with former state-owned enterprises. Engelhard and Eckert (Chapter 10) have demonstrated this in connection with German firms in East Europe. The change agent function of Western firms is effective mainly for two reasons: 1) their knowledge of market economy and management goes way beyond what their Eastern European partners have ever learned before and can ever learn in a reasonable timespan, and 2) their authority is accepted much more readily by the organization members, partly because of their expertise, but also on grounds of their ownership rights, which are viewed with awe and respect as a magic formula for prosperity by people who have been brought up in socialism. West German companies have had the experience that lay-offs in former East German combines were often accepted without much ado when Western capital was involved.

Western experts in Eastern Europe can, however, also encounter resistance and conflict if they handle transformation insensitively. The literature already abounds with cases where German consultants have been unsuccessful in transforming East German enterprises because of their haughty "schoolmaster" attitude. While negotiating the Skoda takeover in the Czech Republic, Volkswagen had the experience that their knowledge for leading the transformation effort was viewed very critically when German experts from the parent company failed to appreciate the feelings of the Skoda management of having to "surrender" to the Germans a symbol of national prestige. In the beginning, the Czechs made many complaints to the insensitive Germans. As Reineke has shown in Chapter 6, this type of behavior on the part of the dominating company is a real barrier for acculturation in East–West mergers and acquisitions.

Transformation Management is Transitory and Limited

Opposite to the view offered by Kilmann et al. (1988) that transformation is ongoing, endless, and forever, the chapters in this volume suggest that corporate transformation in the context of the PCCs is a rather transitory process and limited to a certain stage. The main reason for this conclusion is simply that mold-breaking changes, as proposed in connection with corporate transformation, need to redefine and redraw the boundaries of the system. This is only possible when the process of shifting is limited to some stage or goal of development and stops on reaching this. Of course, if the goal is not exactly defined, then transformation can become an enduring process. And since transformation is not incremental but discontinuous, an enduring process can destabilize the system and lead to its destruction. This is exactly what is happening presently in many PCCs on the corporate and societal level, where ill-defined goals (and insufficient means) are making transformation a hazardous venture ending in chaos and anarchy.

In this way, corporate transformation is different from organizational learning and development and also from planned change. The latter are incremental, continuous, and enduring. They become responsible for the future development and take over once the mold-breaking transformation has reached its end. The boundaries flow into each other. However, this, of course, does not mean that transformation seen as a separate phenomenon cannot once again be triggered by new external or internal initiating forces.

CONCLUDING REMARKS

In this epilogue the findings, as discussed by the authors of this book, were summarized on the basis of issues that characterize corporate transformation and transformation management in the PCCs. However, one could expect that these key themes are capable of defining the phenomenon in general terms.

Corporate transformation may gain importance in the years to come, as environmental discontinuities and shifts in the management paradigm accelerate. Accordingly, management will have to adapt to this kind of change by offering training and adequate organizational structures and processes. Management should prepare for jolts by anticipating or even proactively provoking transformation along the lines described. Chances are that in this way it can be handled in a more efficient manner. The example of transformation management in the context of the Central and East European revolution has made management in general much more sensitive to the phenomenon and the discontinuities than before. Further research can help not only to solve practical problems but also to integrate this field more systematically into management theory.

REFERENCES

Albach, H. (1992). *The Transformation of Firms and Markets. A Network Approach to Economic Transformation Processes in East Germany.* Berlin: WZB.

Bennis, W., Benne, K. & Chin, R. (1961). *The Planning of Change.* New York: Rinehart and Winston.

Davis, S. (1982). Transforming Organisations: The Key to Strategy is Context. *Organisational Dynamics,* Winter: 64–80.

Hammer, M. (1990). Reengineering Work: Don't Automate, Obliterate. *Harvard Business Review,* July/Aug, 4, 104–113.

Kilmann, R. et al. (Eds.) (1988). *Corporate Transformation.* San Francisco: Jossey-Bass.

Quinn, R. & Cameron, K. (Eds.) (1988). *Paradox and Transformation. Toward a Theory of Change in Organization and Management.* Cambridge, MA: Harvard University Press.

Selected Bibliography

Buch, H.F. & Bauer, H.G. (1991). *Transformation in der Wirtschaftsordnung der ehemaligen DDR.* Bonn: Verlag Gesamtdeutsches Institut, Bundesanstalt für gesamtdeutsche Aufgaben.

Dabrowski, J.M. (1994). Untersuchung des Prozesses der Eigentumsgestaltung in der polnischen Wirtschaft. *Zeitschrift für Betriebswirtschaft,* 64, 839–857.

Engelhard, J. (Ed.) (1993). *Ungarn im neuen Europa.* Wiesbaden: Gabler.

Hartwig, K.-H. (1991). *Transformationsprozess in sozialistischen Wirtschaftssystemen.* Berlin: Springer-Verlag.

Hauer, A., Kleinhenz, T., von Schuttenbach, L. (1993). *Der Mittelstand im Transformationsprozes Ostdeutschlands und Osteuropas.* Heidelberg: Physica-Verlag.

Healy, N., M. (1994). The transition economics of Central and Eastern Europe. *Columbia Journal of World Business,* XXIX, 1, 62–71.

Knell, M. & Rider, Ch. (Eds.) (1992). *Socialist Economies in Transformation—Appraisals of the Market Mechanism.* Hants, UK: Edward Elgar.

Lawrence, P. & Vlachoutsicos, Ch. (1993). Joint ventures in Russia: Put the locals in charge. *Harvard Business Review,* 71, 44–54.

McDonald, K.R. (1993). Why privatization is not enough. *Harvard Business Review,* 71, 49–59.

Nurmi, R. & Üksvärav, R. (1993). How Estonian managers experienced the transformation to independence and market economy. *Management International Review,* 33, 171–181.

Quelch, J.A., Joachimsthaler, E. & Neuno, J.L. (1992). After the Wall: Marketing guidelines for Eastern Europe. *Sloan Management Review,* 32, 82–83.

Rondinelli, D.A. (1991). Developing private enterprise in the Czechoslovak Federal Republic—The challenge of economic reform. *Columbia Journal of World Business,* XXVI, 3, 26–36.

Welfens, P.J.J. (1992). Foreign investment in the East European transition. *Management International Review,* 32, 199–218.

Winiecki, J. (1992). *Privatization in Poland A Comparative Perspective.* Tübingen: J.C.B. Mohr.

Index

ISBN 0-89930-840-6

HARDCOVER BAR CODE

DATE DUE

GAYLORD			PRINTED IN U.S.A